REBEL CORRESPONDENT

"MY EXPERIENCES IN THE WAR OF 1860 BRIEFLY TOLD."
BY PRIVATE ARBA F. SHAW COMPANY F - 4TH GEORGIA
CAVALRY, C.S.A.

STEVE PROCKO

Rebel Correspondent

Copyright © 2021
By Steve Procko

ISBN: 978-1-7372834-0-9

All rights reserved
Printed in the United States of America

No part of this book may be used or reproduced in any manner whatsoever without the written permission of the author, except in the case of brief quotations embodied in critical articles and reviews.

Published by
Steve Procko Productions, LLC
Ocala, Florida

www.RebelCorrespondent.com

Cover design: Eric Labacz, labaczdesign.com

WHAT THEY ARE SAYING ABOUT *REBEL CORRESPONDENT*

Steve Procko has uncovered a real treasure! Then, in addition, he has turned it into an even richer treasure! ... It is amazing how much he has expanded on Arba's writings with information about the people, places and events Arba covered, the result of meticulous research. ... Between Arba's writings and Steve Procko's writings, we can all see there is still so very much to learn about people and events in our history.

Ruth Hill Fulton McAllister
Sam Watkins' Great-Granddaughter &
Editor of 2011 "2nd" edition of Company Aytch

Private Arba Shaw's reminiscences are colorful and full of interesting and important details about his wartime experiences. Steve Procko, in assembling Shaw's reminiscences into a complete book, has done students of the American Civil War and Georgia history a favor. A gifted researcher, Procko chased down names and events mentioned by Shaw, adding additional context and detail to the already-rich narrative. The result is a book that any history buff will savor.

Dan Roper
Editor
Georgia Backroads

Having the opportunity to read an advance copy of Rebel Correspondent *was a privilege. Reading through the newspaper articles Private Arba Shaw wrote some years after the war gives one a rare moment in the experience of a young Georgia cavalryman during the Civil War. Author Steve Procko, through his excellent narrative, takes the reader on a rare journey, as recounted by the young soldier's memoirs, with his cavalry unit through many campaigns and skirmishes throughout the South. Also included is much ancillary information by the editor, Mr. Procko, including local historical events and a genealogy of the many persons mentioned by Private Shaw that gives one a virtual playbook of the experience of a private Georgia soldier.*

Gerald W. Flinchum-History Instructor
Kennesaw State University & Emory University
OLLI Adult Education Programs

Private Arba Shaw's account of his experiences with the 4th Georgia Cavalry is a treasure that only grows more precious with the passage of time. Steve Procko does a masterful job of weaving this private soldier's reminiscences into the larger experience of his regiment. Rebel Correspondent *is a well-researched and engaging look at this pivotal event in our nation's history through the eyes of one who lived it.*

John Randolph Poole
Author, *Cracker Cavaliers – The 2nd Georgia Cavalry Under Wheeler and Forres*

ABOUT THE PHOTOS IN THIS BOOK

About the front cover: No photographs have been found of Private Arba F. Shaw as a cavalry soldier. The image used on the front cover is an artistic representation made from an amalgam of unidentified Confederate Civil War cavalry soldier images sourced through the Library of Congress.

When Arba F. Shaw described what he looked like when he enlisted he said, *"When Captain Moore was administering the oath and it came my turn he said to me: 'I don't believe you are old enough.' I said I was 18. He said you don't look to be more than 16. I was 5 ft. 4 in. tall and was beardless."*

About the back cover: The back cover photograph is a composition of an unidentified Union cavalry sergeant wearing a sash that would have been red, based on the 1861 Union army uniform regulations. The original photo is a Sixth-plate tintype, courtesy of the Library of Congress. Arba Shaw identified the man who wounded him on Sept. 5, 1864, as wearing a red sash. *"He had on a red sash. He shot me twice and killed my horse and I shot him or at least my aim was on him and he was shot as could be easily seen, so close were we."*

*For my wife, Lauren,
and our family, almost all of whom
will enthusiastically
acknowledge that they
are not in the demographic
for reading a Civil War book,
but read this one anyway.*

WALKER COUNTY MESSENGER.

Vol. XXIV No. 51   LaFayette, Georgia, Thursday, December 19, 1901. $1 Per Year

MILBURN BUGGIES.

We have the latest and best styles of open and Top Vehicles for business or pleasure.

FIFTY DOLLARS.

FIFTY DOLLARS

is not set cash price on this buggy. It has felt patent steel axles, good hickory wheels with steel tires bolted between every spoke. End springs with the new Barber hanger brace and longitudinal springs underneath. Spring cushion and back covered with genuine leather. Leather Quarter Top. With this we also give a good lamp and a whip.

COME AND SEE THIS BARGAIN.

HARNESS. HARNESS.

MILBURN WAGON CO

F. F. ELLIS, Manager,
912 Market St. Chattanooga, Tenn

W. E. Walker & Co.,

THE UNION STORE!

238 Mont. Ave. — — — Chattanooga, Tenn.

You are always come to a common sense arrangement in strictly business matter. You have heard of W. E. Walker, The Union Store, of course you have, to say so would be an admission that you were not posted. Did y u know this is the cheapest store in the City to

Dry Goods, Notions, Millinery, Ladie's Shirt Waists, Skirts, Wraps, Men and Boys' Clothing, Gents' Furnishings, Boots, Shoes, Hats, Caps, Etc.

Now is the time to get Fine Glassware Free. Tickets with every 25 cent purchase, you get something with every dollars' worth of Tickets. On Monday, Thursday and Saturday every sack between 9:00 and 10:30 o'clock, and Saturday nights between 7 and 8 o'clock we will sell 10 Bars of Electric Soap for 25c, 1 good Broom 10c, one 50 box of Washing Bluing at 2c.

Bargains in Dry Goods Bargain in Clothing.

All wool and Flannel, 10c pr yd.
25 yds Brown Domestic, $1.
Tolde Old Cloth, 10c.
Standard Calico, 4 and 5 5c.
Canton Flannel, 5 to 15c.
Black figured Brocade Sattines, 25 to 35c.
Outing Flannel, 4½ to 12½c.
Bleached Domestic, 4c.

Bargain in Hats.

We trim our Hats to Suit you, and save you 50c to $2.00 on a Hat.
Ladies' trimmed Hats 75c.
Ladies' and Misses' walking Hats for 50c.
Ladies $3 trimmed Hat, $1.50
Ladies $4 trimmed Hats, $2.98.

Bargain in Shoes.

Men's Brogan Shoes, as long as they last, 75c.
Ladies' Dongola Shoes, 98c.
50 pairs ladies' sample shoes, at 98c, size 4½ 5, worth $1.25, at 98c.
Men's W. L. Douglas Shoes, $3 Shirts, 50c to $1.60

This is the place to get Chap, Good School Shoes, 69c to $1.25. Oxford School Shoes, 69c to $1.25. Rubbers of all kinds.

Window Shades, 9c, 3 for 25c.

Men's Jeans Pants, one pair for a customer, 25c.
Men's Black Chevoit Pants, 75c.
Men's Black Beaver Overcoats, with velvet collar, for $2.37.
Men's extra gray chevoits, fancied, French laced, a $6 suit for $3.37.
Men's extra Melton suits in brown and Oxford gray, $7.50.
Men's $12 suits, $10.
Men's boys youth suits, $1.25 each, etc.
Boys' suit coats, a $1.25, at 87c.
Boys' knee pants, 20c.
Boys' Corduroy pants, 49c.

Bargain in Underwear

Children's fleeced union suits, 19c.
Ladies' union suits, 25c.
Men's knit underwear per suit at 10c.
Men's heavy fleeced underwear at 98c.

The second term of the present session will begin January 6th, 1902.

A liberal patronage will be gratefully appreciated by the Principal, who is an energetic and enthusiastic worker in the schoolroom and a deserving man of all the honors given him.

All persons are warned not to buy, fish or otherwise trespass on the lands of the John R. Pike estate under penalty of the law.
W. M. Pike, Ex'r.

As has Washing Bluing for 5c.

Destroyers of High Price and Originators of Half Price. Come to see us   W. E. Walker & Co.

Local Items.

The cold snap brought to a sudden a change and as many a farmer in the thermometer at 8 o'clock a.m. Everyone that Jack Frost could touch went by the board. In the southeast the fellows brought lines of life to man and death to stock.

Western Lodge, No. 91, F. & A. M. will hold its regular annual meeting Saturday until 21st. All the brethren are requested to be on hand at the annual election of officers will occur.
Jas. P. SHATTUCK, W. M.
Jas. E. Rogers, Secretary.

Take Notice.

After December 20 our accounts will be closed in the hands of an officer for collection. We cannot wait longer so please settle.
ORMANDO, JACKSON & SHAW

The Trion Herald contains a petition to the Superior Court from G. T. Myers, O. B. Myers, A. B. Hamilton, Frank Crofts and J. J. Burns to incorporate the Trion Herald Publishing Co. The charter is a broad one, and under it the company can spread its sail in many ways.

Accidentally Shot.

While out hunting Wednesday morning Lee Caldwell, a son of S. J. Caldwell, accidentally shot Albert McBryar, Jr. It is impossible to learn full particulars, but all trust the accident was not very serious.

Thursday's Constitution contained the pictures of our Mercer boys who represented their entities in a debate which occurred at the Friday night. Among them was M. L. Keith, of Trion, who is a member of the Junior class there and who is taking a stand that is reflecting credit upon himself and Walker.

Now that the Christmas season is upon us, these doing their holiday shopping should patronize our local merchants. As is shown by the advertisements that appear in this issue, they have brought elegant lines of holiday goods, embracing presents suitable for every member of the family. Before going elsewhere look over their lines and see if they haven't got just what you want.

The following were elected and installed at the last meeting of A. Laset Lodge, F. and A. M., to fill the office for ensuing Masonic year: Clayton Tatum, W. M.; Jas. B. Tuesday, S. W.; J. D. Stephens, J. W.; J. R. West, Secretary; W. H. Brooks, Treasurer; R. B. Shaw, S. D.; G. L. Stephens, J. D.; J. F. Smith, Chaplain; J. L. Johnson, D. B. McBrier, Stewards; G. C. Baker, Tyler.

Trans Seminary.

The closing exercises of the fall term of Trans school will be Friday and Friday night, December 20th.

All friends and former pupils are cordially invited to attend.

The programme will not be very lengthy, as it is only an intermediate entertainment.

The second term of the present session will begin January 6th, 1902.

A liberal patronage will be gratefully appreciated by the Principal, who is an energetic and enthusiastic worker in the schoolroom and a deserving man of all the honors given him.

ADMIRAL SCHLEY SCORED.

In The Report of the Court of Inquiry.

The verdict in the Schley Court of Inquiry was made public Friday, thus bringing to a close one of the greatest naval investigations in the history of the country.

The findings of the court make a lengthy document, the whole ground being reviewed and Admiral Schley being scored on almost every point by Benham and Ramsay. Although Admiral Dewey signed the report from a matter of form, he gives out a statement in which he makes Admiral Schley a hero.

The verdict in part says: By commanding the engagement on July 5 with the port battery, and turning the Brooklyn around with port helm, Commodore Schley caused her to lose distance and position with the Spanish vessels, especially with the Viscaya and Colon.

The turn of the Brooklyn to starboard was made to avoid getting her into dangerous proximity to the Spanish vessels. The turn was made toward the Texas and caused that vessel to stop and to back her engines to avoid possible collision.

Admiral Schley did injustice to Lieutenant Commander A. C. Hodgson in particular only a portion of the correspondence which passed between them.

Commodore Schley's conduct in connection with the events of the Santiago campaign prior to June 1, 1898, was characterized by vacillation, dilatoriness and lack of enterprise.

His official reports regarding the coal supply and the coaling facilities of the flying squadron were imprudent and misleading.

His conduct during the battle of July 3 was self possessed and he encouraged, in his own manner, his subordinate officers, and men to fight courageously.

ADMIRAL DEWEY'S STATEMENT.

In the opinion of the undersigned the passage from Key West to Cienfuegos was made by the flying squadron with all possible dispatch. Commodore Schley having in view the importance of arriving off Cienfuegos with as much coal as possible in the ships' bunkers.

The blockade of Cienfuegos was effective.

Commodore Schley in passing from Cienfuegos to Santiago, used due diligence and his conduct in this matter was self-possessed in order to obtain information regarding the Spanish squadron from her when she came up.

The passage from Cienfuegos to a point about 22 miles south of Santiago was made with as much dispatch as was possible, while keeping the squadron a unit.

The blockade of Santiago was effective.

Commodore Schley was the senior officer of our squadron off Santiago when the Spanish squad was attempted to escape on the morning of July 3, 1898. He was in absolute command and is entitled to the credit due to such commanding officer for the glorious victory which resulted in the total destruction of the Spanish ships.

GEORGE DEWEY,
Admiral U. S. N.

Rossville Notes.

(Rossville Tribune.)

Miss Clara Smith spent Sunday in LaFayette visiting her parents.
Willie Carroll, of LaFayette, visited relatives here this week.
Messrs W. B. Edge and T. A. Murray have formed a partnership under the style of Murray & Edge, and have opened up a new stock of groceries in H. E. Walt's New York, October 15th, 1901, old stand. They are wide awake business men.

RESOLUTIONS

Of the Crawfish Springs Baptist Sunday School.

Again the grim reaper, Death, has entered our field and with his sickle cut down one of our lambs, conferring another sheaf for the garner of the Great Master above.

Now whereas, it pleased God in the administration of his divine providence on the 20th day of November, 1901, to dissolve the tabernacle of clay that had the immortal spirit of Brother Joseph F. Scott and translated that spirit to a house not made with hands eternal in the heavens.

Resolved 1st, That Crawfish Springs Baptist Sunday School bow in humble submission to the will of Him who doeth all things well.

2nd, That while we keenly feel the loss of Brother Scott's labors and presence, we find consolation in the Christian's hope of a blissful immortality beyond the grave, and that the Lord had need of him in his heavenly kingdom and that he has placed his loved ones who had gone before and were waiting and watching for him.

3rd, That in the death of Bro. Scott, Crawfish Springs Baptist Sunday School has sustained a loss that time alone can overcome.

4th, That we deeply sympathize with the bereaved members of the family and commend them to Him, who alone is able to comfort them in this sad affliction.

5th, That these resolutions be spread upon the minutes of the Sunday School and that copies be furnished the family of Bro. Scott and also the WALKER COUNTY MESSENGER with the request that they be published.

Fraternally submitted,
W. A. Wood,
J. J. Jones,
W. A. Harton,
Committee.

Lightfoot Objects To Time of Enumeration.

What about this for cold weather? Powerful much on those who have to recuperate the children to school in the polling school funds to the benefits. Some may tell why it is that this time of the year is taken of for that purpose? I may be mistaken, but I took it gives a good chance to enumerate twice. For instance, today in the 10th. Now suppose one of our teachers goes out and enumerates a family, tomorrow they move to another district. Then some one will enumerate them there again. Why not select a time, when all teachers make their change? One reason for kicking is that in one district the head personally enumerates at the time required so that we will not have more than 2 our number last year and by the end of January we will probably have over one hundred. Now it right that we furnish a case to teeth that many and be only gets pay for about sixty of them? Why not wait until from the 15th to the 1st of January to enumerate them? LIGHTFOOT.

DURHAM COAL AND COKE COMPANY.

First Mortgage 6 Per Cent Gold Bonds.

The undersigned will receive sealed proposals up to 12 m. on the 27th of December, 1901, for the sale to it of bonds issued under the First Mortgage, dated October 5th, 1899, at a price not exceeding par and accrued interest, to an amount sufficient to use the sum of $3000.37.

CONTINENTAL TRUST COMPANY OF THE CITY OF NEW YORK,
By Henry B. Anson, Secretary.

Subscribe for the MESSENGER

Miller Bros

Seventh and Market Sts.

CHATTANOOGA.

Our store is one a "headquarters." From stock to pit it has been examined with much intelligent care and capacity, attending to our Mail Order Department. If you can not visit our store in person, have no hesitation in ordering goods. Satisfaction guaranteed.

Waists
50c—We are going to sell you what 50c will do in our big Waist Department. A splendid, in made Donnet Waist and Sailors, tan collar and cuffs, the very latest to your under vest suit, or good for any wear—just 75c, 25c.
95c—Now see what it will be. An all wool flannel in solid colors and a dozen. A splendid value.
$1.00—A little higher, you say. Well, grade warrants more. An all wool flannel waist, with tucks, corded with white both in front and back, at $1.
A Mercerized waist, looks like white and wears better, tucked in the tucks, front effect, overlarded buttons. You offer will surprise you, just 92.
$2.00—Silk waists that are worth considered more, are we deuteron, at $1
$2.50—Plain dot flannel waist, in all colors, inches stitched, $1.50.
$2.50—We offer for you a Saxon Dureese, come in oxo, and Yellow in silk effect, hand hemstitched, handsomely made worth $3.00, a great variety of these waists which work last long at this price, $2.50.

Clothing Department

The talk of the rack, a joy to the middle class, and a blessing to the poor. Your choice of actual good shoes, including brown and Oxford Mixture, fine black French checked, a few pure worsted suits in hand cass cheched auteroves-theroid one pattern same piece, all hand, worth $12.00 and $15.00—give mid price, $9.75.
We have no assortment of walking skirts, on two side. There are all wool sherol, double faced, worn good, with thirty two touches and stitched on bottom. See these value, $5.97.
Another $9.97.—In all wool cheviot poppics, black and blue, a $5 boy stock line, handsomely fashioned, a plain, with percales, beautifully tailored. Others are selling this same skirt for $4.00, we offer them for $3.50.

Slippers and Shoes

Ladies' house shoes, with fur trimming or tufts or satin red, browns or blued, 78c, 95c and $1.25. They will cost you at least 20c a pair more elsewhere.
Ladies' shoes or house button cord cushion, 95c.
Ladies' extra button over gaiters, heel quality, 49c.
Ladies' wool slippers, colored's, 50c; bellows, 90c.
Men's boys oak calf sole work shoe, need elsewhere at $1.50, our price, $1.47. Every pair purchased must be better.
Men's kid calf or hid kid shoe, the latest styles, heavy calf-steel soles, $2.50 value; our price $1.97.
Ladies' shoes in toes or Larkins, kid or testing toes, patina finished, 76c value at $1.97.

Flannels and Cottons

Fifty four inch outing flannel, worth 66c, for 30c.
Two hundred pieces of French flannel, all the newest designs with borders, 75c, 60c and 65c.
Best apron gingham 5c in the world for, per yard, 3c.
An exquisite line of Eiderdown for a strong request for robes for the per yard.
A thirty-six inch Percale for dresses, in red and blue, worth 19c, for 12c.

Blankets and Counterpanes

Double-bed blankets in gray, with mercerized red and blue borders. 65c, comfort, special, 47c.
Extra large comforters, covered with mercerized sateen, warmly made, with single or figured lining, our special price, each, 75c.

**Arba F. Shaw Writing of His Experiences
in the Civil War – Circa 1901**
This illustration was created by Arba's
3X great-granddaughter Alyse Keith.

Table of Contents

INTRODUCTION 1

CHAPTER ONE
Rebel Correspondent 8

CHAPTER TWO
Enlistment Day 21

CHAPTER THREE
Going to War 35

CHAPTER FOUR
Life of a Private 56

CHAPTER FIVE
On to Knoxville 76

CHAPTER SIX
East Tennessee 98

CHAPTER SEVEN
The Realities of War 129

CHAPTER EIGHT
Hospitalization and Recovery 168

CHAPTER NINE
Rejoining the Fight 185

CHAPTER TEN
Back to Tennessee 201

CHAPTER ELEVEN
Losing the 4th 235

CHAPTER TWELVE
Endgame 279

CHAPTER THIRTEEN
Afterwards 300

CHAPTER FOURTEEN
The Tale of Two 4ths..313

CHAPTER FIFTEEN
4th Georgia Cavalry, Company F 328

Acknowledgments 349

A Final Note..352

About the Author 354

INTRODUCTION

I LOVE DETECTIVE WORK. Tracing history's mysteries and sleuthing anecdotal stories to separate the wheat from the chaff have become an obsession, which I have lately been threshing into interesting documentaries. I believe this story is one of them.

Recently, I was researching a chain of deadly events that happened in 1864 to folks living in and around the Copper Basin, the tri-state area where Georgia, North Carolina, and Tennessee all shake hands. It was just one incident that illustrates the lawlessness and chaos that existed in the North Georgia mountains at the end of the Civil War.

The Confederate's 4th Georgia Cavalry (Avery) Company D was under the command of Captain William Jefferson Rodgers. Captain Rodgers and about sixty of his men were on patrol just over the Tennessee border looking for bushwhackers and deserters when they came across William Clayton Fain, a lawyer from Morganton, Georgia. Fain, a known Union sympathizer, had been a delegate from Fannin County at the Georgia Secession Convention in January 1861 at the capitol in Milledgeville. He voted against Georgia's secession at the convention and during the war managed to evade conscription by the Confederate Army. By spring 1864 Fain was regularly traveling north into Tennessee with orders to recruit troops from North Georgia for the Union cause.

By April 6, 1864, things had gotten a little too hot for Fain in Morganton, and it was time to "get out of Dodge." He was in the process of moving his family by wagon north to Cleveland, Tennessee, where he was to accept a commission as Colonel in the Union Army. Soon after crossing the Ocoee River on a ferry near Copperhill, Tennessee, Fain and his wife, Margaret S. McLelland Fain, were staying at the home of a man named Alexander Officer near Ducktown, Tennessee.[1]

Fain was surprised and captured by Captain Rodgers and his men. His wife watched in horror as her husband was taken south down the road toward Ellijay, Georgia, along with Henry Robinson, one of Fain's recruits. She secretly trailed behind the group. Three miles south of where he was captured, near Edward's Ferry along the Tennessee-Georgia state line, a shot rang out. Fain fell in the middle of the road, killed execution-style with a bullet to the back of his head. Margaret witnessed her husband's killing. Robinson was tied to a tree further down the road and was shot fifteen to twenty times.

TWENTY-SEVEN-YEAR-OLD MARY CATHERINE Morris Slate was a seamstress at the hotel in Morganton, Georgia, when Captain Rodgers and his company of soldiers rode up, "stopping for refreshments." She recounted in a deposition, given twenty-one years later in April 1885 for Margaret Fain's Widow's Pension, that she was present at the hotel when an excited Rodgers proudly told her that he and his men had recently killed none other than William Clayton Fain.

We know what happened to Fain through eyewitness accounts found in the Widow's Pension Application, which includes the sworn affidavits of several other witnesses in addition to Mary Slate's recollection of the events. Widow's Pension Applications are full of first-person sworn testimonies; though they were clearly created to help in securing the applicant's pension request, they provide some of the few existing written records that help corroborate a story around events such as this one.

THE MORE I FOUND OUT ABOUT CAPTAIN RODGERS, the commander of Company D, the more I wanted to learn about him. As is often the case in searching for lesser-known historical figures, my quest led me down many

---

[1] Margaret Fain, Widow's Pension Application, 1885.

interesting trails and, eventually, to an unknown private who just happened to also become a local newspaper correspondent following the war.

I was trying to put together a timeline for the 4th Georgia Cavalry (Avery). "Avery" stood for Colonel Isaac Wheeler Avery and appears with the name of his regiment so as not to confuse them with another 4th Georgia Cavalry regiment commanded by Colonel Duncan Lamont Clinch, Jr.

That's right. There were actually two 4th Georgia Volunteer Cavalry regiments—how confusing! But wait, there's more! The 4th Georgia Cavalry (Avery) became the 12th Georgia Cavalry in January 1865. I guess the Confederate Army realized that two regiments with the same name wasn't a great idea; perhaps there were too many correspondences coming back with "return to sender" stamps. But all the men of this regiment, after the war was finally over, always referred to themselves as the 4th Georgia Cavalry. There are multiple mentions from around 1885 through the 1930s of a reunion of the brothers-in-arms from Avery's 4th Georgia Cavalry. In this book the 4th Georgia Cavalry always refer to Colonel Avery's 4th Georgia Cavalry Regiment except in a couple of places where Colonel Clinch is mentioned.

One afternoon I stumbled across a passing mention in a post found in a Civil War–themed, old-style computer bulletin board about a newspaper called the *Walker County Messenger*, a northwest Georgia weekly founded in 1878 and still published to this day. The post said one of their local correspondents named Arba F. Shaw had written a series of articles sometime around 1901 on his memories as a Private in Company F of the 4th Georgia Cavalry.

I quickly located an online library of the *Walker County Messenger*, and as I browsed through each issue I began to realize this was a remarkable cache of history. Fifty-five articles were published between December 1901 and February 1903 and eventually titled "My Experiences In the War of the 60's Briefly Told" written by the fifty-four-year-old hand of former Private Arba F. Shaw, the Rebel Correspondent.

Twenty years before Arba Shaw put pen to paper, another soldier's account of his experiences in the Civil War was written by Samuel Rush Watkins of the 1st Tennessee Infantry Regiment (1839-1901). *The Columbian Herald* newspaper in Columbia, Tennessee, serialized Watkins' writings from 1881 to 1882. The column proved so popular that it was published as a critically acclaimed book in 1882 titled *Co. Aytch: Maury Grays First Tennessee Regiment or A Side Show of the Big Show*. Arba Shaw's writings were similar, written between December 1901 and February 1902, then serialized into the *Walker County Messenger*. Whereas Watkins' writing style had a Mark Twain quality to it, Arba Shaw's style is like telling the news from "Lake Wobegon"—except it really happened.

I managed to get digital PDF copies of most of the articles and, using optical character recognition (OCR) software, created rudimentary transcriptions of each article. I had to carefully proof the transcription against each article, correcting the errors the software had created—which were many. I also needed to hunt down a couple of missing articles, which included the critical second to the last one in which Arba comes home after the war is over.

Thankfully, the *Walker County Messenger* was the official "legal organ" of the court system, publishing the public notices of the sheriff, clerk of courts, and judges. Because of this, the county was required to maintain these records going back before 1900 and had leatherbound copies of each year from the beginning of the twentieth century. In early 2020, I was finally able to access these copies and transcribe the missing articles. Surprisingly, because of courthouse security, this was not a simple thing to do in Walker County; it actually required the permission of the Probate Court Judge, for which I am thankful to have received.

Arba F. Shaw produced more than 40,000 words in writing his memories of the war. Up until just a few years ago, you could only access them on microfilm, viewing dim projections in the couple of libraries that maintained copies. With more and more historical newspapers becoming accessible online, the *Walker County Messenger* can now be found in virtual libraries.

As I transcribed the articles, I realized how nice it was to read them all together instead of hunting from newspaper to newspaper. The result is this book. I have made every effort to keep Arba F. Shaw's articles exactly as they were published. The grammatical errors were intentionally kept.

It is also clearly obvious that overt racism was the accepted norm of the time, embraced by almost all white people living in the South. The stories of enslaved individuals presented by Arba, almost casually spoken of as members of another species, are vile, shocking, and cringe-worthy today. He wrote his story over thirty-five years after the events occurred, although the language and culture did not change in the three-and-a-half decades from the time of the events to the time of Arba's writing. Because of this, the writing shows how perfectly acceptable this mindset was in the Jim Crow South of 1901, when a racial system of oppression had become fully entrenched into the landscape.

Arba recounts the lives led by enslaved fellow human beings who had just been granted Emancipation. With the end of the Civil War, these former slaves entered a world that gave them a spark of hope with the beginning of Reconstruction. It was quickly replaced by an oppression that, in many cases, was violently delivered by the very Confederate veterans Arba himself was a part of when he crafted his story.

The vernacular of the time, written in the deep South thirty-six years after the end of the war, is insightful. I have purposely kept the language so the prejudices are present for all to see with one exception—the one and only time through all of his writings when he used a word that I would not allow in this book. The incorrect spellings of names and places were also left as published. I make note in my follow-up recap after each article the corrected spellings where necessary.

So why write a book based on the 120-year-old writings of a Confederate private in a time when this country often feels more racially divided than ever? Because factual history, regardless of the point of view, is important. As I continued my research, it didn't take me long to realize what a truly remarkable memory Arba F. Shaw had in terms of the names, places, and events he had personally experienced so many years before. He produced a historical gem almost 120 years ago that led to my scavenger hunt to find the backstories of the places he visited and the people he mentions.

There are many instances where, in researching the genealogy of a soldier mentioned by Arba, I came across the soldier's descendants, who had nothing more than a question mark about what had happened to their ancestor. Arba was there, an eyewitness to what happened to his fellow soldiers.

His in-depth accounts also help fill in some of the story of the 4th Georgia Cavalry: where they went, who they fought, what battles were won or lost, who was wounded, and who didn't come home. These accounts have great historical value in understanding a regiment for which scant official records exist.

In the 150-plus years since Arba became a lowly private, tens of thousands have followed as young adults who enlisted into the conflict their country found itself engaged in at that particular moment—all of them driven by honor and duty. This is not a book arguing the reasons why Civil War came to be or why today we still haven't quite finished the argument.

This book came about to finish the historical story of the life of a barely eighteen-year-old boy living, fighting, surviving, and, ultimately, finding himself on the losing side in America's Civil War—and then writing about it in his own words.

Rebel Correspondent

Arba Shaw joined the Confederate Army when he was eighteen years and seven days old. He served as a Rebel private for two years, seven months, and seven days until the war ended. He emerged as a changed person, returning to the peaceful farm life he had lived before all the madness.

He wasn't just a farmer; he was also a writer. Thirty-six years later he decided to tell the world about his experiences.

Steve Procko
Blue Ridge, Georgia

CHAPTER ONE
Rebel Correspondent

Walker County Messenger
December 5, 1901
Cooper Heights

Last Saturday morning my right arm was paralyzed again and I will try to write with my left hand so you can read this—it being my first effort. The cause is the result of a wound the Yank officer gave me at Cambellsville, Tenn., on Sept. 5, 1864. He had on a red sash. He shot me twice and killed my horse and I shot him or at least my aim was on him and he was shot as could be easily seen, so close were we.

Last Wednesday at Dr. Hise's Homer Woods and Miss Electa Tucker were made one by Squire John Rogers. Mr. Woods is the son of Rob Woods who has been dead since the 80's and the bride is the charming and youngest daughter of Elder T. C. Tucker, who was so noted in the pulpit in his last years. We hope their journey through life will be strewn with nice laurels that will ever be bright.

We are well pleased with our blacksmith. If he is a swan he is a good one. He has not got his house yet so he can move his wife in.

A. F. Shaw

PUBLISHED IN 1901 IN A LOCAL NEWSPAPER, the *Walker County Messenger*, this small mention of an incident that occurred during the Civil War eventually became a series of fifty-plus articles published over the course of the next fifteen months. It is just one paragraph by a fifty-seven-year-old farmer, writer, and former Rebel private of Company F of the 4th Georgia Cavalry Confederate States Army (CSA).

Imagine the shock of being fired upon and hit twice, his horse shot out from him at close range. Did he hit the Yankee wearing the red sash?

The microsecond snapshot image permanently etched in his brain tells him he did—"So close were we." Oh, and by the way, Miss Electa Tucker and Homer Woods got hitched by 'Squire John Rogers—a new bride and groom beginning their new journey strewn with laurels. Along with the report of an unnamed swan-like blacksmith: Has wife, needs a home.

The first three sentences set

Arba's Mother
Harriet Hardin Shaw
1824-1893

Arba's Grandfather
Amos Shaw
1789-1859

the stage for the remarkable tale yet to come. It's the personal eyewitness account of the Civil War by a former Rebel private more than thirty-five years after it happened. The beginning of the tale is told by the Rebel Correspondent of Cooper Heights, Mr. A. F. Shaw.

KIRJATH ARBA F. SHAW (A. F. Shaw) was born on September 20, 1844, in Walker County, Georgia, to the Reverend William F. Shaw, a primitive Baptist church minister and farmer, and his wife, Harriet Hardin Shaw, a hard-working farmer's wife. The couple had moved to Walker County in 1841, and lived in McLemore's

Cove.² Arba's grandfather Amos Shaw was one of the original settlers arriving in 1838 to the newly formed county. Walker County was formed in 1833, then split from Murray County, which was created in 1832 from Cherokee lands.³ Amos Shaw had twelve brothers and sisters. Julius Clarence Shaw (1894-1958) was descended from one of the brothers, William Wilson Shaw (1792-1870). Julius became the owner of a small textile dye company,⁴ which grew to become Shaw Industries—the world's largest carpet manufacturer.

Arba was the oldest of eleven children and one of the eight children who would survive into adulthood. He recounted the story of his birth in an article published in 1903.

Walker County Messenger
September 25, 1903
Mr. Shaw's Birthday—He Grows Reminiscent

On the 20th I was 59. I first saw daylight at Shaw, Ga., in a log cabin that is standing yet in a fresh field on Uncle Mercer's place. In it I spent, the first three months of my life, then we moved to the place that is yet sacred to us as our old parental home where our brother, J. F. Shaw, lives. In those days it was common to make log houses and puncheon floors because of the absence of saw mills in this country. The puncheons were made of poplar or pine by splitting off slabs as wide as the log would make and about three inches thick, then fastened up on edge in a notch with a glut, then one face hewed straight for the face of the floor.

---

[2] Shaw family genealogy. Genealogy records were sourced through Ancestry.com, which uses National Archives digitized records and State and County Records that include U. S. Census Records 1830-1940, State and County Marriage Records, Birth and Death Records, Cemetery Records, and Property Records. Hereafter when referencing family genealogies for individuals in this book, the source will be designated as family genealogy.

[3] James Alfred Sartain, *History of Walker County, Georgia*, (The A. J. Showalter Company, Dalton, Ga., 1932), 42.

[4] Shaw family genealogy.

Then they were fitted with an axe on the few strong sleepers, say one at each end and one in the middle with a door in one side and a hole in the other for a window, the cracks lined with boards or chinked and daubed and sometimes both and no loft. And it was quite common to make a stick and dirt chimney, but father being somewhat inclined to be a stone cutter, he cut stone and built a chimney. Mother said we moved into the new house when only the front tier of the floor was fitted and two puncheons layed on the back sleepers for the bedstead to stand on. One night she and I, their first born little babe, only three months old, were there alone, father being at his father's that night after a load of corn of which he could haul two loads a day by staying at his father's every other night. On that lonely night she woke up and her pillow had fallen to the ground among a bed of Amos Ryan's hogs that had come there from a mile away to sleep under the house. She got down among the hogs and felt around in the dark and got the pillow.

When the moving was done then to the new ground to clear for crop. The first clearing that had been made on the place was for the crop of 1845 and everything had to come from the stump and when I could first remember at 30 months old he had about 30 acres cleared and an orchard planted. Father had white swelling[5] at that time so he was lame and the first thing I remember him doing was making splits and baskets of the splits and when he got so he could he cut a mulberry tree and split two cuts to make posts for an ash hopper. More anon.

Arba F. Shaw

"KIRJATH ARBA" WAS DEFINITELY AN unusual name for a young boy of the mid-nineteenth century in rural northwest

---

[5] "White Swelling" was a nineteenth century term for tuberculosis of the bone. Christian Fenger, M.D., Tuberculosis of Bones & Joints. Reprinted from the *Journal of the American Medical Association*, October 26, 1889.

Georgia. But you only need to look to his father's occupation as a preacher for a clue.

Arba was a man mentioned in the Old Testament's book of Joshua. He is called the "greatest man among the Anakites." The Bible also states the city of Hebron was in ancient times known to be called "Kirjath-arba." Clearly, just going by the name of "Arba" or "Arby" was simpler.

Arba was a boy during the years leading up to the Civil War. His family were subsistence farmers, growing what they needed and selling what little surplus they had at market. Arba was just sixteen years old at the start of the Civil War in 1861. Many of his cousins joined the fighting early on.

Arba joined as soon as he was eighteen—eighteen years and seven days to be exact. His experiences in the war that he later wrote about spanned from 1862 until the war's end in 1865.

After the Civil War, Arba went home to the place where he was born: in the valley between Pigeon Mountain and Lookout Mountain known as McLemore Cove to the northwest of the Walker County seat of LaFayette, Georgia. His father, the preacher-farmer, his mother, and several of his siblings lived right next door.

McLemore Cove is named after John McLemore,[6] an indigenous Cherokee chief who was the son of a white trader and Cherokee mother. The town's name, "LaFayette," is not pronounced like the name of the famous French Revolutionary War General, but rather "La-FAY-it."

Serendipitously, Arba writes about crossing paths and glancing upon both of his future wives at different times during his accounts of the Civil War.

Arba married his first wife, Amanda M. Bradley, of Ringgold, Georgia, in 1867. She bore him four daughters: Lula Jane, Ida, Sarah Elizabeth, and Hattie. Just over a month after the birth of Hattie on January 2, 1878, Amanda died, perhaps from the lingering effects of childbirth, leaving

---

[6] Sartain, *History of Walker County, Georgia*, 279.

Arba with four young children. Later that same year he married his second wife, Rebecca Frances Johnson, the daughter of the Reverend Joshua Park Johnson II, a primitive Baptist minister living in Dirt Town, a small community in Chatooga County, Georgia, near Little Sand Mountain.[7] His youngest daughter, Hattie Shaw, died at nineteen months old on July 12, 1879, a year and a half after her mother's passing.

In an 1890 Walker County tax digest, Shaw is shown as farming a 94-acre parcel of land, part of parcel numbers 130 and 131.[8] These parcel numbers were from the original plating of 160-acre land parcels from the sixth Georgia land lottery of 1832.

At the beginning of the nineteenth century, the northwest corner of Georgia was the land of the indigenous peoples, mainly composed of the Creek and Cherokee. Their lands were sold out from underneath them in multiple lotteries between 1805 and 1833, and they were sent packing westward on the Trail of Tears. Many northern Georgia counties continued to use the plat numbers from these lotteries in their county land records.

In addition to farming, Arba, using the byline A. F. Shaw, was the "extremely local" correspondent for the *Walker County Messenger* from 1881 until his death in 1909. Shaw reported the news from his small crossroads community located just south of Chattanooga, Tennessee.

The *Walker County Messenger*, a newspaper first published in 1877 in LaFayette, Georgia, was purchased in January 1881 by Nathan Campbell Napier (1834-1902) from the original founder, Augustus McHan (1834-1901).[9] During the Civil War, McHan was captain of Company C, the 39th Georgia Infantry CSA, and was captured in Vicksburg on July 4, 1863. He later became a Baptist minister and founded the *Walker County Messenger*. Napier served as captain of

---

[7] Shaw family genealogy.
[8] Walker County Property Tax Digest – 1890; District 881 Pond Springs Post Office.
[9] Digital Library of Georgia, Georgia Historic Newspapers.

Company K of the 6th Georgia Cavalry CSA and was injured on October 15, 1862, losing his right eye in the Battle of Big Hill in Kentucky.[10]

Published every Thursday under the tutelage of N.C. Napier, the *Walker County Messenger* became an extremely well-edited weekly newspaper that employed an impressive network of local correspondents. It was also the legal newspaper for Walker County, which is probably why the records from the late nineteenth century survive today. By 1907 its masthead boasted 2,300 copies weekly. In the late nineteenth century, the job of being a newspaper "correspondent" for Napier's newspaper in northwest Georgia meant that you would "correspond" to the editor by writing a weekly letter detailing the goings-on in your community. Three weeks after Napier took control of the paper, Arba Shaw's first article appears, published on January 20, 1881.

Walker County Messenger
January 20, 1881
Frick's Gap

There is some revival in our vicinity now in spite of the bad weather. Mr. E. W. Phillips, of Catoosa, sets up a writing and singing school this morning at New Prospect. Hope for good success to him and his patrons. Some oppose singing but that is their own business, but listen and find out what you hear from their children when they sing.

Nothing is being done toward a crop here yet. Great many are not done gathering last year's crop of cotton yet. Farmers are aiming to increase size of cotton crops this year.

Arba F. Shaw

SHAW LIVED IN A COMMUNITY known then as Frick's Gap. In the early 1890s, the name of the area was changed to Cooper's Heights. The name change was reported by A. F.

---

[10] N. C. Napier, Confederate Pension Application, February 11, 1887.

Shaw on August 27, 1891. It was later shortened to Cooper Heights.

Located about twelve and half miles from LaFayette, Georgia, where the newspaper was published, Shaw would go to the Frick's Gap/Cooper Heights post office and mail his correspondence letter approximately every week. It would arrive on the desk of the editor a day or two later, in time for the newspaper's publishing deadline. The *Walker County Messenger* was published on Thursdays until 1903 when it switched to Friday for a few months, then back to Thursday before finally settling on Friday as its publication day. In those days people didn't travel from the rural parts of the county to town at the drop of the hat. Transportation was by horse, or horse and wagon, and the weekly newspapers of the era featured many advertisements of stylish buggies for sale by folks who, undoubtably, are the ancestors of today's car dealers.

Each area correspondent's letters, turned into weekly articles, reported on all of the local items of interest, the minutia of day-to-day life, the births, the deaths, the marriages, life on the farm, and the modern progress of the era that was bringing some big changes to their little communities. The sad reality of life and death hits home as Shaw writes about his daughter Ida and his first wife, Amanda M. Bradley, in 1891.

Walker County Messenger
August 20, 1891
Frick's Gap

Editor Messenger and friends: It is with a sad heart that I record the death of Ida, my second daughter. She was born Oct. 11, 1871 and died Aug. 7, 1891, and was buried in the family graveyard Aug 9. She was down sixteen days, first with typhoid fever, and was doing well when pneumonia set in, and in one week done its deadly work, in spite of all earthly aid.

She was in the likeness of her mother, who has been

dead since Jan. 2, 1878, and for that reason I felt great anxiety in her being spared to me, to keep her form, features, movements and many other turns that she possessed like her mother who too, was the most lovely of all objects of this earth, and which I cherish yet with an increasing love. Ida was a precious jewel to the family, a model for all her associates and to all appearance the center of affection of all that was acquainted with her, and whatever task she found to perform she went at it as if she was happy at the thought of doing good and at the same time everything was done in an expressed manner. It is said she had no enemys on this earth and was never seen to appear unhappy.

A. F. Shaw

As 1901 drew to a close, a week after Arba's first mention of being injured by the Yankee soldier wearing the red sash, the editor of the *Walker County Messenger* must have encouraged him to write his personal account as a Confederate private in Company F of the 4th Georgia Cavalry. It account was written over a period of eleven weeks until February 25, 1902. It was broken down into the fifty-plus articles published through February 12, 1903.

Walker County Messenger
December 12, 1901
Cooper Heights

T. B. Pool is called in again from business on account of a lame back. His looks show that he is a sufferer. His brother in law, Jet Myers is staying with him for a time.

Last week a horse kicked W. A. Broom on one of his legs and he has been unable to walk any since.

Little George, a son of Robert Baker, is bad off again, but we do not understand it to be a repetition of his last falls sickness.

REBEL CORRESPONDENT

Last Saturday I had the pleasure of seeing three of my comrades in arms together. They were Messrs, B. L. Chastain, J. M. Henry and Judge H. P. Lumpkin and I only know of two more in this century—W. M. Brock and Jim Hamilton.

Will say that a little life and notion has come to my maimed arm but it is withered so it has lost its power.

Hamp McGuffey killed the mammoth hawk that had been eating so many hens. Its length from tips of wings was 4 feet and 4 inches. Hamp feels like he has gained the victory.

I have been requested to write some war reminiscences, but as I will have to write from a shattered memory I feel like it would be a poor production.

In the first place I will say that it was a hard task for me to leave a pleasant home where peace and abundant comfort were takin in exchange a miserable out door life where I was liable to be killed any day, but it was a task that for the sake of honor I could not shirk from and now l am glad I performed it and feel like I helped to make one of the bravest armies that ever went to arms and will say that the efficient Editor of the Walker County Messenger was one of as, a captain.

After the war had been going on for a time and all the men that would volunteer without restraint had gone in, the Confederate Government sent out officers to enroll all men and boys aged from 18 to 45 and later from 16 to 60. Then it would call all men to arms from 18 to a named age up and later kept calling until the calls covered all the space from 16 to 60. What lamentation when husbands were called from their dear wives and little ones at home, in thousands of instances parted to meet at the fireside no more, and the young man thinking of his aspirations that were blasted and so many that went away to come no more and many that did return were so injured that their elastic steps was gone and they were maimed for life, some losing an arm, a leg, an eye, or both or many other things.

A. F. Shaw

IN THE DECEMBER 12, 1901, article, Arba "leaves a

pleasant home." The first steps are taken out of the family's farmstead, with a glance back at a mother watching from the door, as he mounts his horse and begins the journey to Dalton, Georgia. A hard task indeed, "for the sake of honor." Recollections of the horrors he witnessed flood back in the last paragraph: "parted to meet at the fireside no more" and "so many that went away to come no more." Arba would witness a lot of "no mores." But he begins with a reunion, getting together with three of the five remaining fellow comrades in arms from the Civil War in times past. They had all made it to the twentieth century; they are the few who at that singular moment in time still remained.

Seventy-five-year-old Benjamin Lafayette Chastain (1825-1906), who Arba referred to as his uncle, was the Sergeant in Company F of the 4th Georgia Cavalry. He fathered nine children and returned to farming in Walker County after the war. The Chastain family was a large one and could be found throughout northern Georgia. One of Benjamin LaFayette Chastain's cousins was Elijah Webb Chastain (1813-1874), who served in Congress prior to the Civil War and was one of the two delegates from Fannin County to the Georgia Secession Convention in 1861. Elijah Webb Chastain was a staunch advocate for secession, in contrast to his fellow Fannin County delegate William Clayton Fain (1824-1864), who was one of the few who voted against secession. In a twist of fate, Fain would be killed execution-style on April 6, 1864, near Ducktown, Tennessee, by members of the 4th Georgia Cavalry. It was Company D, commanded by Captain William Jefferson Rodgers, that was on a mission to find deserters and bushwhackers in the mountains along the Georgia-Tennessee border.[11]

Josiah Moore Henry (1826-1903) was a five-foot, nine-and-one-half-inch-tall, blue-eyed, seventy-five-year-old former private in Company F of the 4th Georgia Cavalry who had been taken as a prisoner of war (POW) in 1864.

---

[11] Chastain family genealogy.

After taking the Oath of Allegiance to the United States in Chattanooga, Tennessee, on March 24, 1864, he went on to father thirteen children, nine of whom survived into adulthood.[12]

Hugh P. Lumpkin (1846-1915) was a fifty-five-year-old former First Lieutenant of Company F of the Floyd Legion State Guards. Before the war he attended Gordon Hall, a private school for boys in Lafayette, Georgia. After the war he became a lawyer and was a close neighbor to Arba in Frick's Gap, later moving to Lafayette, Georgia, where he became a prominent judge.[13]

William M. Brock (1838-1909) was a Private in Company F of the 4th Georgia Cavalry but was wounded at Catlett's Gap, Georgia, on September 17, 1863, and then taken as a POW. He took the Oath of Allegiance to the United States on July 14, 1864, and was released to remain north of the Ohio River for the duration of the war. He returned to Rock Springs, Georgia, after the war as a farmer with a wife and a small family.[14]

JIM HAMILTON WAS A PRIVATE in Company F of the 4th Georgia Cavalry who pretty much disappeared after the war until he is mentioned in this article by Arba in 1901.[15]

Many reunions of former soldiers took place in that era. They all celebrated their survival—lives lived—while reflecting on those whose lives were cut short. They must have still felt the stress and anxiety of going to war, along with the shock of miraculously living through those events—even though they were now fading into the past. But Kirjath Arba F. Shaw's memories were still strong because some memories are burned into the mind's eye and cannot be forgotten.

---

[12] Josiah Moore Henry, Compiled Service Records.
[13] Hugh P. Lumpkin family genealogy.
[14] William Brock, Compiled Service Records.
[15] Jim Hamilton, Compiled Service Records.

This photograph was taken at a 1909 reunion in Dalton, Georgia. It was discovered in an old barn in Whitfield County in 2015. The group was part of the United Confederate Veterans Association, and the local chapter was known as Camp Joseph Johnston Number 34. The names of the veterans are lost to time.

Whitfield-Murray County Historical Society

CHAPTER TWO
Enlistment Day

ARBA'S ACCOUNT OF HIS RECOLLECTIONS from the Civil War starts midway through his column dated December 19, 1901, amid the day-to-day events in Cooper Heights. It's as if he needed to pass on the critical news of his community first, since that was his usual weekly responsibility, before he began the monumental task he was probably not too keen on doing. Since he was a writer with twenty years of experience in December 1901, he was likely aware that he had a historical responsibility to put pen to paper and record the events and his experiences from more than thirty-five years earlier. If he didn't do so, the memories would be forever lost. So once the latest news was out of the way, it begins.

Walker County Messenger
December 19, 1901
Cooper Heights

What cold weather on potatoes and eggs, and how nice on pork in salt.
Last week Mrs. Fanny Meyers, of Chattanooga, visited home folks at the Heights.
Cooper Ramsey is taking in Chattanooga after his fall work is done.
Lon Shaw is a skillful logger for William Moreland. He knocked off one day to visit us at the Heights.
Since Jerry Leath moved to the Kell (Meyers) place last March he has produced and payed $567.10, saying nothing about what was used in his house.
I have for sale a young cow.
Dr. J. J. Johnson has been sick ever since the first of October and is confined to his bed all the time now.

Appendicitis is the cause.

On the 27th day of September 1862, it being the 7th day after my 18th birthday, I enlisted in a new company that was being made up for the 4th Ga., Cavalry under colonel I. W. Avery, but was allowed to stay at home a while and help father gather the crop and on a stated day to report at LaFayette. When I got there the order was to report at Dalton and I with E. A. McClure went by way of M. C. Alexander and he went with us. We stayed the first night with John Dunagin then to Dalton and was mustered in by Captain W. K. Moore who, when the regiment was made, was made Quartermaster and J. E. Helvinston promoted to Captain. The first mustering in was in C. D. McCutchen's law office, he being that day elected 2nd Lieutenant of the company. When Captain Moore was administering the oath and it came my turn he said to me: "I don't believe you are old enough." I said I was 18. He said you don't look to be more than 16. I was 5 ft. 4 in. tall and was beardless. He administered the oath to all the applicants, then we elected officers and we were an organized company known as Co., F. 4 Ga Cav. Then we were given a 10 days leave of absense and we went home. While I was at home I sowed the wheat crop and three of us brothers plowed it in. The 10 days being out we went back and we soon went into quarters at Gordon Springs. There we had fun and a plenty to eat and waited for the company to be made full. Some of us would be away at home on permit most of the time. I went once and H. K. Hamilton being a substitute for, I believe, John Conley, of Rock Spring, sent me by there to get the money. It was $1,700 and on my return I took the money to Mr. Hamilton, and when night came I got lost and wandered half of the night before reaching the west foot of Taylor's Ridge where I put up until morning, then went over to the Springs, money and all all right.

A. F. Shaw

BY SEPTEMBER 1862 THE CIVIL WAR had been underway

for seventeen months. A conflict that had expected to be short was well into its second year. Pride of country in the first few months of the war caused a surge in volunteer enlistments, but casualties had taken their toll on both sides. In August of 1861 the new Confederate government called for 400,000 volunteers to serve for one to three years. In April of 1862 the first Confederate conscription law was passed requiring all able-bodied white men between the ages of 18 and 35 years to enlist; it was extended to men 45 years of age on October of 1862.[16]

The United States prior to the Civil War had a total population of around 31 million people. The population in the North was around 22 million, and the population in the South was around 9 million, of which almost 4 million were slaves.[17] During the approximately three-and-a-half years of the war, a combined total of more than 3 million soldiers fought for both sides, with Union forces outnumbering Confederate forces by almost two to one.[18]

THE EVENTS OF SEPTEMBER 27, 1862, would have been an exciting time for eighteen-year-old Arba. His trip to Dalton, Georgia, approximately thirty-five miles from Cooper Heights, may have been his first trip this far away from home. As he mentions, was but 5' 4" tall and looked very young. The average soldier of the time was 26 years old, 5' 8" tall, weighing around 143 pounds.[19] His travel mates were Ezekiel Andrew McClure—who wouldn't turn eighteen years old until October 30 and probably lied about his age when he enlisted—and Melville C. Alexander, who was then twenty-two years old.

---

[16] William L. Shaw, "The Confederate Conscription and Exemption Acts," *The American Journal of Legal History*, 6(4), (October 1962), 368-405.
[17] 1860 United States Census.
[18] American Battlefield Trust – Army populations and statistics.
[19] Ibid.

Colonel Isaac Wheeler Avery, Jr., age 25, commanded the 4th Georgia Cavalry.

Photograph estimated to have been made between
Fall 1862 and Spring 1863.
*Carte De Visite by J. H. Van Stavoren; Nashville, Tennessee
David Wynn Vaughan Collection*

Arba mentions that the three of them stayed a night on the way to Dalton, Georgia, at the home of John Dunagin [*sic*], who was likely John Brice Dunagan (1836-1900), then living near Ringgold in Catoosa County, Georgia.

On the next day, September 27, 1862, they all enlisted in Dalton with the 4th Georgia Cavalry, commanded by Lieutenant Colonel Isaac W. Avery who had a few days earlier been promoted from Captain. Arba and his friends were all sworn in by newly commissioned Captains William Kilpatrick Moore (1830-1895), a Virginia native, and Cicereo Decatur McCutchen (1824-1898)—both local Dalton attorneys until then. McCutchen would later resign his commission on April 17, 1864, when he was elected to the Georgia Senate from the 43rd District. After the war they both became judges in Dalton. Joseph E. Helvenston was born in Effingham County, Georgia, in 1825 and had moved to nearby Whitfield County to marry Keziah Ann Davis in 1852.[20]

Isaac Wheeler Avery, Jr. was born in St. Augustine, Florida, on May 2, 1837. At eighteen years old he was a legislative correspondent in Milledgeville for two of Georgia's largest newspapers. He studied law at Oglethorpe University and was admitted to the bar in 1860, becoming a member of the firm of Lloyd & Owens in Savannah.

At twenty-four years old he entered the service on May 21, 1861, as a Private in the Oglethorpe Light Infantry, which was Company B of the 8th Georgia Infantry in which he fought in the first battle of Manassas.

On January 10, 1862, Avery became a Captain and was given orders to organize Company I of the 23rd Georgia Cavalry Battalion with soldiers raised mainly out of Whitfield County. He called the new company the "Georgia Mountain Dragoons." The officers were Avery as Captain; William L. Cook, 1st Lieutenant; D. Jackson Owens, 2nd

---

[20] William K. Moore, Cicero D. McCutchen, Joseph E. Helvenston, Harrison E. Hamilton; Compiled Service Records.

Lieutenant; and Hughes H. Burke, 3rd Lieutenant. Avery gave a little information on the history of the Dragoons in a newspaper account in 1888.[21]

> *The nucleus of the regiment was a scouting company, called the Georgia Mountain Dragoons, organized November 1, 1861, and offered by (myself as captain, W. L. Cook, 1st lieutenant, D. J. Owen, 2d lieutenant and H. H. Burk, 3rd lieutenant. This independent troop, raised mainly in Whitfield county, had an active service, sharing the campaigns in Kentucky and Tennessee and among other battles taking part in the bloody struggles of Shiloh and Perryville. In August, 1862 the company was increased to a battalion of five companies, known as the Twenty-third Battalion Georgia Cavalry, with Captain Avery promoted to lieutenant colonel, lieutenant Cook to captain of the original company, and four other companies, commanded by Jeff Johnson of Bartow county, G. B. May of Murray county, C. D. McCutchen of Whitfield county - whose company was largely from Walker County - and D. J. Owen.*
>
> *I. W. Avery*
> **North Georgia Citizen**
> ***August 8, 1888***

WHILE HE WAS IN THE PROCESS of manning the "nucleus" of his regiment, Avery published in the *Southern Confederacy*, an Atlanta paper, on January 26, 1862, the following notice:

> *My cavalry company, now in camp at Dalton, Ga., will leave for Bowling Green, Ky., on Saturday, the 1st day Of February, 1862. I can take 115 men and lack a few to fill that number.*
> *My corps will be the solitary body of Georgians among the*

---

[21] *North Georgia Citizen*, "Fourth Georgia Cavalry - Proceedings of the Meeting of the Cavalry on the 17th Instant - Letter from Colonel Avery," August 8, 1888.

thousands of troops in that whole Western department and our chance for distinction will be brilliant and unexceptional. We will be in the division of Major General Hardee - a true son of Georgia, who will favor us, his own State countrymen.

I have complete equipments - Tents, Camp Equipage, Saddles, Bridles, Saddle Bags, etc., for my whole Company. Each member will get a Bounty of $50 begin with; $50 a year for Clothing and $24 per month for wages of men and horse, and I will furnish a fine Uniform.

The South needs every man who can wield a sword; and to those who wish to serve in our time of peril, who thirst for the need due to patriotism, and crave the martial distinction to be won at the post of danger, will find so better chance than in my Corps.

**Apply by letter, or come in person to Dalton, Georgia, ready for service.
I. W. AVERY, Captain M.D.**

AFTER LEAVING DALTON IN FEBRUARY 1862, the Georgia Mountain Dragoons traveled north and then west, eventually ending up near Shiloh, Tennessee, in April 1862. In an article in the *Dalton Citizen* on March 30, 1911, Company I's First Lieutenant Augustus C. Gunz recounted:

Arriving at Nashville, we were ordered to stop and await Gen A. S. Johnston falling back to Nashville. Here we had active service in the fall of Fort Donaldson. Feb. 14, 1862, which caused us to evacuate Nashville. The army went to Corinth, Miss., arriving there about the 1st of March.

On the 6th and 7th days of April, 1862, this company took part in the bloody struggle at the Battle of Shiloh. Gen. Albert Sidney Johnston commanding, lost his life in the battle, Gen. Beauregard taking command. Shortly afterwards his health failing, Gen. Bragg took command of the army.

The evacuation of Corinth, Miss. caused us to fall back to Tupelo, Miss. Here the Kentucky campaign was planned.

From Tupelo we were ordered to report at Chattanooga, Tenn., to Gen Bragg, who, on seeing the condition of the men and horses, ordered the company to North Georgia to recruit up and remount the troop.

Our camp was at Cumberland Shed, in Murray county, Georgia.

The Dalton Citizen
March 30, 1911
A. C. Gunz
First Lieutenant Co. I,
4th Georgia Cavalry,
Army Tenn, C. S. A.

THE GEORGIA MOUNTAIN DRAGOONS were held up in Nashville for the fall of Fort Donelson located about seventy miles to the northwest on the Cumberland River. The battle was a loss for the Confederates with the capture of more than 12,000 men. It was in this battle that General Ulysses S. Grant received the nickname "Unconditional Surrender" Grant. After Fort Donelson, the Confederates, including the Dragoons, retreated south to Corinth, Mississippi.

When the Dragoons fought at the Battle of Shiloh on April 6 and 7, 1862, it was a unit composed of four officers and eighty men. They were directly under the Third Army Corps commanded by Major General Thomas C. Hindman, who was also wounded at Shiloh when an artillery shell struck his horse. Avery's Georgia Mountain Dragoons were part of Brigadier General Sterling A. M. Wood's Third Brigade.[22] Wood was also wounded and dragged by his horse in the battle. General Albert Sidney Johnston, as mentioned by Lieutenant Gunz, died on April 6, 1862, when he was wounded in the right knee. The ball clipped an artery,

---

[22] Joseph T. Derry, A. M., *School History of the United States: Story of the Confederate War, etc., Confederate Military History, a library of Confederate States Military History,* Volume 6, Georgia, 37.

and Johnston bled to death[23] over the course of an hour when no one thought to apply a tourniquet to his wounded leg. It is said that he was carrying a tourniquet in his pocket.[24]

The Georgia Mountain Dragoons penetrated enemy lines on reconnaissance near Corinth, Mississippi, in May of 1862. General Pierre Gustave Toutant-Beauregard (P.G.T. Beauregard) complimented him by special order for valuable scouting, obtaining necessary information at the General's request.

In June 1862 Captain Avery was captured by Union forces[25] during another reconnaissance mission but was soon exchanged and returned to the Dragoons, who then made their way back to Dalton, Georgia. Throughout the second half of 1862, Avery's Dragoons became the 23rd Battalion Georgia Cavalry, and he spent much of his time raising troops. He continuously ran advertisements in the *Southern Confederacy* newspaper with the headline: "Cavalry Recruits Wanted"—with everything furnished but the horses.

One of Avery's original recruits was James E. Burton of Chattooga County, Georgia, who enlisted with his brother Benjamin F. Burton in the Mountain Dragoons in January 1862.[26] When the company expanded into a regiment, James E. Burton had his eighteen-year-old son, John R. Burton, enlist. All three Burtons were in Company I together, but that didn't last very long.

Benjamin F. Burton was captured during the battle of Chickamauga in September 1863. As a POW he was sent to Camp Douglas at Chicago, Illinois, escaped in June 1864,

---

[23] William Preston Johnston, *The Life of Albert Sidney Johnston*, (New York: D. Appleton and Company, 1878).
[24] "Ocean Algae Brings Sea Change in Battle Dressings," *The Washington Post,* (May 7, 2001), Military medical historian Colonel Robert J. T. Joy, *"Johnston had a tourniquet in his pocket, but didn't think it was worthwhile."*
[25] "Capture of Capt. Avery," *Southern Confederacy*, (Atlanta), 2/101 (June 13, 1862), 2.
[26] Burton family genealogy and Compiled Service Records.

and was recaptured two months later and sent to Camp Chase in Columbus, Illinois, where he remained until the end of the war.

James E. Burton was listed as a POW, took his oath of allegiance in Nashville, Tennessee, on January 10, 1864, and then was released. He was likely captured soon after the Battle of Knoxville in November 1863, and then shipped to Nashville with other POWs. Upon his release he would have had no idea where the 4th Georgia Cavalry was so he likely headed south toward home into northwest Georgia. What befell James after this is not too clear, although he is listed in the muster rolls of November 27, 1864, as wounded. Another unsubstantiated account has him possibly being killed by Gatewood's Scouts in September or October 1864 at or near Naomi Crossroads, Walker County, Georgia, for being a deserter. John P. Gatewood was a notorious Rebel guerrilla who patrolled the North Georgia Mountains performing vigilante justice and terrorizing the local populations regardless of their political sympathies.

Private James E. Burton's portrait from the period gives a good representation of the uniform Colonel Avery furnished to enlisted soldiers of the 4th Georgia Cavalry. A single-breasted frock coat of Georgia Cadet gray, with a skirt extending one half of the distance from the top of the hip to the bend of the knee. The buttons were yellow metal, the same shape and devices as used for Officers of Infantry, but five-eighths of an inch in diameter for a large size. For the sword belt, a waist belt of plain black leather, not less than one-and-one-half inches nor more than two inches wide, was worn.[27] By October 1862 the 23rd Battalion grew to eight companies: Company A under Captain William L. Cook, Company B under Captain Reuben R. Keith, Company C under Captain Isaac W. Avery, Company D under Captain

---

[27] February 15, 1861, Adjutant General's Office, Milledgeville, Georgia, General Order No. 4, Uniform and Dress of the Army of Georgia.

Rebel Correspondent

James E. Burton was a forty-one-year-old farmer from Chattooga County when he enlisted in Company I of the Georgia Mountain Dragoons along with his brother Benjamin in January 1862.

He is pictured here in what would have been a standard issue Georgia Cavalry Private's uniform.
6th plate tintype, Lamar Williams Collection

Jefferson Johnson, Company E under Captain George B. May, Company F under Captain William Jefferson Rodgers, Company G under Captain Joseph R. Helvenston and Company H under Captain R.E. Kingsley.[28]

From September 17 through September 19, 1862, one of the bloodiest battles in American history raged to a draw at Antietam Creek near Sharpsburg, Maryland. Confederate General Robert E. Lee retreated back into Virginia, and the Union claimed it as a victory. Five days later on September 22, 1862, in Washington, D. C., President Abraham Lincoln issued an executive order warning that he would emancipate all of the slaves in any state that did not end the rebellion against the Union by January 1, 1863.

Also on September 22, 1862, just five days before Arba would enlist, Avery was promoted to the rank of Lieutenant Colonel. By the beginning of 1863 a total of eleven companies had been formed from the original corps of the 23rd Battalion. The original Dragoons Company I became Company I.[29] All the additional men who had been recruited became the 4th Georgia Cavalry. Gordon Springs, where the 4th Georgia Cavalry was initially camped, was located about eight miles west of Dalton nestled in Taylor's Ridge.

H. K. Hamilton was actually Harrison E. Hamilton, also of Company F, and served as a "substitute soldier" for John Fletcher Conley (1827-1917). Conley was a prominent, respected Walker County citizen who lived in the same farmhouse for eighty years. Hamilton left Company F, listed as sick at Resaca, Georgia, on September 1, 1863, and was recorded as absent without official leave (AWOL) on April 19, 1864.[30]

The practice of hiring a substitute to take one's place

---

[28] Georgia 4th/12th Cavalry, Compiled Service Records.
[29] Colonel Isaac W. Avery, the 4th Georgia Cavalry, and 12th Georgia Cavalry; Compiled Service Records.
[30] Harrison E. Hamilton, Compiled Service Records.

was allowed in the early part of the Civil War by the Confederacy. The Confederate conscription law allowed a draftee to hire someone who was exempt from service due to their profession or trade or to hire a foreign national. The practice of hiring a mercenary replacement had been around since the American Revolution.

Over time, hiring someone to take your place in the ranks became resented because the price was more than the average soldier could afford, causing some to claim: "This is a rich man's war and a poor man's fight."[31] In John Fletcher Conley's case, in addition to the $1,700 he paid to Harrison E. Hamilton, he would have also likely paid a fee to the Confederate government for the right to provide Hamilton to them in his place.

By December 1863 the Confederate Congress did away with the law allowing substitutes. In fact, men who had hired substitutes early in the conflict became once again subject to conscription. Several cases against this policy change were argued in Confederate State Supreme Courts; the final ruling upheld the Confederate government change to prevent the use of substitute soldiers.[32]

Researching the history of the 4th Georgia Cavalry can be confusing because there were actually two separate regiments under that same name: one regiment was raised in South Georgia under the command of Colonel Duncan L. Clinch, Jr. and the other regiment was formed in North Georgia under the command of then Lieutenant Colonel Isaac W. Avery, Jr. To additionally confuse matters, in January 1865, Avery's 4th Georgia Cavalry was renamed the 12th Georgia Cavalry. For veterans of Avery's unit such as Arba F. Shaw and his band of brothers, it would forever be known to them as the 4th Georgia Cavalry. For

---

[31] Congressman Scott Ferris; Oklahoma 6th District, *U. S. House Congressional Record*, (September 2, 1918).
[32] Margaret Wood, *Civil War Conscription Laws*, Library of Congress, (November 15, 2012).

historians, it is referred to as the "4th Georgia Cavalry (Avery's)". When researching the records today, all of Avery's unit is found listed under the 12th Cavalry.

Arba's article dated December 19, 1901, ends as he is mustered into Company F, beginning his Civil War journey. But after reviewing the first half of the column, the reader is left wondering if he sold his young cow, and if he received a fair price.

CHAPTER THREE
Going to War

COVERING THE PERIOD FROM January 1, 1863 through April 1, 1863, these five articles tell the story of Arba Shaw's first taste of life in the army. This would have been a very exciting time for a young soldier traveling from home and seeing new sites—perhaps the longest trip away from Walker County of his entire life.

January 9, 1902
"GOING INTO WAR.
Mr. Shaw Writes of Some of His Experiences"[33]

We left Gordon Springs, as I remember, Jan 1st 1863, but the day before I was one of a detail to go to Dalton with Tom Wilson, Co. F's. wagoner, to get rations for our journey, and that night by permit I stayed with a cousin, A. Hamilton, and when I got to the Springs the company had been ordered to Fayetteville, Tenn., and I got on their tracks and went on.

The first one of the company I overtook was J. M. Henry

---

[33] In the first two articles published on December 12, 1901, and December 19, 1901, the beginning of Arba's account was included at the end of his regular weekly article reporting on events in Cooper Heights. At the beginning of 1902 his account of his war experiences became its own individual article. The headlines for the next few articles reflected on where Shaw was in his story: "Going To War, Mr. Shaw Writes Of Some Of His Experiences" and "More Experiences, Of Camp Life During The War Interestingly Told." Finally, by February 6. 1902, they settled on "My Experiences In The War of 1860 Briefly Told." Two weeks later on February 20, 1902, it was "My Experiences In The War of the 60's Briefly Told." On October 2,1902, it was again modified to "My Experiences In The War of the Sixties." Then on January 15,1903, the editors changed again to "My Experiences In The War of the Sixties Briefly Told," the headline that remained until the last article published on February 12, 1903.

swapping horses with one old man Louis Williams on the Alabama Road and my attention was called to the conditions in the trade. Then Mr. Henry and I went on and caught up in a few miles and we began to realize that we were going into war.

The first night we camped at the Thomas Payne Spring, 1 1/2 miles to the southwest of Ringgold. At that spring I saw the girl that became my first wife and laid claim to her, that being the only time I ever saw her until 1867. At the first sight I did not learn her name. I only knew her by her manner of walk.

The second day we went to Chattanooga, Tenn., and camped on the foot of Lookout Mt. in the then a forest, but now a suburb of that city near where the Chattanooga Medicine factory is, where Theadfords Black Draught is prepared. That night it rained hard and all of us got up, made fires and stood by them until day. Now we were getting acquainted with war.

On the 3rd we went to Kelley's ferry crossed on a pontoon bridge and camped below at Pryor's. On the 4th day We went through Jasper, Tenn., and camped at the foot of the famous Cumberland Mt. in Sequachee Valley.

The 5th day we were all day crossing the Cumberland Mt. where we saw large orchards of the largest and tallest apple trees that I ever have seen, and that night we camped at the west foot of the mountain. The 6th day we went through Deckerd and Winchester on to Salem on what was then known as the Fayetteville branch R.R., and camped again. On the 7th we went into quarters at Fayetteville, Tenn.

A. F. Shaw

JANUARY 1, 1863, WAS AN IMPORTANT date in the history of Civil War events. This date is when the Emancipation Proclamation took effect. Lincoln had issued his preliminary notice 100 days earlier on September 22, 1862, which would free enslaved individuals in any state that did not end its rebellion against the Union by January 1, 1863. The day passed, and none of the ten Confederate states paid much attention to Lincoln's warning. So, according to the laws of the North, those who were enslaved in Confederate states were all free.

The Emancipation Proclamation did leave things a bit unclear in the four slave states of Kentucky, Maryland, Delaware, and Missouri, which were not in the Confederacy, as well as in Union occupied parts of the Confederate states. It would take until the ratification of the Thirteenth Amendment to the Constitution in January 1865 to end legal slavery throughout the United States. The South would return to the Union, and the new way of life set forth in the U.S. Constitution at the war's end would be in effect. "Juneteenth"—or June 19, 1865—celebrated this emancipation in what was then faraway Texas, which was thought of as the last part of the country to officially proclaim the freedom of enslaved people. However, it really took until December 1865 when Delaware and Kentucky ratified the Thirteenth Amendment for slavery to be officially abolished.

But for Arba Shaw, there was likely no awareness of the tremendous importance of January 1, 1863, other than it marked the day his fellow soldiers finally left the Gordon Springs encampment where the 4th Georgia Cavalry had gathered. On the day before, New Year's Eve, Arba accompanied Company F's wagoner Private Thomas P. Wilson (1839-1918) over to Dalton to pick up supplies. Wilson, who had joined at the same time as Arba, didn't last long in the company. After becoming sick on September 21, 1863, at Chickamauga, he was dropped from the rolls and declared AWOL in April 1864.[34]

By New Year's Day, Arba had to catch up with his company, racing up the road from the house of A. Hamilton, one of his many cousins, until he came across his friend Josiah Moore Henry trading for a horse with "old man Louis [sic] Williams" whose actual homestead is found marked on

---

[34] Private Thomas P. Wilson, Compiled Service Records.

an 1864 hand-drawn map currently in the Library of Congress.

On his first night he mentions crossing paths with Amanda M. Bradley, who would become his first wife in 1867, at Thomas Payne Spring. He did not know her name but "knew her from the manner of her walk."

The cavalry covers the ninety-six miles on horseback from Gordon Springs, Georgia, to the new headquarters in Fayetteville, Tennessee, in seven days. Although not a tremendously fast pace for men on horseback, they had to maneuver the large regiment composed of men, horses, wagons, and more across the Tennessee River, as well as the Cumberland Mountains for the first time.

January 23, 1902
"MORE EXPERIENCES.
Of Camp Life During The War Interestingly Told"

We went into quarters south of the Elk river and about 3/4 a mile a little east of south of Fayetteville, which was on the north side of the river in Lincoln Co, Tenn. To go to the town from the quarters we had to cross the river on a famous bridge made of cut limestone and banistered with stone. On top of the banisters were broad stones for pedestrians to walk on if they could keep their heads balanced. It was built on arched pillars that were there to stay through the storms and high waters.

When we got there several companies had beat us there and were in their new tents and tents were ready for all of us to put up as we needed them. Tents up we were ready to respond to the requirements of our superiors in office and we were detailed to camp guard, picket drill, forage and soon we had not been there long until more of the boys came in and joined us and two I call to mind were Uncle Ben Chastain and J. D. Fricks.

We had not been there many days when there came one of those rainy days. We all made the best we could of it and in the evening it was my turn to get wood for the night at

REBEL CORRESPONDENT

which I got wet as a rag, and about sun down I was detailed with a few others to report to Col. Avery's headquarters in Fayetteville.

When there he told the Lieutenant in charge to take us seven miles north west to a certain brick church and picket and scout that section. As we started we met a blizzard and the rain turned to snow about 3 or 4 inches deep and when we got there I made an effort to dismount and was so be numbed I fell to the snow. My clothing being wet they were frozen hard through to my body.

We went first to a stiff old man, and stiff he was, who had plenty of the comforts of life and lots of darkies and asked him to let us stay around his fires that night. He said, "No you can't stay," and we had not learned A then or we would have stayed any how. When we found be would not consent we did not know what to do. He told us we could stay in the brick church where there was a stove. Then we wanted an ax to cut wood and he would not let us have any but an old beater as dull as a stone hammer and when we got to the church it was in a grove of large beech trees and there was no chance for wood only to get it oft of an 18 inch beech log about 16 feet long as hard as beech ever gets with that old beater by only the light of the snow.

A. F. Shaw

THE OLD STONE BRIDGE IN FAYETTEVILLE, Tennessee, was a 450' long stone arch bridge over the Elk River. The bridge would survive for more than 100 years after Arba visited it. It was finally destroyed in a flood in 1969, although parts of the ruins still remain.

According to the records of the 4th Georgia Cavalry at its start, it comprised eleven companies (A through L with no company J). A POW named Captain John D. Ashton is listed as a member of Company M. However, Ashton was captured in Summerville, Georgia, on September 10, 1863, and was paroled after the war on May 17, 1865, in Albany, Georgia. So this listing is likely an error in the records as there are no other men listed as part of a Company M.

THE 4TH GEORGIA CAVALRY MADE it to a camp based south of Fayetteville, Tennessee, and the men trained there for the first time. The first few months were spent in training to be a soldier—boot camp for the 4th Georgia Cavalry. Day-to-day life would have included picketing, guard duty, and foraging.

Picketing is the process in which a soldier, or a small unit of soldiers, moves on a line forward of a position to provide warning of an enemy advance. Guard duty was the serious business of maintaining control of the camp boundaries. Foraging was equally serious as the soldier needed to provide food for his horse.

A group of soldiers would go on foraging detail, specifically to find enough food for the company's horses and, often when rations were low, for meals for the men themselves. To accomplish this, soldiers went to the nearby farms and seized whatever they needed for their company. If they needed horses, they sometimes had foraging documents drawn up to show to the unfortunate farmer to make their seizing of his assets an officially government sanctioned event. To the subsistence farmer of the day, what was being taken were the crops, livestock, and food stocks they needed for themselves to survive.

As the Civil War progressed, hunger became a part of life for citizens with farms in the middle of it all.

THE 4TH GEORGIA CAVALRY
(Later renamed the 12th Georgia Cavalry - January 1865)

Colonel Isaac W. Avery (1837-1897)
Lieutenant Colonel William L. Cook (1823-1907)
Major D. Jackson Owen (1830-?)
Major Augustus R. Stewart (1838-1909)
Lieutenant Benjamin H. Newton - ASJ (Adjutant)
Captain William K. Moore - AQM
Captain Joseph Stones - ACS
Major James B. Edelen - Surgeon (1829-?)
Jasper N. Smith - Assistant Surgeon (1830-?)

Company A
Captain Reuben R. Keith (1822-1864)

Company B
Captain George B. May

Company C
Captain Jefferson Johnson (1826-?) *Company I*
Captain Hugh Houston Burke (1825-1879)

Company D
Captain William Jefferson Rogers (1820-?)

Company E
Captain Olin Wellborn

Company F
Captain Joseph E. Helvenston (1825-1863)
Captain Felix G. Horne (1836-1893)

Company G
Captain Roswell Erasmus Kingsley (1837-1876)
Captain William R. Logan (1832-1876)

Company H
Captain James H. Graham (1829-?)

Company I
Captain Hugh Houston Burke (1825-1879)

Company K
Captain A. C. Bradshaw
Captain Peter W. Stewart

Company L
Captain Leonard B. Anderson (1839-?)
Captain James C. N. Foote (1820-?)

Steve Procko

February 6, 1902
MY EXPERIENCES
In the War of 1860 Briefly Told.

Some of the boys kindled a fire in the stove, and some beat enough off of the beech log to make a good fire and down we went to sleep with nothing to eat. I was the only wet one and soon got too cold and did not sleep any that night so I got up. The wood was burned down and I went out to beat on the beech log some more. I would get so cold I would take in the little handful I had beat off and run in and throw it in the stove and in a few minutes it would burn down and then to the old beater and log again the rest of the night.

The next morning we moved out to an old-time school house, much wiser than we were the night before, with a decision in our minds that by angling long sticks of wood and pushing them up they would do to burn in that old time, broad fire place and the stiff old man could keep his good axes and his beater too. The snow was frozen hard and lay several days. We made good fires and the house was ample roomy for us. We scouted the country and found plenty of good peasants that would feed us and our horses too. Don't remember how long we were there or who all was in the crew, but H. Beneyfield, of Chattanooga, and a Mr. Kent were there. Kent was bad sick part of the time. He was a feeble man at best and from that exposure I took pneumonia from the severe cold that it caused.

We reported back to quarters and I was feeling awful tough and one night I was on camp guard and my fever was so high that it seemed like I could not live if I did not get some water to drink. I went twice to a nearby pond, broke the ice but the water was so cold that what little I could drink did not quench that awful thirst. I worried through the night and next morning reported sick and was hauled to the hospital in Fayetteville and the fever changed to typhoid. Then I had a job that lasted till cool weather the next fall.

In the hospital there was lots of sickness. Father came

to see me when I was sick and when I got better an old retired Dr. McKinney, who lived across the street from the hospital, invited two of us boys to his house every night to eat pot-liquor from turnip greens with cornbread crumbled in. We thought it was the best stuff we ever eat. I wish I could remember the other boy's name. The Drs' cook was one of the good old time aunties and her husband belonged to a farmer five miles away and when he came in one Wednesday night we two boys were at supper. He said, "What are these two men in here for?" O, day's sick a eatin' dey supper. He said, "Good God amity! I say sick a eatin' dey supper."

The hospital fare was simply the yellowest cornbread I ever saw and beef, and Pinkney White was our cook. He did the best he could, but he, like all cooks, could not cook such as he had to make it good to sick men. He lived and died in east Armurchie valley. Drs'. Smith and Saxton were our physicians at Fayetteville.

A. F. Shaw

ARBA'S ILLNESS, WHICH HE CALLED both pneumonia and typhoid, likely came from exposure to the elements and poor drinking water during his round trips as a courier running between Pulaski, Tennessee, and the commands position in Salem, Tennessee. Doctor Jasper N. Smith was the Assistant Surgeon to the 4th Georgia Cavalry, serving the regiment through January 1864.[35]

During the Civil War death by disease was a greater threat than losing one's life in battle.[36] Most of the soldiers were leaving home and traveling for the first time, and living with other soldiers in unsanitary conditions. It was an era when the transmission of disease was not yet understood. Louis Pasteur's work on germ theory was happening at the

---

[35] Jasper N. Smith, Compiled Service Records.
[36] Civil War Casualties – American Battlefield Trust statistics.

same time the war was being fought. Joseph Lister's work on antisepsis and asepsis wouldn't be published until 1867. A rudimentary vaccine for smallpox existed at that time; but, though available, it was not readily accepted or even understood by the masses and could not even be assessed as safe for use. As a result, two out of three deaths in the camps were caused by disease. Many soldiers died of measles (rubeola), which was and still is one of the most highly contagious of all the infectious diseases.[37]

Dr. Charles Clinton McKinney (1788-1864) was a seventy-five-year-old retired physician who lived across the street from the Fayetteville, Tennessee, hospital on South Elk Avenue where Arba and his fellow soldiers were being treated.[38] The home he built in Fayetteville (circa 1820-1825) sported the first indoor bathroom in town.[39] It is one of the oldest structures still standing in Fayetteville today (that is, the house—not sure about the original bathroom).

McKinney served as a surgeon in the War of 1812 with Andrew Jackson, namely, the part of the war Jackson was waging in Louisiana with the indigenous Creek peoples. On March 27, 1814, the war with the Creek came to a head at the Battle of Horseshoe Bend in Central Alabama, near present-day Dadeville. Sam Houston, the future Texas statesman, was a third lieutenant in Jackson's army. During a bayonet charge, Houston was wounded in the upper thigh by a Creek arrow. Family history says that Dr. McKinney, who was stationed north of the battlefield in Talladega, Alabama, was the surgeon tasked with the removal of the arrow, although other accounts claim that Houston had a fellow soldier just "pull out the arrow." Houston suffered from the

---

[37] Centers for Disease Control and Prevention – Measles (Rubeola).
[38] Young family story on their ancestor Dr. Charles Clinton McKinney posted at "Generations of Care" web blog; Lincoln Health System; Huntsville, Alabama.
[39] The Fayetteville-Lincoln County Chamber of Commerce, *Historic Homes of Fayetteville, Tennessee*.

effects of the wound the rest of his life, hobbling on a cane or crutch.

While in the hospital in Fayetteville, Arba mentions H. Beneyfield [*sic*], actually the forty-year-old Private William H. Bennerfield of Company I. As previously noted, this company was known as the Georgia Mountain Dragoons, having been formed in Whitfield County, Georgia, of men from the Chattanooga area. Bennerfield's military records show him as "Captured 12 Dec 63 Kingston, Tenn" along with "1 Horse valued $300.00." He was transferred to a Union Army prison in Rock Island, Illinois, where he would remain until the end of the war.[40]

Rock Island Prison, a Union prison located on government-owned land surrounded by the Mississippi River between Moline, Illinois, and Davenport, Iowa, was built on twelve acres of the 946 acres that comprise the island. In December 1863, even though construction was not finished, it began to receive Confederate prisoners. Private Bennerfield arrived at Rock Island Prison on January 6, 1864. In the one month leading up to his arrival, the prison ranks had swelled to more than 5,000 prisoners. During its time of operation, Rock Island Prison contained more than 12,000 Confederate soldiers, of which almost 2,000 died due to poor sanitation, malnutrition, and diseases including scurvy and smallpox, which were rampant.

Private Bennerfield signed his Oath of Allegiance to the United States on June 22, 1865, upon his release from Rock Island Prison. Most Confederate soldiers signed the Oath of Allegiance to the United States at the secession of hostilities after General Robert E. Lee's surrender. The actual words varied from document to document, but they usually affirmed that the signee would "faithfully support, protect, and defend the Constitution of the United States and the Union of States," and that they would "abide by and faithfully support all laws and proclamations during the existing rebellion with reference to the emancipation of

---

[40] William H. Bennerfield, Compiled Service Records.

slaves." There also might have been additional wording regarding the signee's agreement of not "taking up arms against the United States."

There was also an oath called an "Ironclad Oath," which when taken made this claim: "I have never voluntarily borne arms against the United States." This represented a problem for a lot of citizens after the war because no former Rebel soldier or Southern citizen could hold federal, state, or local office, or serve in the military under the provisions of the oath. Former Confederate citizens had to petition the President of the United States for a pardon. It wasn't until 1884 when Congress passed legislation removing all of the restrictive portions of the Ironclad Oath.[41]

February 20, 1902
MY EXPERIENCES
In the War of 1860 Briefly Told.

As soon as I was able to mount my horse from a suitable stump I began to beg Dr Smith to let me go to the command, but he kept me in a few days longer. Mean while it had moved to a place 20 miles west, called Melville, and soon after I reported there. Co F., was ordered 20 miles west of that place to Pulaski in Giles Co. Tenn, where we performed various duties that others could tell more about than I could. There is where I formed my first acquaintance with my much esteemed old chum and comrade, Bob Trundel.

When Co. F, went to Pulaski, the rest of the command came back to Salem, as I remember 20 miles east of Fayetteville. I was the regular courier to bear the dispatches from Capt. Helvington to Col. Avery, a distance of 60 miles; it being the order for me to make the round trip in three

---

[41] *Thirty-Seventh Congress of the United States*, "Oath of office for all persons of civil, military or naval department of the public service – Chapter CXXVIII – An Act to prescribe an Oath of Office, and for other Purposes," January 2, 1862.

days. Sometimes the waters would get up so I could not make the rounds in the specified time and the mud was so bad that it took the hair off of my horse's legs to the knees and hocks. The first day I would make the trip to Fayetteville and get my rations with Dr. Smith and horse feed at the hospital. When I got there one night the doctor was out of corn and he said I would have to go to the government cribs at the depot and get corn where there was a row of cribs by the side of the railroad possibly 300 yards long where the farmers had put up the tenth of the corn for the use of the army. I went and got a big armful and the guard saw me about the time I started with it and he took after me and I made as good time as possible and when I got to the end of the R. R, I made a leap from the turn table and did not step far enough and slipped back into the pit under the table in the black mud. There he caught me. He said, what are you taking this corn for. I said to feed my horse. He said yon must not lake this corn, it belongs to the government. I said I belong to the government too and was a courier to Col. Avery and by that time he recognized me in the dusk of the evening, then he said you are all right, go on.

One day at Pulaski I was off duty and Bill Meek and I went to the guard house where Ben Baley was on guard. Ben had a long beard and had on a large long nubia and he was clawing around his neck like he would take the hide and hair and Bill having been in the army a long time knew what was the matter. He said, "Ben what is the matter. Ben said by the way I don't know. Bill said I bet you are full of gray backs and Ben took off his nubia then and there and the whooee at the gray backs! The first that Co. F., had seen. As soon as Ben got off guard be got out his razor and shaved, put on clean clothes and hunted somebody to wash and scald the gray backs to death.

One morning while we were there there was a train of government wagons drove up and stopped in the street and Tom Thumb was with them and in walking with the average man he would have to walk two steps and ran three to keep up. He looked to be about 30 inches tall. He had a full long *beard of auburn hue. He was such a show to us we would follow around after him and when he went in the stores he was too low to see on top of the counters. I saw him put his hands on the edge of the counter and tiptoe to see on top.*

A. F. Shaw

After getting over his bout of typhoid, Arba returned to his duty as a courier for Colonel Avery and Captain Helvenston in March 1863.

The scourge of soldiers on both sides—ranging from the most famous general to the lowly private—was body lice. These dangerous pests went by many slang names but "gray back" was the term mentioned by Arba. The name was also used by Federal soldiers when referring to their Confederate counterparts for obvious reasons. The lack of hygiene also meant that "gray backs" could have a deadly effect by carrying typhoid rapidly through companies in the field. Later wars came up with their own terms for the common louse. They were known as "cooties" in the trenches of battle during World War I—which, without a doubt, is a great answer to file away in the event you find yourself immersed in a modern trivia game.

The "nubia" was a knitted head scarf and not part of the official uniform. Nevertheless, it surely provided some comfort to cavalry soldiers much like a bandana would for mopping sweat. It was also the perfect place for a "gray back" to build a comfortable home.

Robert Thompson Trundle[42] (1844-1917) of Company E was born in Tennessee and was wounded on July 21, 1864. He appears on the registry of the Floyd House and Ocmulgee Hospitals in Macon, Georgia, on October 28, 1864. The description of his injuries states: "US ball entering 4 inches above right nipple and emerging at inferior angle scapula wounding lung." He survived his injuries and married

---

[42] Robert T. Trundle, Compiled Service Records and family genealogy.

Margaret Ann Williams on September 12, 1867. He farmed in Wood Station, Catoosa County, Georgia, and he and his wife had twelve children, nine who survived into adulthood.

William A. Meek from Company I was also part of Captain Benjamin F. White, Jr.'s Artillery Battery, which traveled with the 4th Georgia Cavalry regiment, as was Benjamin W. Baily or Bailey (1824-1904) of Arba's Company F. According to Bailey's military records, he "left sick at Rosville, Georgia Sept 25, 1863" and then "Dropt [sic] in obedience to Orders for Desertion April 19, 1864."[43] All that was left behind may have been his nubia.

March 6, 1902
MY EXPERIENCES
In the War of 1860 Briefly Told.

Courier duty was all I had to perform while the company stayed at Pulaski. In the early spring the regiment, being fully grown to 12 large companies, moved to Mud Creek, 5 or 6 miles south of Pulaski, and Co. F resumed its respective place in the rank where we drilled until the last days of March.

One morning after a morning rain, we were off drill and John Fricks, my old mess mate said lets go and catch a mess of fish. We went and he caught three and I two—all yellow cat from 12 to 15 inches long. Some little boys were out hunting and their dogs ran a hare into a drift where we were fishing. We helped them catch it and bought it from them. Then we went to a turnip patch and asked for a mess of salad, got it and went back to camps and boiled the salad and fried the fish and rabbit. What a supper we had that night. That made me reflect back on the past.

But a sad reverse was awaiting us. The good times closed to an end. With the wagon train complete, an ambulance, a full Corps of officers and 12 large companies all strung out it looked like a considerable army and yet we

---

[43] William A. Meek, Compiled Service Records.

had no weapons of war. Now the time had come. We left the camps on Mud Creek and started to Fayetteville where we drew on the 1st day of April 1863 a full supply of Belgian rifles and long sabres and 40 rounds of ammunition and canteens and haversacks and I reckon saddles and spurs too—don't remember. On our way to Fayetteville I saw our Major Owen's fine spirited horse rear up, fall back on the Major and ruin him, so he was not with us any more.

Now were ready for war. We went to McMinville and on the way I saw the first blood shed by gun shot in the regt. One of the boys in another company in dismounting, shot himself through the foot. I saw him get down. He got down on the right hand side and had the gun musle turned down instead of up.

While we were about in the vicinity of McMinville and Smithville, I don't know when or how, we were joined in with 4 other regiments which made Cruse's bridage. And there was a battery of artillery to be manned and it was done in part, if not all, by men in the brigade that by misfortune lost their horses. Two of them went from Co. F—Jessie Smith and John D. Fricks. Smith soon died out of measles and Fricks lived through and made as good a soldier as ever went to arms and stayed with us to the bitter end and acted his part in many a hard fought battle. He has been dead more than 15 years of paralysis. May peace ever be to his ashes. He was a hero in the truest sense and right here I want to say that Newton Powell was with us in the same White's battery to the final roll call.

It does not occur to me now that Cruse's brigade was at first composed of Ga., Regiments. I can't call to memory what states all the regiments were from, but later it was composed of the 1, 2, 3, 4, and 6. Ga. regiments.

A. F. Shaw

AS HE ENTERED THE FOURTH MONTH of being a soldier, Arba and the rest of the 4th Georgia Cavalry hadn't actually experienced battle yet. It must have seemed like a fun camping trip with more than a thousand men tightly packed into the same campground. Some of the gunfire he had been exposed to actually resulted in the accidental wounding of the now "unhappy campers" by their own weapons. Because not only were the men of the 4th Georgia Cavalry learning to be soldiers, they were also busy inventing new analogies–which is how the term "shooting yourself in the foot" clearly originated, or not.

They were all still green and learning how to handle their brand new long sabers and Belgian rifles. With the blockade affecting the ability of Confederate forces to import weapons, by spring 1863 the Belgian rifle issued to Arba likely came from captured arms.

As unlucky events continued to mount, Arba was witness to the accident that befell Major Daniel Jackson Owen on April 4, 1863. Owen was a 2nd Lieutenant in Company A of the 23rd Battalion Georgia Cavalry, which was Isaac Avery's original unit in January 10, 1862. When it became Company I of the 4th Georgia Cavalry, Owen was elected Captain on September 22, 1862. On January 30, 1863, Owen was promoted to Major with these words: "Approved under the Constitutional authority vested in the President." Owen's injury, which occurred as he was preparing his men to march to the front, resulted in a dislocation of his left hip. On January 30, 1864, a board of three surgeons in Atlanta, Georgia, submitted a letter stating "we have carefully examined said officer and find him wholy [sic] incapable of performing the duties of a soldier because of dislocation of his left hip."[44]

Owen had to resign his commission due to this disability on February 18, 1864. He was succeeded as Major by the twenty-five-year-old Augustus R. Stewart[45] from Jackson County, Alabama, who at the start of the war was a citizen of Ringgold, Georgia, and who was then a Captain in Company K. Colonel Isaac Avery wrote the recommendation to

---

[44] Daniel Jackson Owen, Compiled Service Records.
[45] Augustus R. Stewart, Compiled Service Records.

promote Stewart on March 23, 1864: "Approved and respectfully forwarded. I know this officer to be a most excellent one, and ernestly [sic] recommend the promotion as richly merited."[46]

Owen filed for a Confederate Pension living in Worth County, Georgia, in 1888.[47] His personal account of the incident stated that "while in command of the regiment on the way to the front—my horse became unmanageable reared up and fell back on me crushing my hole [sic] left hip rendering left leg almost useless leaving me cripple for life." His doctor's affidavit stated that "the head of his left femur was fractured and after healing his leg was three inches shorter making locomotion very difficult." He started applying for a soldier's pension in 1888 and was granted a yearly pension of fifty dollars, which he filed for yearly and received through 1897.

Jesse W. Smith[48] of Company F succumbed to measles, according to Arba. Smith was thirty-seven years old when he mustered in on December 15, 1862, in Dalton, Georgia; he was one of Arba's neighbors in Walker County. His military records are sparse, with only a mention of his mustering in. However, someone was searching for him through the Commissioner of Pensions in 1914 when an additional notation was made. Perhaps when he died in spring 1863 he was buried with no record in an unknown grave in East Tennessee, which was common during the war, so his wife was trying to apply for a widow's pension fifty years later.

Finally, in April 1863, the 4th Georgia Cavalry was ready for war. The regiment initially met up with the 2nd, 3rd, and 4th Georgia Cavalry and the 7th Alabama Cavalry to form Crews' brigade between McMinville and Smithville, Tennessee.

---

[46] Major Daniel Jackson Owen, Compiled Service Records.
[47] Daniel Jackson Owen Pension Applications 1888-1897.
[48] Jesse W. Smith, Compiled Service Records.

REBEL CORRESPONDENT

Thirty-four-year-old Colonel Charles Constantine Crews (1829-1887) was in command of these regiments as well as several artillery batteries. Crews was the eldest in a family of eight children and had several brothers also fighting in the war. His younger brother Captain Fleming Jordon Crews (1841-1905) succeeded him as a First Lieutenant commanding Company A, 2nd Georgia Cavalry, when Charles was promoted to Colonel to command the brigade. In 1864 Fleming was promoted to Captain. Lt. Colonel James Mortimer Crews (1835-1898) then commanded the 3rd Tennessee Cavalry. Dr. Leonidas Crews (1831-1903) was an Assistant Surgeon in a Confederate hospital. Private George T. Crews (1838-1863) of Company K, 35th Georgia Regiment, died of pneumonia in January 1863 at Richmond General Hospital Number 17 in Richmond, Virginia.

Colonel Charles Constantine Crews (1829-1887)
Confederate Military History 1899

Prior to the war Colonel Charles Constantine Crews was both an attorney and a doctor. He became a lawyer after passing exams at age 18 years in 1847. Then he went to medical school starting in 1853 at the Medical College of Louisiana, the precursor to the Tulane University of Medicine, and graduated in 1859.

Crews first enlisted for the war as the Captain of Company A, 2nd Georgia Cavalry, in March 1862 as part of Colonel Winburn J. Lawton's Regiment, Georgia Cavalry under the command of General Nathan Bedford Forest. He was captured by Union forces of the 23rd Kentucky Infantry and later exchanged in October 1862 near Glasgow, Kentucky. He was also wounded several times in battle. In February 1863 he was severely wounded in the hip in action near Dover, Tennessee. He was wounded again at the war's end and was disabled from his wounds in April 1865.[49] After the East Tennessee Campaign on January 8, 1864, he is mentioned multiple times in a report by General William T. Martin (1823-1910) that "Col. C.C. Crews deserves mention for his skill and bravery on this occasion."[50]

In December 1863, prior to the Knoxville Campaign, Crews' Brigade's makeup would change to the 1st, 2nd, 3rd, 4th, and 6th Georgia Cavalry along with some Horse Artillery Batteries. From the original founding of Crews' Brigade command in January 1863 through the end of the war, the makeup of the different cavalry regiments that comprised the brigade would be shuffled slightly. But the 4th Georgia Cavalry was in Crews' brigade through the entire war with the exception of the Atlanta Campaign when Brigadier General Alfred Iverson, Jr. was its commander. For the Atlanta Campaign under Iverson, Crews reverted to his original command, the 2nd Georgia Cavalry.

To confuse the chain of command a little further, in official War Department correspondence during 1863 occasionally Colonel Avery's 4th Georgia Cavalry was listed as being commanded by Colonel Duncan Lamont Clinch.

The officers in all of the regiments in Crews' own brigade petitioned the War Department in December 1863 to promote Crews to Brigadier General. The petition received endorsements by General William T. Martin and John T. Morgan; however, because Crews wasn't commanding a brigade in the middle of 1864, the promotion was tabled. But Crews returned to command the brigade when Wheeler went into Tennessee in August 1864. By 1865 General Joseph E. Johnston (1807-1891) endorsed the promotion as well.

---

[49] Charles Constantine Crews, Compiled Service Records and family genealogy.
[50] W. C. Dodson, *Campaigns of Wheeler and His Cavalry 1862-1865,* (Hudgins Publishing Company, Atlanta, Georgia, 1899), 149.

However, since the war was coming to an end and with the Confederate War Department in disarray, the promotion was never formally approved.

After the war Crews went back to practicing medicine. He was also the treasurer of the Bainbridge, Cuthbert, and Columbus Railroad Company, which was to have run a north-to-south line through southwest Georgia in 1869. However, the plan was abandoned. He moved to Texas in 1875, where he spent some time raising cattle and horses. In June 1879 he moved to New Mexico territory where he engaged in shipping and hauling ore.[51] Throughout his time in Texas and New Mexico, he continued practicing medicine. Crews died of pneumonia in Hillsboro, New Mexico territory, in 1887.

Colonel Charles Constantine Crews House in Hillsboro, New Mexico – 2016

His private medical practice was located in the two front rooms.
CC BT-SA 4.0 – Creative Commons

---

[51] Ralph Emerson Twichell, *The Leading Facts of New Mexico History*, Volume 4, (Cedar Rapids, IA, Torch Press, 1917), 279.

CHAPTER FOUR
LIFE OF A PRIVATE

March 20, 1902
MY EXPERIENCES
In the War of 1860 Briefly Told

We stayed along in front of the enemy's lines picketing, scouting, foraging, and drilling on an east and west line south of Murfreesboro.

The siege of Vicksburg was on and that seemed to retard the advance of the army in Tennessee against us. We moved from place to place. I remember one place we gathered corn in a field that had been sown in wheat. In the standing corn, I reckon it was in May, the wheat was in boot and about knee high. As I remember we went next, to Duck River and stayed there many days. I saw blue grass with the seed stalks more than two feet tall, the land was so rich. It was there I saw two of Co. F's. best men wrestle one fall; one was all they agreed on at the start. It was fairly done and both seemed to be satisfied. They were Rube Ransom and Hiram Loyd. Both men are dead now, but they have sons and I believe widows living in this county. As to which man fell on the bottom it strikes me that it was Loyd, I am not sure.

While on Duck River we would get a kind of large mussel from 3 to 6 inches long out of the river, crack off the hulls, fry and eat the meat. The boys called them oysters.

I. D. (Dave) Allen, now of Chattanooga, was our forage master. He would take the wagons out every day and bring in corn in the shuck for the horses. One day he told me it took 110 bushels per day to feed all the horses of the regiment.

The next place we went to was Flat Creek near Wall's

Cross Roads. There we did a lot of heavy scouting and picketing. Our meat there for a while was pickled hog jaws, as salty as the salt could make them, and they had the hair all on them. It rained a great deal when we were there. The camp was along the side of the creek and the land was a cedar glade full of lime stone and how muddy it would get. Then we had left our tents and had no way of sheltering and we had it to take. Our picket post was half mile north at Walls X roads where the growth was white and red oak, very large. There we killed a pair of bull snakes respectively 8 and 9 feet long. One of then hung out of a hole that had been out high in a hollow tree and stuck its head out over Ben Baley's head. Some of the boys said look what a snake. Ben looked up saw it and went away with the velocity of a bird apparently. Bob Springfield took his saber and cut off the snakes head as it hung.

The night before that it rained hard all night and R. F. (Frank) Shaw and I were on picket together. The rain was a lullaby and I would go to sleep on my horse as wet as I was. When we were off duty I would put my saddle between two of the ridges on one of the huge white oaks at the X roads and wrapping up with my blanket and siting on the saddle, lean against the tree and would soon be off in sweet repose. The next day the sun shone so we could dry out our clothes.

While at that place I boiled poke root in a black smith shop to wash in for the itch and when I applied the remedy it was worse than the disease, It put me in such a rage I just went into the slack tub as near all over as I could.

A. F. Shaw

AS THE WAR ENTERED MAY 1863, back in the east Stonewall Jackson would die on May 10, eight days after being shot by friendly fire at Chancellorsville, Virginia. In the west, the men of the 4th Georgia Cavalry continued their training and were becoming soldiers, drilling in the area south of Murfreesboro, Tennessee. Most of the energy of the Union Army was focused on the siege of Vicksburg, which by the middle of May was just beginning to percolate, so the 4th Georgia Cavalry used that time to get ready.

Company F's Sergeant Reuben Jefferson Ransom (1825-1873) ended up sick with "Biles," a gallbladder illness, and left the company after the battle of Chickamauga in September 1863. His rank was reduced to Private on November 1, 1863, and he was dropped as AWOL on April 19, 1864.[52]

Lieutenant Isaac David Allen (1829-1910), the company's forage master, would later become a retail grocer in LaFayette, Georgia, and then in Chattanooga, Tennessee, after the war. Clearly, the lessons learned in foraging supplies for an army trained him well for his future occupation. He married Elizabeth Vickery before the war in 1854. They had six children.[53]

First Lieutenant Isaac David Allen and His Wife, Elizabeth Vickery Allen Circa 1905

Benjamin W. Bailey (1825-1904) and Robert B. Springfield were both privates in Company F. Bailey was born in Tennessee in November 1824. Bailey would be left sick at Rosville, Georgia, on September 25, 1863, and would not return, being dropped as AWOL on April 19, 1864.[54] Springfield originally enlisted on August 1, 1861, in Knoxville, Tennessee under Captain Gillespie, who may have been Captain Henry C. Gillespie of Company C of the 5th Battalion (McClellans) Tennessee Cavalry, who was in Knoxville at the time. Somehow he ended up with the 4th Georgia's Company F and would serve out the war in this unit.[55]

---

[52] Reuben Jefferson Ransom, Compiled Service Records.
[53] Isaac David Allen, Compiled Service Records.
[54] Benjamin W. Bailey, Compiled Service Records.
[55] Robert B. Springfield, Compiled Service Records.

March 27, 1902
MY EXPERIENCES
In the War of 1860 Briefly Told.

One camp I forgot. It was the little village called Auburn. There was a grist mill there run by horse power, the horses being lead up on a round table and hitched to beams behind and when they pulled the table would turn and the horses would only walk in the same place all day long. The table was level and about 20 feet across.

It was there we were hurried into line the first time for a fight. It proved to be a heavy scout of blue coats. They went back and did not give us any fight.

At Auburn one morning Colonel Avery marched us out on dress parade and had us to fire off our guns against the side of a ridge across a field. He gave the command ready, aim, fire.

Back to Flat creek the land was fine—lots of good wheat said to make 40 bushels per acre and it was taming when I left. I was unwell all the time from my attack at Fayetteville and one day I was one of a detail to go to a field of clover to oat with scythes and haul in to feed our horses. The cutting was too much for me in my condition. I soon became so bloated and weak that I was unfit for service and Capt. Helvingston sent me to the hospital. J. M. Henry was also sick and the captain sent him too. We went to Shelbyville, then the ambulance went back and we boarded a car for Chattanooga. We stayed there 48 hours, then the doctors sent us to Ringgold, and in 48 hours more they sent me to Cherokee Spring, two miles east of Ringgold, where I stayed three weeks. The treatment was turpentine, quinine and tincture of iron. I felt like I would die if I did not get water and one night, after the nurses had turned in for the night, I went to the bucket determined to drink my fill of water that had been denied me so long. Accordingly I layed the spoon handle dipper on the shelf, turned up the bucket and drank as long as I could bold my breath, rested and then drank all I wanted of that good sulphur water, then went back to my bunk, covered up and was soon in too deep a sleep to dream and slept on until Dr. Bateman came around the next morning making out his list of fares and prescriptions. He roused me up and said: "How do you feel this morning?" "Lots Better" Next he noticed that I was wet all over as water and he said:

"What made you so wet?"

"Sweat."

"What made you sweat so?"

I then told l him about the big drink of water and he said: "You fool, it will kill you." I said I had rather die satisfied than to famish to death—it was enough to be hungry. The doctor was pleased and told me to say what I wanted to eat and I should have it if it would do for me to eat. That night the bloat all sweated out through the pores and I was prostrated—was a living skeleton. Then in a few days I began to gain strength and he gave me a furlough and father came after me. I got home July 11th 1863.

While I was at Cherokee Spring there were three Enterken brothers in a room opposite my room. Two had measles, the other was their nurse. One was better and could put on his clothes and walk out with safety in fair weather. One evening there was a heavy rain and wind and he was in the hall and got damp and in 24 hours be died. He first took a violent headache, became unconscious and died that way.

A. F. Shaw

ARBA CLEARLY HAD NOT RECOVERED from his bout with what he called typhoid from March 1863, and he ended up sick again along with Josiah M. Henry. Together they were sent to the hospital by Captain Joseph E. Helvenston. The more than 110-mile trip must have been difficult by means of ambulance and train to Shellbyville, then to Chattanooga, Tennessee, then to Ringgold, Georgia, and finally to the hospital at Cherokee Springs, Georgia. A treatment of turpentine, quinine, and tincture of iron was often prescribed but was not a cure. The cause was contaminated water, which was produced very easily by a cavalry regiment totaling a thousand men and horses.

The Confederate Army had built a 500-bed hospital next to the healing waters of Cherokee Springs. The sulfur water was considered beneficial for treating patients with chronic diarrhea and dysentery. Situated on approximately thirty acres, the hospital was divided into three wards made up of tents. Each ward was separate with a broad street in the center. In addition, there was a laundry "wash-house," bathing house, bakery, kitchen, and convalescent dining room.

In a diary published in 1866, nurse Kate Cumming commented on her visit to Cherokee Springs, which occurred just over a month after Arba was there as a patient: "There is a fine bakery, and convalescent kitchen, in which are large boilers for cooking. The convalescent-dining room, which is new, is covered and open on the sides. A horn calls the patients to their meals, which has quite a romantic sound, like old feudal times... Take the hospital all together, I don't see how it could be more perfect."

In addition to the rudimentary medicines available at the time, the hospital was using food as a medicine as well. As Cumming noted: "The surgeons put down on their books what kind of diet they want, and the head nurse copies it, and hands it to the steward, who makes a register of the number of men. The head cook has a list of the articles which come under the different classes of diet, and distributes them accordingly."

Cumming also wrote that she observed the goal of the hospital staff was to be as well supplied as any hotel in the South. In her Thursday, August 13, 1863, diary entry, she noted, "General Bragg is in this hospital sick...Mrs. Bragg is with the general."[56]

Dr. Robert Parker Bateman (1831-1877) was the physician who treated Arba at Cherokee Springs. Bateman had received his medical degree from the University of

---

[56] Kate Cumming, *Kate: A Journal of Hospital Life in the Confederate Army of Tennessee – From the Battle of Shiloh to the End of the War*, (J. P. Morgan, 1866), 83.

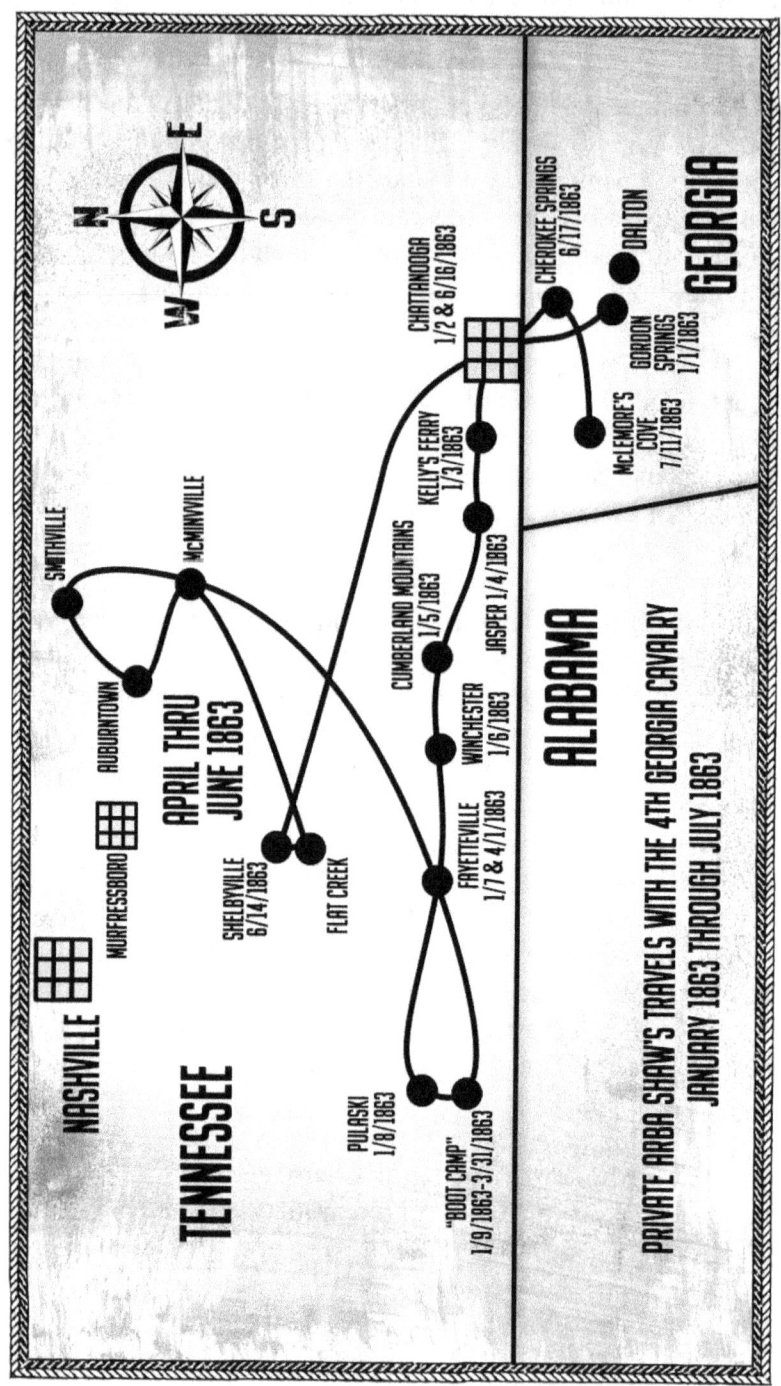

Nashville in 1852. He then practiced medicine just south of Nashville in Nolensville, Tennessee, until the beginning of the war. He initially had enlisted as a captain of Company C of the 4th Tennessee Infantry from May 15, 1861, until he resigned his commission on October 23, 1861. At the beginning of 1862 he was appointed Assistant Surgeon with the rank of Captain by the Provisional Army of the Confederate States. He reported to the 25th Louisiana Infantry as a surgeon on November 16, 1862. In May 1863 he was relieved from field service and ordered to report for hospital duty in Chattanooga, Tennessee. Finally, on May 20, 1863, he was ordered to Cherokee Springs, Georgia, arriving right around the time when Arba and Henry arrived there. After the war Bateman practiced medicine in Memphis, Tennessee, through 1877. In the spring of 1877 his health took a turn for the worst; it's likely he was suffering from tuberculosis so he traveled to Hot Springs, Arkansas. On June 13, 1877, Dr. Robert Parker Bateman inhaled some chloroform and then shot and killed himself. He left a wife and twelve-year-old son. Dr. Bateman is buried in Shelby County, Tennessee.[57]

The three Entreken brothers who had the measles, who Arba encountered at Cherokee Springs, were actually a larger group of rubella infected brothers and cousins. The records from the time show Private Thomas Talley Entrekin (1832-1920) and his brother Private John M. Entrekin (1846-1924)—both from Haralson, Coweta County, Georgia—were at the hospital in Cherokee Springs. Seventeen-year-old John was the brother with the measles, as he recounted in his pension application of August 1898; his older brother, thirty-one-year-old Thomas, must have been the one caring for him. The two brothers were part of Company H of the 4th Georgia Cavalry so Arba would have known them well.[58]

Also at Cherokee Springs hospital were three of Thomas

---

[57] Dr. Robert Parker Bateman, Compiled Service Records and Bateman family genealogy.
[58] Thomas Talley Entrekin, John M. Entrekin; Compiled Service Records.

and John's Entrekin cousins from Marion County, Mississippi, who were part of Company B of the 18th Alabama Regular Infantry—all in the same Alabama company. These three of five brothers—Privates William Bryant Entrekin (1821-1863), David L. Entrekin (1837-1863), and James Marshall Entrekin (1840-1864) —had been admitted to the hospital on May 25, 1863, in a sad sort of family reunion with their Georgia cousins; everyone except Thomas was suffering from rubella. Forty-two-year-old William would die on July 11, 1863, and twenty-six-year-old David would die on August 20, 1863, both from the measles—victims to the statistic that more soldiers died of illness than in battle during the Civil War.

The two other Mississippi-born Company B, 18th Alabama Regular Infantry, Enterkin brothers who were not hospitalized were Sherrard Entrekin (1832-1864) and Daniel Stanford Entrekin (1843-1916). Sherrard would die on May 20, 1864, at Atlanta Medical College Hospital, the location of present-day Grady Hospital; he is buried in a mass grave of unknown Confederate soldiers at Oakland Cemetery in Atlanta, Georgia. James would die on August 7, 1864, at Catoosa Springs, Georgia, after being killed in action. Of the five brothers, only one, Daniel, survived the war. [59]

In a letter to James Entrekin's wife Susannah Rice (1837-1915), who was at the time pregnant with their fourth child, Mary Matilda, on the day her husband died, Daniel, James's brother, wrote[60]:

8 August 1864
Dear Sister,
I seat myself to drop you a few lines which I will inform you that I am yet alive and well. Much hoping these few lines may come safe to home and find you well. Susanah it is with pain that I have to drop you these lines which will

---

[59] William Bryant Entrekin, David L. Entrekin, James Marshall Entrekin, Sherrard Entrekin, Daniel Stanford Entrekin; Compiled Service Records and Entrekin family genealogy.
[60] Original letter by Daniel Stanford Entrekin to his sister-in-law Susannah Rice Entrekin held by Entrekin descendants, August 8, 1864.

inform you that James is dead, he was killed yesterday evening shot dead on the battlefield. I am sorry that I was not present at the time. I saw him last night when he was brought out to be buried. He was shot in the breast about the left nipple and it came out about the right shoulder... out in the country. I suppose that he spoke after he was shot but I can't learn what he said only he said he was prepared to die. There was a lieutenant belong to another regiment that was right with him was all that was near enough to him to know what he said and I have not seen him yet. The yankees charged the picket line in front of the brigade on our right end broke the line and our company was sent to their assistance. They was deployed out five or six steps apart and he was standing behind a big tree shooting when he was shot. I can say one thing for him he lived and died a brave man and died discharging his duty. It seems like it is more than I can bear. That is four brothers I have lost in a little more than twelve months and now I am left alone. There is one thing that comforts me and that is to think he is gone to a better world than this. Susan I have got all his things but there is nothing worth sending out that I could send in a letter except seven dollars and a half of money. I have got his knife... is a little money owed to him in the company. I will get it if I can and send it to you in the next letter. I would send the money in this letter but hear that yankees was about to take Mobile and I am afraid it will not go. You must excuse my short letter and bad writing for my heart is so full I can't write. I want this to go to mother without delay. I would write her one but it is more than I can bear now. I want to see you all very bad. It seems like I can't hardly stay here now. My relatives is all gone but I have plenty of friends here but they ain't much satisfaction to me now. James was buried as chance would allow it. He was put in the grave with one of his friends that fell near him about the same time. So I must close, write soon. Nothing more at present, only remain your loving brother till death. Goodby for this time, I hope not for always.

D. S. Entrekin

Arba convalesced at Cherokee Springs for just a couple of weeks. Even with the hospital's then state-of-the-art use of "diet as a medicine," he had lost a frightening amount of weight during his illness and recovery.

Up north in Pennsylvania, the Battle of Gettysburg raged in the first three days of July 1863, with its massive casualty count of more than 50,000 men on both sides. The news of the Union win at Gettysburg would have been arriving to North Georgia just as a feeble Private Arba Shaw was ready for his father to come and pick him up so he could go home to continue his recovery. It must have seemed a million miles away.

April 3, 1902
MY EXPERIENCES
In the War of 1860 Briefly Told.

At home Sunday July 11th, 1863 on a 30 days furlow. I was not able to be up but a few minutes at a time when father came after me and the Dr. told him he could take me, but it would kill me. But not so, did not hurt me. He hauled me in a carriage and I lay down nearly all the time. I could walk with a stick at home, there was plenty to eat and I felt like eating. When I first got weighed my weight was 90 pounds. After being at home a week I gained a pound every day for the next 42 days When my furlow was out I could get on a horse from a stump and go to Dr. T.Y. Park's. He gave me an invalid's certificate for 30 days more and that took me almost to the battle of Chickamauga. When I reported for duty the regimental surgeon told me to stay out a while, which I did.

The first night after the fight at the Gower's ford I stayed at the court house in LaFayette, and all I could get to eat was a pumpkin about the size of my head which I cooked in a borrowed pot at the northwest corner of the house. I had no grease to go with the pumpkin and did not relish it much. I went into a lot near the old Methodist church house to pull some grass for my horse and it was there I found the pumpkin.

That night some of the boys, J. H. McWhorter, and, I believe, John Biggerstaff and others, brought to the court house our good brave Captain Helvingston. He was shot dead in the fight at the Gower's ford and at the same time Jack Boss' horse became uncontrollable in the charge and kept going and he was killed. Boss was captured and stayed in prison to the end. The Captain was taken home to his dear wife in Whitfield county.

The next day I started toward the battlefield of Chickamauga, and on Sunday, the twentieth of September, there was a killing frost, and the cool, bracing air and the fierceness of the battle prompted me to go and see how the boys were getting along. I found them at the Glass, now Stott's mill, coming out of the fight. They had been in it right that day (Sunday). That night we camped along between the Crawfish Creek and the road running east from the old Glass home, and the next morning by twilight we were in our saddles and going down the LaFayette road in a lively canter toward the battlefield, all wondering what was to pay. We forded the Chickamauga at the Lee and Gordon mill and kept on west, went across the Mission Ridge at the Milwee hollow, then turned south. We soon began to find what for. There was a command of yankee cavalry that stayed at father's Sunday night and the general pressed him in to pilot them to Crawfish, and at the Owen's ford they met the Johnny pickets, who gave them a little spat. Then the blue coats decided to cross over to the Chattanooga valley road and go to Chattanooga, but Wheeler wanted that wagon train, and he got it at what is now known as the Henry switch on the Chattanooga Southern in one and a half miles of where I live. I was one of the detail to burn their wagons. We captured lots of men and mules, and that night by permit

from Colonel Cruse, commanding brigade, I stayed at home.
A. F. Shaw

AFTER ARBA WAS RELEASED FROM Cherokee Springs hospital and taken home by his father, Reverend William M. Shaw (1821-1890), he was given an additional furlough extension from T. Y. Park. This was likely Walker County native Dr. Alonzo Thomas Clement Park (1832-1919). Park, who had received his "physician certification" in 1859, had enlisted as a Private in September 1861 in the Company I of the 35th Georgia Infantry. He was detailed as a medical attendant in Fredericksburg, Virginia. He was wounded in June 1862 and placed on medical furlough. In March 1863 he was appointed a hospital steward and assigned to a hospital in Chattanooga, Tennessee.[61] Dr. Park was likely conveniently close to the Reverend William Shaw's farmstead when Arba needed to extend his furlough.

IN THE MORE THAN TWO MONTHS that Arba was on medical furlough from the 4th Georgia Cavalry, they had been on picket duty in Middle Tennessee with the major action at Vicksburg occurring to the west. This would change at the beginning of September 1863 with skirmishing in northeastern Alabama with continuing action into northwestern Georgia. It would be the 4th Georgia Cavalry's opening act in their involvement in the Battle of Chickamauga.

When Arba rejoined his unit in LaFayette, Georgia, on September 17, 1863, fighting was happening right in his own backyard of McClemore's Cove. Early in the morning at around 4 a.m. on Pigeon Mountain at Catlett's Gap near Gowan's (Gower's) Ford, which is midway between Lafayette and Arba's home to the west, Captain Joseph E. Helvenston and several other Company F men charged on horseback over the pickets of Union General William Babcock Hazen's brigade.

---

[61] Dr. Alonzo Thomas Clement Park, Compiled Service Records.

Hazen would later write that "the attack was so sudden that the horsemen were upon us, and some passed us and

Catlett's Gap 2020 – View to the Northwest With Lookout Mountain in the Distance

Photo by the author

were captured before they could check their horses. The pickets instantly took cover, while I sought the friendly shelter of a field of high corn. The affair was over in almost an instant, with a repulse and a loss to the enemy of one captain and several men."[62]

The one enemy captain General Hazen referred to was Captain Joseph E. Helvenston (1825-1863), who had mustered in most of Company F's men back in Dalton in December 1863.

Helvenston's body was returned to his widow, Keziah Ann Davis (1837-1863), and their three children for burial in Whitfield County, Georgia. Keziah herself died less than three months later on December 12, 1863. They are both likely buried at the Davis-Helvenston family cemetery west of Dalton, Georgia. Their grandmother Eliza Davis[63] raised

---

[62] William Babcock Hazen, *A Narrative of Military Service*, (Boston, Ticknor and Company, 1885), 120.
[63] Joseph E. Helvenston, Compiled Service Records and Helvenston family genealogy.

the Helvenston children.

The other men captured included Enoch Judson Boss (1825-1903), whose horse charged uncontrollably past the pickets, leading to his capture. Boss was held as a POW at Camp Douglas in Chicago, Illinois, until after the war. He was released on June 15, 1865.[64] The sixty-acre camp, located on the south side of Chicago in today's Bronzeville neighborhood, was named to honor Stephen A. Douglas, Abraham Lincoln's Illinois rival in the 1860 presidential election who died on June 3, 1861. The Douglas residence was nearby.

Originally an enlistment training camp for Union regiments raised in Chicago, Camp Douglas, along with Rock Island Prison 180 miles to the west, became notorious POW prisons. The reason for the location near the city of Chicago was because the city was a transportation hub with a network of railroads that allowed for easy movement of prisoners from where they were captured in the South. Like Rock Island Prison, overcrowding was the major problem at Camp Douglas. There were sixty-four prison barracks, each twenty-four by ninety feet long designed to hold ninety-five prisoners with the camp's capacity totaling 6,000 prisoners. As the war progressed, the barracks averaged 189 prisoners and the total population would be around 12,000 prisoners. Disease was prevalent. More than 40,000 prisoners would pass through the camp during its four years of operations, and the death toll from disease was estimated to be more 4,400 lives.[65]

A neighbor of Arba's, Boss would return to farm at Pond Spring, Georgia, after the war. William Brock (1839-1909) was wounded in this skirmish; though he wasn't captured at Catlett's Gap, he was captured on July 14, 1864, in Chattanooga, Tennessee, where he signed an Oath of Allegiance. He was released with orders to remain north of

---

[64] Enoch Judson Boss, Compiled Service Records.
[65] Andreas, A. T., *History of Chicago: From the Earliest Period to the Present Time*, (Chicago, The A.T. Andreas Company, 1885), "Camp Douglas," Volume II, 300-310.

the Ohio River until after the war, after which he returned to life as a farmer in Walker County, Georgia.[66]

April 10, 1902
MY EXPERIENCES
In the War of 1860 Briefly Told.

At home again. What a sad reverse! When I was last at home this settlement was in its prime. The farms all under good fences, the fields laden with corn and clover, the garner full to the overflow with good wheat, and abundance of fine stock of all kinds needed, and when I came back after the battle what did I see. The whole valley was one sea of deep dust and not a sign of a fence to be seen and the corn and all the stock was gone and not a chicken was left to crow for day. They poured the wheat in the dust for their horses to eat.

The next day I stayed at home and mother washed and dried my clothes and the following day (Wednesday) I started to hunt my command. Struck up with Jack Towns, our ambulance driver. He was in the ambulance and was going to the command and we went by way of Crawfish, then to Sanders McFarland that night, where a part of the regiment was camped. In the crowd was Tige, as we called him. His name was Brumbalo. In a saber combat he whipped seven yankees. He was a stout, active, large man, well drilled with the saber.

The evening I left home (Wednesday) I found a United States horse hitched in a hollow, south east of where we burned the wagon train at the Henry Switch. He had on a cavalry saddle and a gun with revolving cylinder. It was a good five shooter. The horse had been hitched there 48 hours without food or drink. Uncle Billy Mathis was pressed in on Monday to protect the yankees and it was this horse they furnished him to ride. We left camp at McFarland's, came up the dry valley road south west, found the command on a

---

[66] William Brock, Compiled Service Records and Brock family genealogy.

move and that Thursday night camped up the creek west of old Lookout church. The next morning as we were forming to start on the famous raid Wheeler made then around the Federal army in 1863, I fell out and stayed about home with the convalescents until Wheeler went around, which took about fourteen days as I remember. By this time cool weather had come and I was ready for duty. Now one year of my war experience had passed and my regiment had been in lots of fights and yet I had not fired a gun in battle, but the time was now close at hand. We convalescents went to meet Wheeler as he came off of his raid. We were in camp at Cherokee Springs and went through LaFayette to go to Galesville, Alabama, by Blue Pond. We had one cannon with us and the horses failed to pull it up Lookout Mountain, so we boys unlimbered the gun and rolled it up the bad places. We met the command on Sand Mountain.

A. F. Shaw

THE STOUT, SABER-BEARING Brumbalo [*sic*], nicknamed "Tige" was forty-one-year-old Sergeant Calvin Hamilton Brumbelow (1822-1864). Brumbelow had three brothers and a teenage son serving in different regiments of the Confederate Army. His three brothers would survive the war, but "Tige" was captured just two months later, near Kingston, Tennessee, and would die of measles on February 8, 1864, at Rock Island Prison. He is buried just south of the prison barracks in grave number 402.[67] His son John Brumbelow of Company B, 6th Georgia Infantry, had already been killed in action on June 10, 1862.[68]

The Battle of Chickamauga would start the next day on Friday, September 18, 1863. By Sunday, Arba was part of the cleanup detail "capturing lots of men and mules." Less than a week after leaving, he returned home to find the

---

[67] Calvin Hamilton Brumbelow, Compiled Service Records and Brumbelow family genealogy.
[68] John Brumbelow, Compiled Service Records.

valley completely changed from a week earlier as Union forces had razed everything. It must have been very emotional as he walked up to the front door of the farmstead, hoping for the best but fearing the worst. His family was very lucky to survive.

It was also very lucky that Arba was still convalescing with other wounded members of his unit to the south so he didn't fight in Joseph Wheeler's Raid. The bloody battle at Chickamauga had thinned out both armies. The Union Army of the Cumberland was down to around 35,000 soldiers from an original force of 48,000 troops. The Rebel Army of Tennessee was down to around 47,500 soldiers from an original force of 66,000 troops. The Union Army withdrew to Chattanooga, Tennessee, while Wheeler maneuvered around the Union forces coming down through the Sequatchie Valley north of Chattanooga, inflicting damage on the Union supply lines. Wheeler looped back down into Alabama where the rest of the 4th Georgia Cavalry would meet them.[69]

April 17, 1902
MY EXPERIENCES
In the War of 1860 Briefly Told.

The Sand Mountain was then in its virgin state and was the most pleasant looking country I saw during all of my travels.

When we met the command we waited for our company to come and then we fell in our respective places. We took a left-hand road and came off of the mountain at Lebanon, Alabama, as I remember, four miles north of where We crossed Wills Valley as we went. That night I helped our butcherman, Boatright, butcher a beef for the fourth Georgia. He was so well up to the business that I was hardly known in the dressing. His knife would fly fast and the strokes were long, so it was but a few minutes until it was

---

[69] American Battlefield Trust – Battle of Chickamauga.

ready to issue to the companies. It was guessed at and divided, bones not being considered. Often we would hear the complaint, "My piece is all bone," and many other things were said. The issuing Sergeant had to turn a deaf ear to the complaints and do the best he could. The next morning we started, we knew not where, and, as I remember, we went back to the Blue Pond road we had just went over. Don't remember all the camping places, but one night we camped at Rinehart's, near Trion Factory, and it seems the next day we passed through LaFayette and filed right and crossed Taylor's Ridge at the Mattox gap, then went north.

We camped one night in the hill country, near Tunnel Hill, Ga., and it rained all night and we made fires and stood and turned around before them. There was always somebody that could start a fire—no matter how hard it rained. The next day we went to Red Clay on the line between Georgia and Tennessee. We camped on the bank of a creek that was as red as the clay. We stayed there two or three days and it stayed red all the time. When time to leave we saddled, mounted, formed and marched out, and about the time we got straightened out the line halted and the air being sharp and cold we were not long making a decision to make fires to warm by. The officers giving order not to burn rails, the fence was torn down to get the pieces and we would break rails that were not very stout so we only burned pieces at last.

At last we moved on a forced march up in East Tennessee. We crossed the Tellico river. It was as clear as a crystal almost, and was possibly less than 100 yards wide. Now we are going up the south bank of the Tennessee river and we soon stopped to feed and cook and eat for the last time in three days.

A. F. Shaw

WITNESS THE FLASHING KNIVES of Whitfield County, Georgia's five-foot, ten-inch tall "regimental butcher" Private Nathaniel C. Boatwright of Company A as he does his magic with the foraged beef the soldiers manage to find.

The job of butcher was an important one for more than 1,000 men who made up the 4th Georgia. Boatwright made it through the war unscathed and was with the cavalry regiment through surrender; he signed his Oath of Allegiance in Chattanooga, Tennessee, on May 21, 1865. He married Sarah Jane Harp (1839-1881) in 1857, and they had eight children together. After the war Boatwright returned to his family and life as a farmer in Murray County, Georgia, but later moved to an area southeast of present-day Dallas-Fort Worth, Texas, around 1880. He lived there until his death in June 1901.[70]

IT WAS NOW LATE OCTOBER 1863, and the 4th Georgia Cavalry was to become part of Lieutenant General James Longstreet's Corps in Brigadier General John T. Morgan's First Division as part of Colonel Charles C. Crews' 2nd Brigade.

Shortly after, in early November, Confederate General Braxton Bragg sent Longstreet's Corps toward Knoxville to tangle with Union Major General Ambrose Burnside. In doing so, it reduced the size of the Rebel forces remaining around Chattanooga. With that, Private Arba F. Shaw and Company F began their march to the northeast, crossing back through Georgia and on into Tennessee on their way toward Knoxville.

---

[70] Nathaniel C. Boatwright, Compiled Service Records and Boatwright family genealogy.

CHAPTER FIVE
ON TO KNOXVILLE

April 24, 1902
MY EXPERIENCES
In the War of 1860 Briefly Told.

Up the south back of Tennessee river, just above Tilico river, the land was as fine as any I ever saw. We went in the fields to get corn. It was not one or two stalks in a hill, but it was in bunches and the one I went to had eight stalks and as much corn on them as my horse would eat. The field was in the bend of the river just below the ford. We crossed that night. The bottom of the river was rocky, the water about belly deep to the horses and swift.

We started at dusk, and we passed White's battery, and one of the artillery boys, Bill Hambrie, got a cannon cartridge of powder. It was in a sack, and about a quart of it, and as we came in sight by some means it caught fire and burned his eyes out and all the hair off his head.

After we crossed the river we went on in the direction of Maryville. It was then only a prospective town. I only remember a few shanties with daub chimneys. Some of them were finished out with a barrel. There was a grade there for a railroad, and between there and Knoxville the timber of a bridge had been put up, but a little way from Maryville. Now we are in for it. When we topped the hill south of the bridge the yanks on top of the hill north of the creek saw us and began shooting cannon at us, and the skirmishers in the swamp along the north side were shooting at us. We were not long in facing in line and counting off 1, 2, 3, 4, and 1, 2 and 4, dismounting to fight and to the rear with the horses. All ready, Colonel Avery in front gave the command forward *march, and down that long hill in an open field at a regulation step, Colonel and his orderly, Sam Latimer, in front mounted, and at every step we met heavy charges of grape and canister and minnie balls from the yanks in (the bushy swamp, and strange to say that Harrison Dalton was the only man hurt. As we went down the hill a piece of shell struck him on the breast on his testament in the breast pocket. The testament saved his life. Dalton was about two steps directly behind me. Somebody cared for him. We went on to the creek, where Latimer's horse was shot. The creek was eddy at that place and deep, and we filed to the right up to the bridge where it was shallow and crossed. By that time we got the first sight of the yanks that shot so much in the swamp. They saw we were on the flank move, and they came out and gave us room. By the time we got sight of them they were too far to shoot at, and we kept our ammunition, but went on and crossed a lane. Lieutenant G. D. Allen, was in front of me, A yank shot at him as he jumped off of the bank into the road and the ball cut out a notch in the top rail of the fence and passed on. My right hand was only far enough above for safety. On across the lane and the hollow, and up on top of the hill where their line of battle had been, but they were all gone. Then the Texas rangers came in mounted, raised the rebel yell, and gave them a send on to Knoxville, and we went back to our horses and camped for the night.*

The next morning we started on toward Knoxville, but did not go far until there came an order along back the line for about face, and about faced seemingly all at once, and we went to and crossed the Holston river below Knoxville a few miles. It was real cold weather, and the place we went in we had to jump our horses off of a straight-up bank, four or five feet above the water and light in water as deep as the bank was high. We stayed on and all took the ducking together. The water was deep and swift, and weak horses failed to get across unless they could swim to land.

A. F. Shaw

Steve Procko

It was November 1, 1863, as the 4th Georgia Cavalry stepped back into Tennessee along the route of what was known as the Cleveland Highway, today called Georgia State Road 71 that turns into Tennessee State Road 60. The Tellico River is to this day a pristine river located in the remote mountains of East Tennessee.

A tragic accident of the soldier in White's Battery named Bill Hambrie finds no mention in the historic record of the horribly wounded soldier. In fact, Captain White's Battery Horse Artillery has only sparse records remaining today. Traveling along with Crew's and Russell's Brigades were two-horse artillery batteries: Captain White's from Tennessee and Captain Wiggins' from Arkansas.

Throughout Arba's account of his experience in the Civil War, Captain White's Artillery Battery is mentioned the most often. During the Civil War horse artillery was used on both sides. These batteries were quick to move with the cavalry units and also provided a method for transporting men and not leaving them behind if they were to lose their horse or mule to injury or death during battle or from day-to-day life of the cavalry in motion. The horse artillery soldiers were trained to quickly dismount and deploy their artillery as needed, and to just as quickly remount and move on. In White's Battery there would have been two-wheeled caissons or carriages with light cannons or howitzers attached, along with artillery crew riding the horses or men riding in the wagons when necessary.

At FIVE-FOOT-EIGHT-AND-THREE-QUARTERS-inch tall with black hair, brown eyes, and a dark complexion, Captain Benjamin Franklin White, Jr. is himself enigmatic.[71]

He first enlists as a Captain of Company H, 4th Tennessee Infantry, on May 15, 1861. But his time with this company is short; he resigns on September 28, 1861, by special order number 174 accepted by the Confederate

---

[71] Captain Benjamin Franklin White, Jr., Compiled Service Records.

Secretary of War.

A week later he pops up as a Senior First Lieutenant in Captain Crains' Tennessee Battery. Captain Walter O. Crain was from Louisiana, had been a U.S. naval cadet in Annapolis, Maryland, in 1849, and now was an artillery battery commander. Plus, to add drama to White's new predicament, Captain Crain had just been ordered to Nashville to take the command of Nelson's Artillery.

White had been busy recruiting and is clearly restless, looking to command his own battery. With great ambition, he posts a letter dated October 18, 1861, to Major General Leonidas Polk, the second cousin to former President James K. Polk. "I went to East Tennessee but found a large number of the men in the section still union in sentiment & consequently opposed to the war," he wrote. "I was told a day or two ago by the Major of Col Lewis Regt now stationed in Lafayette, that I could get a company of one hundred men in Georgia from his neighborhood, in a very short time...I am very anxious to get into some more active service."[72] But apparently no decision is made by his superiors as to who would replace Crain until spring 1862.

White, on April 15, 1862, posts another letter to Adjutant General Thomas Jordan protesting the looming appointment of another officer to take command of what was formerly Crains' Light Battery. "As Senior First Lieutenant under Captain W. O. Crain, there has been no opportunity allowed me for my commanding officers to judge whether I was competent to command a light battery or not," he wrote. "The company has been raised to its present strength primarily by my exertions at considerable sacrifice. I cannot think it just that the road to promotion should be effectively bound against me, when I had every reason to expect such reward as my works here mentions. The men composing the company, some of whom are old United States soldiers, here shown Lt. not much confidence and disdain, and though not

---

[72] Letter from B. F. White, Jr. to Major General Polk; Memphis, October 18, 1861.

conscripted here expressed a desire for me to succeed to the command.[73]"

His lobbying must have been successful because in November 1862 White's Battery is first reported as part of General John A. Wharton's Cavalry Brigade of Major General Joseph Wheeler's Corps. White's name is also mentioned as being part of the infamous Christmas raid into Kentucky in December 1862 by Brigadier General John Hunt Morgan. A Federal Report created after the raid stated: "White's name is supposed to be Robinson, formerly a Kentuckian."[74]

In Captain White's Battery of Horse Artillery, almost all the soldiers first came from a large group of Texas cavalry, including the Texas Rangers in late 1862, followed by Alabama, Georgia, and Tennessee Cavalry soldiers through most of 1863. Most all the members came from other companies, no doubt because they lost the primary means of transportation to a cavalry soldier—their horse. As a result, only about ten percent of the soldiers were actual recruits and volunteers.

IN THE BEGINNING OF 1863 WHITE'S (Tennessee) Battery was again part of General John B. Wharton's Division of Wheeler's Corps, seeing battles as the year progressed at Shelbyville, Tennessee, and Chickamauga, Georgia, to name a few.

A document to Union headquarters by U. S. Brigadier General Thomas J. Wood to U. S. Assistant Adjutant-General Captain P. P. Oldershaw from Gordon's Mills dated Saturday, September 12, 1863, reported on a brigade of Rebel deserters: "Another deserter, who was brought in with these men, reports himself belonging to White's battery,

---

[73] Letter from B. F. White, Jr. to Colonel Thomas Jordan AG; Corinth, Mississippi, April 15, 1862.
[74] *Tennesseans in the Civil War: A Military History of Confederate and Union Units with Available Rosters of Personnel, Volumes 1 and 2*, (Nashville, Tennessee, Civil War Centennial Commission, 1964, 1965).

attached to one of Forrest's brigades of cavalry. He says he killed Captain White this morning, two hours before day, and made his escape. The captain had drawn his pistol to shoot him, when he seized a gun and shot him. This man says he left Rome, Ga., with his battery Thursday morning (September 10), and the brigade to which it is attached, coming up by the way of Dalton."[75]

Of the deserters, there is a record of three deserters around the date of September 15, 1863, in Rome, Georgia, from White's Battery: Private J. S. Mathis, formerly of the 11th Georgia Cavalry; Private John Neal, formerly of Company H, 4th Georgia Cavalry; and Private R. T. Snow, a volunteer who came over the lines around September 13, 1863, and two weeks later joined the Union Army's 5th Kentucky Battery. Snow looks to be the most likely suspect as he and two other soldiers—Bugler Thomas G. Leverett and Private Richard K. Melton—had been thrown in jail at Rome, Georgia, on August 28, 1863, for some unreported charge, something Captain White would no doubt have been extremely unhappy about.

Contrary to the Union field report of the time, Captain B. F. White, Jr. was not killed. Records show him on a sixty-day surgical leave of absence around this time, followed by duty as provost marshal in Milledgeville, Georgia, in December 1863. So it is clear he was undergoing medical rehabilitation. That's the reason why White's Battery was under the command of twenty-nine-year-old Lieutenant Arthur William Pue, Jr. as part of Longstreet's army of approximately 17,000 Rebel soldiers as it began moving toward Knoxville, Tennessee, in Arba Shaw's account.

---

[75] *The War of the Rebellion: A Compilation of Official Records of the Union and Confederate Armies,* (Washington, Government Printing Office, 1890), sr. 1, vol. xxx, pt3, 582. Hereafter this source will be designated as *OR.*

By the end of December 1863 both the 4th Georgia Cavalry and White's Horse Artillery Battery were part two cavalry brigades that comprised the First Division Cavalry Corps under Brigadier General John T. Morgan.[76]

First Division Cavalry Corps
(Knoxville Campaign) Brigadier General John T. Morgan

First Brigade Colonel Alfred Russell	1st Alabama - Col William W. Allen 3rd Alabama - Col James Hagan 4th Alabama - Col Alfred Russell 7th Alabama - Col James C. Malone Jr. 51st Alabama - Maj James Y. Dye
Second Brigade Colonel Charles C. Crews	1st Georgia - Lt Col Samuel W. Davitte 2nd Georgia - Lt Col Francis M. Ison 3rd Georgia - Col Robert Thompson 4th Georgia (Avery's) Lt. Col. William C. Cook 6th Georgia - Col John R. Hart
Horse Artillery	Wiggins' (Arkansas) Battery Lt. J. P. Bryant White's (Tennessee) Battery

TWENTY-THREE-YEAR-OLD PRIVATE SAMUEL Carpenter Latimore (1840-1901) of Company E was from Monroe County, Tennessee, and was on detached service as Colonel Isaac Avery's orderly through most of the war.[77]

---

[76] *OR*, sr. 1, vol. XXXII, pt2, 643.
[77] Samuel Carpenter Latimore, Compiled Service Records.

Private Harrison Dalton, also of Company E, had just turned thirty-eight years old as his company moved into Tennessee. He was walking directly in front of Arba when he got hit in the Bible, which was conveniently in his breast pocket. His horse was also shot. He made it through the end of 1863 but had had enough so disappeared, to be later dropped from the rolls for desertion on May 1, 1864.[78]

May 1, 1902
MY EXPERIENCES
In the War of 1860 Briefly Told.

The weak horses could not stand the pressure of the main current of the river and they would wash down into the deep eddy water below, rider and all, and lodge on an island. Some of the horses failed to get there but the men all swam to the island and were ferried out. I saw one man that lost his horse start on the swim with his overcoat on. He did not go far til he pulled off his overcoat and swam on and left it. I was uneasy for my part, as I could not swim, but my plan was fixed. It was to do like those that stayed with their horses—just fall off to one side and hold to the saddle or mane and let the horse take me to the island, In the main current the horses would turn their heads almost direct up the stream so as to breast the current which would strike them about the lower part of the neck. I got across all right and like all the rest was wet all over to begin with; the first thing to do on the starting across was to take a dive and as we got across we would stop and make fires and thaw up and dry.

This is the place where I got the cabbage head that broke my three days fast. It was about the size of a man's head. I cut it in two and said: "Boys, some of you can have half of this cabbage if you want it," and my wife's great uncle, George Wimpee, a 1st Ga. man, said: "I will take it."

---

[78] Harrison Dalton, Compiled Service Records.

I gave it to him and then and there by the fire we ate all of it raw. It was a solid white head.

While we were there it was easy to see why East Tennessee could flood the market so with her corn. She has a plat of large rivers and they all have an immense quantity of the best of bottom land that never fails—only when it does drown out.

Back to the cabbage eating from there we went to surround Burnside in Knoxville. Longstreet's corps was all ready there when we arrived and the place was surrounded and the firing of the skirmishers was constant. Every day we went up in the morning, dismounted and marched up to the N. W. commons and lay down in the edge of the woods and the yanks would shell the woods and cut limbs off of the trees and we would have to dodge to keep them from falling on us. We stayed all day expecting any minute to be ordered to charge the place, but the order never came. We retired for the night a few miles away but were back by times the next morning and lay there all day at the same place. The cannon balls and shells would pass over and bury in the hill just across the hollow behind us and we did as the day before and went out at night to camp and feed.

A. F. Shaw

Thirty-three-year-old Private George Washington Wimpee (1830-1903) of Company G, 1st Georgia Cavalry, was from Rome, Floyd County, Georgia, and was Arba Shaw's great uncle from his mother's family. Wimpee's company was also known as the Highland Rangers commanded by Captain John L. Kerr, a tailor from Rome, Georgia.

On April 12, 1862, Wimpee, along with three of his brothers—William (1811-1892), David Henry (1835-?), and Matthew A. (1829-1913)—were training in the gloomy drizzle of the early morning at Camp McDonald, which was located at Big Shanty, the future Kennesaw, Georgia.

Suddenly, a bugle cry went out, and the four brothers quickly raced away on horseback. They were the first in hot pursuit of a locomotive by the name of "The General," which was at that moment being hijacked northward by Union spy James J. Andrews and a well-organized band of raiders. The Wimpee brothers were quickly left in "The General's" steam. The raiders' goal was to take out the telegraph lines and bridges all the way to Chattanooga. "The General" traveled at high speeds of over 75 miles north, only to be abandoned by its hijackers two miles north of Ringgold, Georgia, once the locomotive lost steam pressure. Andrews was captured soon after and hung as a spy in Atlanta on June 1, 1862.[79]

In November 1863 three of the four Wimpee brothers—David, George, and Matt—were part of Colonel Charles Crews' Second Brigade, along with Arba, making their way toward Knoxville, Tennessee. After the war George W. Wimpee and his son William F. Wimpee did quite well for themselves as agricultural inventors. First came the father and son "improved Colter and Plow," which was awarded patent number 202,688 on April 23, 1878. William would go on to receive patent number 288,865 on November 20, 1883, for a new and improved fruit picker.[80]

May 8, 1902
MY EXPERIENCES
In the War of 1860 Briefly Told.

I begin this chapter with the 3rd day at Knoxville. It was raining that morning before day and we would start long enough before day to get to the commons by day. How dark it was that morning and drizzling rain fell all day.

---

[79] George Magruder Battey, Jr., *A History of Rome and Floyd County, State of Georgia, United States of America: Including Numerous Incidents of More Than Local Interest, 1540-1922*, (Atlanta, Ga., Webb and Vary Company, 1922), Volume 1, 150.
[80] Wimpee family genealogy.

On the day before the commissary man failed to find any rations for us but some of the boys that were out of line found a stray pig and brought it in in small pieces. Jim McCracken's mess got its head and cooked it in a flared camp kettle and when bugle called to saddle up, I saddled and went to McCracken's fire. He was in the act of pouring out the water and grease that cooked out of the pig head and I said: "Let me have that grease." "Allright," he said, so I ran my fingers under it and made my breakfast out of it. It was cool and I felt as well all day as if I had eaten a square meal, but for that I would have done without a bite two days.

As I said above it drizzled rain all day and we lay and shivered in line in the same place all day until dark when Longstreet's infantry charged and we, under the command, started too, but never went far til we were called off. When the charge was begun there was an enormous fire started and in two or three minutes it was sufficient to light up the whole country around. Afterwards we learned that the yanks had fired their commissary. Reckon they thought when the rebels raised the yell and started that nothing would stop them, but when Longstreet's men got to the barrier they had outside of the fortifications, they saw they could not take them without too great a sacrifice and wisely concluded to go back.

We went to our horses and I believe we started that night to Kingston, Tenn. Anyway we marched the next day and all the next night until the break of day, at which time we ran onto the pickets of our men—some of the 3rd Confederate. Uncle Henry Hardin was one and he spoke. I knew his voice and asked him how far it was to the yankeys. He said it was not far and we were getting in a hurry. About that time Lieutenant Dave Allen was ordered to cut off so many men of Co. F. and picket and scout on our left flank and our little band started off in a dim settlement road. It was not good light yet and we ran right into the yank's picket post, but they were all in a stampeed and the last men going out of sight when we got to the camp. I well remember an expression uncle Ben Chastain made when it was light enough to see. The yanks were on a high long ridge and the Johnneys at the foot. He said: "Boys, they have got the deadwood on us today; we will get the worst of it.

A. F. Shaw

The timing of the 4th Georgia Cavalry in and around Knoxville, Tennessee, would have been about November 16-17, 1863, when the siege of Knoxville began. The area that Arba mentions, the N. W. commons, was most likely around what was known to the Rebels as Fort Loudon, but Union forces would rename it as Fort Sanders after U. S. Colonel William Sanders (1833-1863) who was killed there on November 18. Coincidentally, Sanders, who was appointed Brigadier General but never confirmed by the U. S. Senate, was killed by a rebel sharpshooter under the command of Rebel Colonel Edward Porter Alexander (1835-1910), who was Sander's roommate at West Point during his time there between 1852 through 1856.[81]

Just after the 4th Georgia Cavalry began taking part in the siege of Knoxville, Tennessee, President Abraham Lincoln was standing among a crowd of about 15,000 people in Gettysburg, Pennsylvania, on November 19, 1863. It was just four and a half months after the Union forces turned back the Confederate armies in what was arguably the bloodiest three-day battle in American history—a turning point in the war. His Gettysburg Address was to consecrate hallowed ground for the burial of Union soldiers. The speech lasted between two and three minutes. Just 272 words in ten sentences. Future historians would consider it as one of the finest speeches ever delivered by an American President.

Four days later, the Battle of Chattanooga began in

---

[81] Gary W. Gallagher, *Fighting the Confederacy: The Personal Recollections of General Edward Porter Alexander*, (University of North Carolina Press, 1989), 8.

Chattanooga, Tennessee, on November 23, 1863. General Ulysses S. Grant seized the offensive against diminished Confederate forces under the command of General Braxton Bragg (1817-1876). Bragg had sent General James Longstreet (1821-1904) with 17,000 troops to Knoxville, leaving about 49,000 troops at Chattanooga when Grant began his assault with his army of more than 72,000 troops. Two months earlier, Bragg must have been feeling very much in control of the region after thrashing Union forces at the Battle of Chickamauga. He thought he had the Yankees on their heels, which was partly true as their supply lines had been blocked and they were starving. Then along came Grant, and by November 25 the Rebels were defeated and retreating toward Dalton, Georgia. On November 29 Bragg resigned his commission and would be replaced by General Joseph E. Johnston (1807-1891), setting the stage for the Atlanta Campaign in 1864.

EARLIER ON THAT SAME DAY of Bragg's resignation back in Knoxville, during the freezing early morning hours, Rebel luck was just as bad with a disastrous attack by Longstreet's forces on Fort Sanders. The debacle was carried out by three brigades from Major General Lafayette McLaws' (1821-1897) Infantry Division. Humphrey's Brigade was led by Brigadier General Benjamin Humphreys (1808-1882) and was composed of the 13th, 17th, 18th, and 21st Mississippi Infantry. Bryan's Brigade was led by Brigadier General Goode Bryan (1811-1885) and was composed of the 10th, 50th, 51st, and 53rd Georgia Cavalry. Wofford's Brigade was composed of the 16th, 18th, and 24th Georgia Infantry as well as Cobb's Georgia Legion and the 4th Battalion Georgia Sharpshooters under the command of Colonel Solon Zachary Ruff (1830-1863). The twenty-minute attack with the Rebels standing in a moat-like ditch in front of the steep, slippery walls of the fort while bullets rained down from above was unsuccessful, forcing the Rebels to quickly retreat; 813 men were killed on the Confederate side, including Colonel Ruff. More than 200 Confederate soldiers were captured in the ditch in front of the fort in the chaos of the retreat. Through it all, there were only 13 Union casualties.[82]

Longstreet removed McLaw from his command after the attack for neglect of duty. With the unsuccessful attack on Fort Sanders, the siege of Knoxville came to an end. By mid-December 1863 Longstreet withdrew to the northeast around Rogersville, Tennessee, to prepare for the winter.

May 15, 1902
MY EXPERIENCES
In the War of 1860 Briefly Told.

The yanks left the post judging from every appearance at the first signal of the pickets. Some had not gotten up, some were cooking and others were eating. At any rate we had a picnic—that is, our little squad. There were lots of good fires to warm us and all the good things we wished for to eat already prepared and still steaming and, sure enough, coffee too. Just imagine what a set of men would do for the like of that who had marched a day and night hungry and cold. There was plenty for our horses too.

We hunted over the camps and got us good saddles, bridles, halters, blankets, dog tents, frying pans, half gallon camp kettles, saddle pockets and anything else that we could utilize and all the rations and horse feed we could afford to burden our horses with. We kept out pickets all the time and about 4 p.m. it proved to be as Uncle Ben said. They had the deadwood on us and we got what Patty gave the drum—a good beating. We fell back, it seems to me, a few miles and camped a day or two, and when we did start right, we in 22 hours went, as I remember, 80 miles and that took us to Blaine's cross roads 18 miles north from Knoxville where we had two or three days rest. The 4th Ga. camped on a rich,

---

[82] David J. Eicher, *The Longest Night: A Military History of the Civil War*, (New York: Simon & Schuster, 2001), 616.

north face of a hill where there was fine red oak timber. J. C. Palmer being one of Co. F's. ax bearers, dismounted and marked a tree of his choice, then went to unsaddle and hitch his horse—In the meantime uncle Hiram Loyd got ready for the ax first, picked it up, commenced to cut the marked tree Palmer said, "That is my tree, Loyd. Look round where I marked it." Loyd said, "I will rassle with you for it." "All right" Palmer said, so Loyd came down the hill and Palmer went up to meet him. Palmer took advantage, gave a quick snatch and trip and sent Loyd down the hill a rolling. Palmer well knew that if Loyd got hold of him that it would be Loyd's tree as he was small and slender and Loyd was large. Loyd got up and ran Palmer a piece, then came back saying: "I would as soon try to catch a grey hound as Palmer and I will desert after this." And the morning we left there was the last time we saw him in the war.

At that place is where I first distinctly remember seeing the 6th Ga. She had captured a wagon train and was all rigged up in new blue caped overcoats. As to a space after leaving Blaine's cross roads I do not remember, but we went up toward Virginia. The 6th was a new regiment commanded by the brave little Colonel Hart, of Summerville, Ga.

A. F. Shaw

COMPANY F'S AXE-BEARING, twenty-one-year-old Private Joshua C. Palmer was born in South Carolina but was farming in Enon Grove, Heard County, Georgia, southwest of Atlanta with his father and mother at the start of the war. He was enlisted in Dalton by then Captain S. Jackson Owen in October 1862. After the fateful "rassling" match with Hiram Loyd in November 1863, he did indeed disappear from the 4th Georgia, probably returning home where he married at the war's end. In the late 1860s he, his wife, and their young daughter moved to Texas where he lived until 1914.[83]

---

[83] Joshua C. Palmer, Compiled Service Records and family genealogy.

Rebel Correspondent

The 4th Georgia Cavalry seems to have been toward the rear of the action on the northwest side of Knoxville during the attack on Fort Sanders. They then moved westward toward Kingston, Tennessee, before a rapid eighty-mile gallop northeast, placing them at Blaine's Crossroads eighteen miles northeast of Knoxville. This major intersection of several roads was named after Robert Blaine, who operated a tavern, a stagecoach stop, a post office, a medical dispensary, and a store named Shields' Station beginning in the 1830s.

THE LOCATION OF ARBA AND the 4th Georgia Cavalry in December 1863 is a little hard to pin down. Through his account, Blaine's Crossroads was reached on December 10, 1863. According to a soldier in the 6th Georgia Cavalry's account, it was December 16.[84] Records then show the 4th's Company G on wagon guard detail at Bulls Gap, Tennessee, for three weeks, which takes that company through the end of December.[85] Major General William T. Martin's report of January 8, 1864, mentions that the 4th Georgia was on detached service at Kingston, Tennessee, through December 30.[86] The rest of Crews' Brigade fought and skirmished east of Knoxville at Russellville, Mossy Creek, Strawberry Plains, and New Market during December.[87]

But it was at Blaine's Crossroads on either December 10 or the 16 that Arba mentions the 6th Georgia Cavalry for the first time. Arba's future editor at the *Walker County Messenger* was Captain N. C. Napier of the 6th's Company. K. Shaw's observation of the newly minted 6th Georgia Cavalry's soldiers dressed in recently captured Union blue-caped overcoats must have been confusing, and perhaps a

---

[84] J. W. Minnich, "The Cavalry at Knoxville," *Confederate Veteran Magazine*, vol. 32, 10-12.
[85] Company G, 4th Georgia Cavalry, Compiled Service Records.
[86] *OR*, sr. 1, vol. XXXI, pt1, 547.
[87] Minnich, "The Cavalry at Knoxville," *Confederate Veteran Magazine*, vol. 32, 10-12.

little dangerous. After all, one would not want to be mistaken for the enemy. Or perhaps there was another motive.

Their commander, Colonel John R. Hart, was a thirty-seven-year-old Granville, North Carolina, native. He was a

Private Curtis Green (1840-1926)
*1/6 plate ambrotype, Unknown photographer
David Wynn Vaughn Collection*

minister and an opinionated, passionate officer with questionable judgment. In August 1864 while Atlanta was falling, he challenged a fellow officer, Colonel James P. Brownlow of the 1st Tennessee Cavalry, to a duel. In a February 1865 letter to Georgia Governor Joseph E. Brown (1821-1894), even as the South's chances for victory were all but eliminated, Hart wrote that "if the time should ever come, when Georgia should take her cause into her own hands then my sword, my all sir—is at your service."[88]

PLAYING DRESS-UP WITH THE ENEMY'S uniforms was not an unusual tactic, but the 6th Georgia kept getting caught doing it. Private Curtis Green was born in December 1840 near Cave Springs, Georgia. He enlisted in June 1861, transferred to Smith's Legion Georgia Cavalry in May 1862, and was captured at the start of 1863 in Danville, Kentucky. He was exchanged shortly after his capture and soon transferred to the 6th Georgia Cavalry's Company K. The 6th's Company K was commanded by Lieutenant J. J. O'Neil, who tasked his men with scouting. Soon Private Green was wearing—yes, you guessed it—a distinctive blue colored uniform. "They dressed in blue and went through great perils,[89]" said Green.

Near Rome, Georgia, in September 1863, Green was captured by Union forces, who did not take kindly to his choice of attire and charged him as a spy. He was convicted and sentence to death; he was to be shot on October 4, 1864. The night before his execution he escaped his prison cell. With the help of a spoon, he had been digging the dirt floor of his jail cell, creating an opening large enough to crawl through. Clearly, this was larger than a salad spoon. He promptly got to the nearby Oostenaula River, jumped in, and floated to freedom. He was in North Carolina with his commander Colonel Hart and the rest of the 6th Georgia Cavalry at war's end. He then rode west on his horse and did not stop until he arrived in Texas.

---

[88] Confidential Letter from Colonel John A. Hart to Georgia Governor Joesph E. Brown; Madison, Georgia, February 15, 1865.
[89] Curtis Green, *Confederate Veteran Magazine*, vol. 2, 164.

In June 1866 he married Martha "Mattie" Lee (1843-1867). She died tragically during the birth of their first child in 1867. Green married a second time in January 1870 to Amanda Ellen Ross (1854-1931). They had twelve children. He farmed in Coryell, Texas, until his death in 1926.[90]

BY APRIL 1865 BOTH UNION AND REBEL forces were trying to stop the ugly incidents that were still occurring on both sides now that the war was over. It was hard to just turn off the machine of war with Rebel anger and frustration running high; clearly, the 6th Georgia was not immune. Hart would find himself indicted for murder and on June 21, 1865, and held in prison at Fort Pulaski near Savannah, Georgia. The charge came from an incident in which Hart reportedly allowed two men under his command in the 6th's Company G—Sergeant William Riley Johnson and Private James C. Millican—to murder Captain John McGuire of the 175th New York and a Confederate deserter name Howell on April 15, 1865, at Wilson, North Carolina. Not surprisingly, the men of the 6th Georgia Cavalry were roaming the countryside around Wilson dressed in Union blue uniforms.[91]

Colonel Hart, who became an attorney himself after the war, employed an attorney from the law firm of Madison and Morgan of Savannah named A. Porter. On June 5, 1865, Porter forwarded a letter from Colonel John Byne Walker (1805-1884) of Madison, Georgia, to Union General Henry Warner Birge, who policed the district around Savannah after the end of the war:

Col Hart of the 6th Georgia Cavalry is in your city under arrest charged with allowing two of his command to murder two federal prisoners at Nelson, North Carolina. Col Hart has a wife & 3 children living in our country & the Col has always maintained character for Integrity Bravery and Humanity. If he has any sort of showing we believe that he

---

[90] Curtis Green, Compiled Service Records and family genealogy.
[91] Mark H. Dunkelman, *Marching with Sherman: Through Georgia and the Carolinas with the 154th New York*, (LSU Press, 2012), Chapter 13.

will prove his entire innocence of the charges against him, He will be enabled to show that at Wilson NC he Paroled 19 prisoners, & ordered to Virginia two who intend to be paroled, the seargent [sic] & one private who had these two men in charge returned to Col Hart and reported that the two prisoners had attempted to make their escape in the evening of the same day & they were forced to shoot them. Col Hart reported this fact to his superior officer, General Allen, and desired the General take charge of the case. At this time the Confederacy was entering the dissolving scene & nothing could be done by General Allen, & thus it stood until a few days ago when an arrest was ordered from Atlanta.[92]

Two weeks later on June 17, 1865, at General Birge's recommendation, attorney Porter followed up with Union General Quincy Adams Gilmore in Hart's defense. "Col. Hart reported this fact about the killing of the two Federal soldiers by the guard who were sent off with them to his, Col. Hart's superior officer and desired General Allen to take charge of the case to have an investigation at once, but unfortunately at that very time the Confederacy was entering the dissolving I fear nothing could be done by Gen'l Allen. You will see at once my Dear Sir how difficult it would be for Col. Hart in the absence of all material witnesses to prove his innocence."[93]

General Gilmore responded, "Write to A. Porter lwy. and inform him that a fair trial will be awarded to Col. Hart & that he will not be forced of required to 'prove his innocence' but will be regarded as innocent until proved to be guilty."[94]

On August 2, 1865, Hart lobbied for a change of venue for his trial to Georgia as many of his men, who would be needed to appear in his defense at a trial, would be at a great inconvenience

---

[92] Letter from Colonel John Byne of Madison Morgan City, Ga., to Walker A. Porter, Esqr., June 5, 1865.

[93] Letter from A. Porter, Savannah; Letter to General Quincy Adams Gilmore, June 17, 1865.

[94] Letter from A. Porter, Savannah; Letter to General Quincy Adams Gilmore follow-up by General Gilmore written in the margins of the original letter, June 17, 1865.

financially to have to travel to South Carolina.[95] Six days later, his request was returned by Provost Marshall General Benjamin W. Thompson at Hilton Head, South Carolina, with the recommendation that he be tried in Georgia where he and his witnesses resided. There are no records of a trial or final outcome. Apparently, the charges against him were dropped.

After 1865 Hart started a law practice in Thomaston, Georgia, where he lived with his wife and four children, but he had both personal and financial difficulties and ultimately moved to northwest Georgia. He also worked as an agent and writer for *The Constitution* in Atlanta, which was at the time had the 4th's Colonel Isaac W. Avery as its editor.

In October 1877 Hart barged into the office of the Cedartown Express in Floyd County and verbally denounced the editor over something published that he disagreed with. The next day, the editor's stepson Fletcher Smith, a well-known printer and bookbinder from Rome, Georgia, attacked Hart and beat him severely with a stick.[96] The injuries were not considered serious at the time, but they ultimately resulted in his death on June 1, 1878. He was penniless. In 1886 soldiers from the 6th Georgia raised funds for their leader's tombstone in Rome, Georgia.[97]

But in December 1863 Colonel John R. Hart was in Knoxville, Tennessee, leading his men of the 6th Georgia Cavalry onward, with some curiously wearing Union blue while crossing paths with Private Arba F. Shaw and the 4th Georgia Cavalry. They all moved on from Blaine's Crossing, Tennessee, toward the icy, snowy winter of 1863 to be spent in the eastern Tennessee mountains skirmishing with the Yanks and living in survival mode.

---

[95] Letter by Prisoner John R. Hart from Hilton Head, South Carolina, to Major Burger AAG, August 2, 1865.
[96] *Rome Weekly Courier* (Rome, Ga., October 10, 1877), "Difficulty in Cedartown," 3.
[97] Hart's tombstone in the Myrtle Hill Cemetery; Rome, Georgia, reads: "*John R. Hart, Col. 6th Ga. Cav. C.S.A., Erected by Comrades & Friends Aug. 6, 1886.*"

**Col. John R. Hart (1826-1878)
commanded the 6th Georgia Cavalry.**

*Carte De Visite by Webster & Brother, Louisville, KY
David Wynn Vaughan Collection*

CHAPTER SIX
EAST TENNESSEE

May 22, 1902
MY EXPERIENCES
In the War of 1860 Briefly Told.

On our way we were at Dandridge and several other towns. Saversville, Moose Creek, Moss Creek, Morristown, Rogersville, Bulls Gap and I don't know where all else.

Now we are in a country of mixed politics—the blue and the gray. The blue had been protected by the men that wore the blue when they invaded that section and took largely of the stuff of the southern sympathizers and when we went we had to live off of those who had been protected. I remember we had a spat across the French Broad late one evening and while we were in the spat, some one of the 4th said: "What regiment do you belong to, Yank?" and one said but I don't remember what he said, and the Yank said; "What regiment do you belong to Johnny?" and Johnny said the "bloody 4th Ga." but night soon fell and no body was hurt on our side of the river and don't reckon there was on the other side and we went on our way. One thing I noted. It rained on the night of the 29th of October and the next morning the Smokey Mountains were capped with snow and stayed so until the winter was gone.

We were in Martin's Division which wintered there. Wheeler was in Georgia that winter with the balance of his corps. We had many hard trials that winter as we were continually skirmishing and sometimes had a stiff little fight. I wish I could give an accurate account of the winter's proceedings but it has been too long. We were poorly clad and the winter was so cold that the ice was 21 inches thick on the ponds, and the creeks were frozen over so hard that the wagons and artillery crossed on the ice and where we traveled the surface of the earth would get smooth and slick almost as the ice and I saw lots of Longstreet's men on that frozen ground barefooted. We had to forage on horse back and go armed. The most of the time we forded the French broad river many days on forage detail. The river was too wide and deep to wagon across, it was said to be 440 yards wide and when we got across we often would have to hunt in the caves and thickets to find the corn and meat where it was hid and sometimes we could not find it and we had to do without until we could find it. Sometimes we would ask children where their father was and some would say, "In the army," and some would say, "Gone over the river to get salt." The truth is lots of them were hid out and once in a while a bushwhacker would molest us.

One day Bill Turket was on picket and the snow was deep and a little boy and girl were plodding along the road toward him. Bill said, "Halt," but they kept coming. Bill said "I'll shoot if you don't stop." Then they stopped. Bill said, "Who comes there?" and the response was "Jake and Hallie." Bill talked with them a while and sent them back.

One day we went to a ford on the bank of a small river and camped after dark and as we were camping two shots was fired into our camps from the nearby rough heights, supposed to be by bushwhackers, but the two shots was all the demonstration they made. The next morning we forded the river and that put us into a fine well equipped farm and on passing by the residence we saw some battle soon about the house and the people there said the rebs shot the holes across the river and across the field which was between the river and the house. The yanks were at the house and two of them were shot through the plank wall of the well dairy house. Don't remember what command the Johnnys belonged to. Will tell you more about the well dairy in the following August, 1864.

A. F. Shaw

EAST TENNESSEE WAS A COUNTRY of mixed politics. The Southern sympathizers had had all their food, livestock, and other valuables taken by the Blue; now the Northern sympathizers would suffer the same fate at the hands of the Gray. In fact, Tennessee was the last state to secede from the Union; its eastern counties leaned toward the Union point of view through most of the war.[98] After Tennessee voted to secede, the state held another convention in June 1861 at the courthouse in Greene County where they unsuccessfully petitioned the state legislature to allow East Tennessee to become its own state.[99]

Arba backtracks the timeline from the siege of Knoxville, which ended in mid-December 1863, to October 29 when the first snow covered the Smokey Mountains and remained all through the winter. It was foreboding of the misery yet to come—a deep freeze in East Tennessee.

Knoxville did not go the way the Confederates would have liked. Food was now scarce, and it was difficult to rely on those citizens of "mixed politics" to help. There were skirmishes with the Union forces that remained east of Knoxville as well as guerrilla "bushwhackers" who could also have been masking as Union scouts. By the end of 1863, the 4th Georgia Cavalry was trying to survive in the harshness of winter. They had been on detached service from Crews' Brigade for much of December 1863 in Kingston, Tennessee.[100] They would rejoin the rest of the brigade around January 1, 1864.

TO THE SOUTH IN MACON, GEORGIA, sixteen-year-old

---

[98] Daniel W. Crofts, *Reluctant Confederates: Upper South Unionists in the Secession Crisis*, (University of North Carolina Press, 2014), 149.
[99] Eric Russell Lacy, *Vanquished Volunteers: East Tennessee Sectionalism from Statehood to Secession* (Johnson City, Tenn.: East Tennessee State University Press, 1965), 122-126.
[100] John Randolph Poole, *Cracker Cavaliers: The 2nd Georgia Cavalry Under Wheeler and Forrest,* (Mercer University Press, 2000), 106.

Rebel Correspondent

Leroy Wiley Gresham (1847-1865), an invalid who had had his leg crushed when a chimney collapsed on him and was also suffering from tuberculosis, was making daily entries in his diary.[101] The teen recorded his impressions of the war and the experiences of living with his ailments, as well as meticulous daily weather statistics from the beginning of the conflict until his death at eighteen years of age on June 18, 1865. On January 2, 1864, he recorded: "Cold still and bitter cold. At Day the Mercury on the back porch stood at 7 degrees + at Breakfast time 11 degrees at noon 29 degrees." This was 300 miles south of the Smokey Mountains where the temperature was likely below zero degrees.

ARBA MENTIONS THAT SOME OF THE INFANTRY was walking barefoot on frozen ground. The command gave permission to exchange shoes for the better ones their captured prisoners were wearing. In the cavalry, foraging for food for both soldiers and their mounts became the all-consuming focus. The bitter cold was taking its toll.

The New York Times reported:

Our losses by the enemy gaining possession of East Tennessee, says a correspondent of the Atlanta Intelligencer, are incalculable. We are not only deprived of the vast flour mills of that country, which previously supplied the whole army, but also of vast machine shops and depots, which we had extensively organized at Knoxville. Beside this, we are now entirely cut off from the coal, iron and copper mines of that region, which were worth millions to us. The copper rolling mills at Cleveland, which were superintended by Col. Peet, the Government agent, and which were burnt by the enemy, formerly turned out 6,000 pounds of copper per day. Over three millions of pounds had been delivered to the Government. This was the only copper rolling mill in the country, and which kept us supplied in copper for caps and

---

[101] Janet Elizabeth Croon, *The War Outside My Window – The Civil War Diary of LeRoy Wiley Grisham 1860-1865,* (Savas Beatie LLC, 2018), 278.

cannon. This is among our losses by the battle of Chattanooga, which are spoken of as merely resulting in a few thousand men and thirty-eight cannon.[102]

ARBA RECOUNTS THEN SIXTEEN-YEAR-OLD Private Joseph William (Bill) Turkett (1846-1917) enjoying a light-hearted moment with two young kids in the heavy snow while on picket. Turkett enlisted in Dalton, Georgia, on September 20, 1862, and was a member of Company A, which was primarily made of men from Whitfield County, Georgia. Turkett had been captured on April 21, 1863, at McMinnville, Tennessee, but was lucky enough to be paroled just five days later at Murfreesboro and returned to the 4th Georgia Cavalry. It was perhaps his age that allowed for his early parole and prevented him from being shipped to the Union prisons to the north.

In 1860 Turkett was living in Tilton, Georgia, though he was born south of Atlanta in Henry County, Georgia, in February 1846. He married his first wife, Martha Ellender Pepper (1845-1885), in 1867, and they had seven children. After the death of Martha in February 1885, he married his second wife, Delila Hicks (1850-1921), in November 1885. They had four children. After the war he became a farmer and lived in Georgia, Mississippi, and then Texas until his death in Iowa Park, Texas, in March 1917.[103]

AT THE END OF 1863 the *Richmond Enquirer* reported: "The Confederate Army in East Tennessee has gone into winter quarters; Longstreet's men are said to be without shoes, despite the fact that the weather is extremely cold and the mountains are covered with snow; 300 cases of smallpox are reported among the Yankee prisoners at Danville."[104]

---

[102] *The New York Times*, reporting on an *Atlanta Intelligencer* article, December 21, 1863.
[103] Joseph William Turkett, Compiled Service Records and family genealogy.
[104] *Richmond Enquirer*, Monday, December 25, 1863.

May 29, 1902
MY EXPERIENCES
In the War of 1860 Briefly Told.

From the battle scarred dairy we went on in a hurry, and though we did not know the cause, we soon learned what was the matter. We soon crossed a creek with high banks. We crossed on an old time wooden bridge, and soon the chief officer begun to send out flank scouts of which it fell my lot to be one, and there were orders for an advance guard and skirmishers. Then we began to expect a spat and, sure enough, the intention was to charge the guard of a large cattle corral the yanks had, and the spat went our way. We drove the fine herd back and appropriated them to our own use. It was said there were 2,200 of them. The wooden bridge, we thought, was not sufficient to bear up the cattle that would be on it at once, and we made them ford the creek above. It was dusk when the cattle got to the creek, but we kept them moving until they crossed the river, then they were where we and Longstreet's men could take care of them, and we did, and they were our beef and the yanks had to make other arrangements.

One day Company F was sent to a specified place on the bank of a river to scout and picket and, of course, we, like all the rest of Adam's race, would eat when we could get it and feed our horses, too, and we had to get it or do without. We would hunt and find corn and shell a part and grind it in the mill that stood by our camp. Thus we had bread and decided that it was not good to live on bread alone, and there came a two hundred pound fat biter, and the decision of the court was that his life should pay the penalty. Accordingly, the very large wash pot that was in the midst of our camp was set up and filled with water and a fire soon made the water scalding hot. Now for the execution of the sentence. The hog was fine and made us all the meat we wanted the few days we stayed there.

Steve Procko

The first time we looked out for corn after we camped there we went to an old man's house. He was of small size and looked to be 76 or 80, and the only person living with him was a 6 or 7-year-old granddaughter. He had about as much corn in one room of his house as we and our horses would eat at supper and breakfast, but the old man was so humble, and the little granddaughter so little, we left him his corn and went somewhere else to get it. I often think of that old man and little child, and am glad we had conscience enough to leave his corn.

After our time was out there we were entered back to the command, and soon we were on another trip. J. D. Allen, our lieutenant, was in command. We were under the same orders—scout the country and picket, and we had to look out as usual for number one or starve. This time we were in the hill country, but the land was good and we were obliged to intrude on the protected ones for our subsistence.

We found scant allowance of corn and some wheat and no meat. We were camped by a well to-do farmer and he was a blacksmith too. He had some grown daughters, and their mother was as spry as the daughters, and the father was out somewhere in hiding. One evening I went to the house to buy some poultry, of which they had an abundance of turkeys, chickens and guineas, and she said, "If you have any greenback I'll sell you some chickens." I said "I have no greenbacks, but I've got Confederate money." She said she would not have it, and when I found my pleading was in vain I told her that if she would not have my money, nor would not give me any chickens, I would take them. I went back to camp and it was dark in a few minutes, and the boys all being pressed with hunger it was not hard to get help, and one went with. I made a grab for two on the roost in the crack of the fence by the yard gate. One got away but I gave the other to my chum, and by that time the woman and children were coming out of the house to catch and put up the chickens.

A. F. Shaw

Rebel Correspondent

June 5, 1902
MY EXPERIENCES
In the War of 1860 Briefly Told.

My chum took the chicken I caught and when the lights came out he ran off to the camp and I was not satisfied with one. I watched the lights and they went into an old-time log barn and went to catching chickens and I went to the wall and reached through and pulled out another and went to the camp and dressed and cooked them before I slept and and had them ready for our messmates when they came off duty the next morning. I told them to eat and ask no question and we ate.

We stayed there one more day and the morning we left Lieut. Allen took a table full of us to the same house and ordered breakfast for us and when we sat down the lady seemed in a some what bad humor and was giving the fellow that stole her choice saddle mare down the country. Lieut. Allen, in his peculiar manner of expression, got her fired up and she, shaking her index finger at him said: "You are the very rascal that stole her," and many other hard speeches and the Lieutenant got so mad that he got up from the table and never ate any breakfast. The rest of us ate and went out to the front veranda and he was standing out there with his mouth poked out and J. H. McWhorter said, "Dave, she was rather getting onto your good feelings, wasn't she?" Dave said, "Yes, no — shall talk to me that way."

We told them we were going to leave that morning and went back to camp. We were late getting off and the camp was not in sight of the house and mean time the father had been put on notice of our departure and came in from his lair before we got off. When we got ready to go the Lieutenant took a detail with him and went to the house bent on some sort of revenge—don't know what —but when they got there he met the man of the house, arrested him and said: "Get in the road and go with us." All he could do was to obey orders and he went and his wife and three grown daughters came pouring out of the house squalling to the top of their strength. The Lieutenant would make the man go fast enough to keep out of their reach until they went about three miles through the mud and water when they were exhausted and gave up the chase and soon the Lieutenant released the man and let him go back to his home. When Wheeler made his raid, in 1864 I saw the same man and was talking about that circumstance and he said he was glad he did what he did, because it made his wife more careful in her talk. He said she would talk too much in spite of all he could say.

We went into camp, as I remember, four miles north of Morristown near a paper mill. It was then dilapidated by the soldiers before we got there. We camped north of the mill on a west slope in a cedar thicket. There is where Henry Odum thrashed Alvis Loyd with a cedar brush because Alvis was sick and would not get up and cook supper. Alvis got up and what he did for Odum was a plenty and when we left that camp Alvis deserted us.

It was there we saw Longstreet's men surround a field and send in drivers and catch all the rabbits there were in it. There could not one get away. The paper mill was run by two over shot water wheels. The owner said one was 70 feet tall and the other 100 feet tall. The mill was built at the base of a high bluff.

I believe it was at Morristown that Longstreet's men had a fight that lasted, as I remember, all one evening and till about 9 o'clock in the night. And then it rained and how they split the loblolly the next day as they marched.

A. F. Shaw

As THE MIND-NUMBING COLD of January 1864 continued, it was a miserable time for the Johnnies in East Tennessee. Staying warm and trying to find food were the two most important things on their minds. The losses experienced by the Confederate Army in late 1863 set the stage for what was to come in 1864. There was no way for Arba and his comrades to know the dire situation they were soon to face; for them the experience of wintering in East Tennessee at the foot of the Smokey Mountains was literally frozen in time.

IN A REPORT TO CONFEDERATE HEADQUARTERS from his winter quarters in Russellville in East Tennessee dated January 19, 1864, Lieutenant General James Longstreet wrote: "We only got some few arms and a little ammunition. Our infantry was not in the condition to pursue, half of our men being without shoes. Our cavalry is almost as badly off for want of clothing, and the horses are without shoes, or nearly half of them."[105]

Longstreet followed up on January 21, 1864, with a message to Ira Roe Foster (1811-1885), the Quartermaster General for the State of Georgia, in Atlanta: "There are five Georgia brigades in this army—Wofford's, G. T. Anderson's, Bryan's, Benning's and Crews' cavalry brigade. They are all alike in excessive need of shoes, clothing of all kinds, and blankets. All that you can send will be thankfully received." And then again the next day he wrote that "for want of shoes and clothing our infantry cannot go on."[106]

Quartermaster Foster, a veteran of the Seminole War of 1836, was appointed to the position at the start of the war in May 1861 by his good friend Georgia Governor Joseph E. Brown. He worked diligently throughout the war to supply clothing, boots, and blankets to Georgia's soldiers. His efforts were not entirely successful, with Georgia's soldiers being chronically in need of supplies throughout the war.[107]

---

[105] *OR*, sr. 1, vol. xxxii, pt1, 94.
[106] *OR*, sr. 1, vol. xxxii, pt2, 597-598.
[107] William Harris Bragg, *Joe Browns Army: The Georgia State Line*, 1862-1865, (Mercer University Press, 1987), 51.

STEVE PROCKO

June 12, 1902
MY EXPERIENCES
In the War of 1860 Briefly Told.

As I remember, it was in the vicinity of Morristown, and possibly the night the battle was there, that two Johnnies were bushwhacked on the same post. I believe one fell dead on the spot and the other was mortally wounded so he died before the next night. There was only one man at a time on that post. I was told that the two murdered men were 6th Ga. men.

Anyway the next evening was the 4th Ga's time to picket at that place and the bushwhacker post was the one I was placed on about early dusk and that gave me time to make an ample survey of the advantages and disadvantages. The post was on top of a ridge with an old turned out field on my right with saplings grown up and on the left were open woods of large leafy saplings and trees and no shrubbery to keep the winds from blowing the leaves away. The earth was moist and the whacker could come noiselessly upon the left and see a man on a horse by having the advantage of the light opening on the other side and shoot him off from a very short range. There was a very dark, lowering cloud both nights. I noticed that on looking to the right over the old field I could see the top of the saplings while down below a level of my eyes was total darkness and on the left was where the danger was. The bushwhacker could see me by looking up and where he was it was the blackest of dark to one on horseback, Just before my first watch was out my horse gave a hiss and looked into the dense dark woods and right then I reined my horse and retreated back north to the foot of the ride where there were leafy woods on both sides of the road and deep mud in the road and when the relief came the other man was left there and when I went back on my second watch the sentinel was still there and they all made that the post until day when we went back to the top of the ridge.

As I went to my post that evening I saw the bed on the yard fence with the blood on it from the man that was mortally wounded the night before and he was dead.

At another time there was a detailed Scout (that means one, two or more men from each company in the regiment and some commissioned officers and uncommissioned to command) put on guards and take-off. We were sent across the French Broad at Newport. It was my time to be detailed again. I often thought Shaw was a mighty handy name anyhow. Anyway I went and when we got to the river the mush ice was floating down in bergs and we had to watch and not let it catch our horses. They were heavy and the water was swift and up on the sides of the horses and if a berg struck a horse it would take horse and man before it to the shoal below and into the deep eddy. All across safe into Newport and on south to and across the Pigeon river in Cockeco county, then camped that night some of us went to a house, ordered supper and were eating. Meanwhile some one lifted a rich hive of bees. When it was gone one man that could handle cuss words in an expert way rode to the gate and ordered us out. We got out before we were done eating supper. Later it was found out that "to-do" at the gate was a cut and dried signal. Those who went in the house were to attract the attention of the inmates while the ones out were getting the bees. When the signal came some of the boys said, "Boys, the Lieutenant is calling and we must go," and all got out right now. He was not a Lieutenant; it was a sham to get some honey and so understood by some that were eating.

And that night after we all got down to sprawls and were asleep there fell on us a deep snow. The first I knew of it I roused up and moved my hat. (I would always cover my head with my hat.) When I moved, whoop! the snow fell all over my face and head. I brushed it away the best I could, pulled up my blanket over my head and was soon into dream land again and when day came I was as warm under two blankets and the snow cover as if I had been in a feather bed under a heap of quilts.

A. F. Shaw

Steve Procko

June 19, 1902
MY EXPERIENCES
In the War of 1860 Briefly Told.

One night there was a heavy detail (or a strong chain picket and my partner was Sam Goddard and the weather was cold and the day sentinel had a fire by a small stump. It was burned down bellow the surface and when the wind blew it would blaze up. Sam got pot down over the fire to warm and I said, "and, the first thing you know a Yank will send you a whistler." He said, "I don't care; I'm going to warm." Sure enough at that very moment one called by. Sam mounted and gave his mule a lift with his spurs and away he went and we both fell back 75 or 100 yards from the chain line. Where we stopped was on top of a small hill and where we were at first was down in a low basin by a fill of the East Tennessee R. R , not far south of Rogersville. The relief guard would go along the chain and would miss us because we were out of line and Sam and I stayed in our saddles all that cold windy night when the ground was frozen. The pickets fired all along the lines, but Sam and I kept our ammunition. The Yanks had a chain picket parallel with ours and by being quiet we could frequently hear a yank make a noise. We hear a cough, a stamp on the ground and sometimes a voice. About the break of day there came a man from yankeedom along the railroad and we held him up and took him up to Gen. Martin's headquarters. We did not know but what he was a spy. Don't know what became of him.

We were then in a flatwoods country and it was all so marked up with saw log roads that we could not know which was the original way. Don't remember how or when we left that place or where we went next.

At another time the command was on a move and it fell my turn to go on detached duty that day as advance guard, under Lieut. Allen. He counted and cutoff all in his count and said, "Come on, boys, and we went without any happenings *of note until almost camping time. When we were riding up between a creek and a large field we saw a house a little distance ahead of us and three men ran from the house up the hill across the field into a clump of woods on the upper side and on the bluff of another creek. We threw the fence and took after them but they beat us to the woods and were safe, and as we were hunting for them we found three large new boxes and, of course, we, as soldiers, had to see what was in them. We opened them. One had nice bed quilts and good U. S. and homemade blankets and another had wearing apparel—shoes, boots, hats, caps, homemade and U. S. and the third was full of what we all loved the best—bacon and hams. They were divided among us. Three fell to my share and we did not take much of the other stuff. From that find we turned back to the camp on another small creek at a small village, don't remember the name, but one thing I do remember—there was a pile of onions at a store house that had been frozen and were rotting. That night, with nothing to feed on, the order was rest the next day and I proposed to some of my chums to go up the creek foraging. They agreed, so we saddled up and rode up a trail along that creek several miles before we saw any sign of a settlement but at last we were rewarded. There had never been a Yank or Reb there. The crib was full of nice corn and four or five stacks of nice fodder in the lot. Of course our faces were hard by this time. We filled our forage sacks and got as much fodder as we could take and went back to camp and that aroused the major in command of the regiment. He sent his orderly to me and ordered me to report to him at once. I went, but I felt mighty little, and when I got there he said, "Good morning, Shaw." I saluted him and said good morning. The Major said, "Shaw, I want to know where you got that corn and fodder," I told him where and how to go and he said, "All right, I will send a detail after some for the regiment." Then he said, "I want enough of yours to feed my horse." Of course he got it and I then felt like I was growing back what he had scared off of my growth. We stayed there until the next morning and I don't know where we went next.*

A. F. Shaw

BUSHWHACKERS AND UNION SCOUTS nibbled at Longstreet's army's edges, testing their resolve. The military records of the 6th Georgia Cavalry record Private John Coleman as being killed in action near Sevierville, Tennessee, on January 27, 1864.[108] He is perhaps one of the two murdered 6th Georgia men in Arba's account. Coleman had enlisted just a few months earlier, on September 1, 1863, in Walker County, Georgia, and was a member of Company H. The date recorded in the official military records for Private Coleman could be incorrect, with the actual date of his death a week to ten days earlier.

A CHAIN PICKET CONSISTS of a string of posts with a couple of men, each with a chain of sentries out in front of each post constantly on the alert ready to fight at a moment's notice. Arba's partner was nineteen-year-old private Samuel William Goddard (1844-1933) of Company C from Floyd County, Georgia. Goddard would return to farming after the war, living the rest of his life in Floyd County. He married Martha "Mattie" Morgan in October 1870, and they had four children. Goddard was perhaps the longest living member of the 4th Georgia Cavalry, living to the age of ninety-nine years before his death in August, 1933.[109]

Foraging was still an important activity, and sometimes it wasn't only food that was found. It must have raised spirits immensely when they found a cache of Union boots and blankets.

---

[108] Private John Coleman, Compiled Service Records.
[109] Goddard family genealogy.

June 26, 1902
MY EXPERIENCES
In the War of 1860 Briefly Told.

Often Jim McCracken, of Company F, would say, "Boys, we are going to draw women some of these times," and one morning he and some others were going to report at headquarters and didn't know what for, and when they got in sight they saw some women standing around headquarters, and Jim said, "By heavens, boys, I've been telling you all the time we would draw women, and now the time has come."

One day we went across the French Broad on a forage detail and we could not find anything and we had to go back without anything, and three or four of us stopped for supper with a man that lives on the foothills south of the river. From all the surroundings, he seemed to be well to do, and we asked him if he had any com, and he said not. We believed he had corn hid out in a near by cedar thicket. We went back to camp and the horses gnawed bark for supper and breakfast, and the next morning we went back to that cedar thicket, and in it was one of the largest of cedar brush heaps. On investigation we found a large pen of corn, more than we could use in one day. It was hard to hide corn from soldiers, anyhow, especially cavalry. They know how to deploy and hunt.

Not long after this find we were ordered out in force to meet the yankees, and away we went all in a hurry, artillery and all, and as usual the demand was for advance guard and scouts on the right and left, and again it was my turn to go on the wing. Our little band did what was ordered for it to do, but we did not find anybody to fight, but the command did, and got a good flogging, too. J. D. Fricks told me the yanks charged them and were all mixed up with White's battery and tried to take it, but the Johnnies managed to save the battery. We went back to the same camp, as I remember, and it seems to me that some other command got between us and these yanks and had time to fortify, and when the yanks came they got a flogging. I was on the battle ground after that and saw saplings from small size up to eight inches that were shot down with minnie balls. I am like John Fricks. He said he did not like to tell that without a witness to prove it, yet there are living witnesses. Don't think there was any artillery used in that battle. As I remember it was south of the French Broad and our camp was on the north side.

And soon after the above occurred, General Martin, with his division, started after the same routed yanks, and went driving them toward Knoxville, and there were women and children standing on the sidewalk in Dandridge to greet our coming, and there was a small girl among them with a white rabbit in a cage, the first I ever saw. We went on and were soon met by the yanks. They had crossed the river and were ready to meet us again.

Their skirmishers fired on our advance. We halted, formed line of battle; the officers called for volunteers to skirmish, and soon there was enough on the way. I had not fired a gun at a man and I stepped out in the line, too. We deployed and went forward to where we had a full view of their situation. There was a large hollow between us, they on the southwest and we on the north east. The others went to work as soon as they got there, but as to me—what about shooting at a man? But they were shooting at me and I resolved to go to work and after the first shot my nerves quieted and I worked on with as deliberate precision as the other boys that had been in lots of such like places. We kept up the skirmish some time. Meantime we asked the yanks to quit shooting and lets talk awhile.

A. F. Shaw

A Correction.

Ed. Messenger Will you please publish the following letter from Dr. Wm. R. Cole. He is right in the statement he makes in his letter—I had forgotten how it was and wrote it differently.

Rebel Correspondent

A. F. Shaw

Jackson, Tenn., June 30, '02.

A. F. Shaw, Dear Comrade:—I see in the last issue of the *Walker County Messenger* in your recollections of the war, you mentioned a battle close to Dandridge, Tenn., where we got the worst end of the fight. I happened to be in the fight and was assistant surgeon in White's Battery which you mentioned. We lost two pieces of our battery in that fight and several of our boys in the battery taken prisoners and two of our men by the name of Nelson were killed. I think they once belonged to the 4th Ga. Cavalry before they joined the battery. Col. Avery charged the yanks and kept them from taking more of our guns.

We came back and camped on the other side of the French Broad that night, and I think next day we went back and occupied the battlefield. I found two men from the 4th Indiana Cavalry who had been wounded by our battery. I took a piece of shell out of one of them and some canister shot out of the other. They both got well and were paroled and went back to Knoxville. I have met a yankee soldier who was in the same company with the two boys I operated on in that fight. He told me he was through the war and in all the fights in East Tennessee. I told him I was in all of the fights in East Tennessee. Some of our boys on the 1. C. R. R. called my name, (Dr. Cole). He came to me and asked if I was a surgeon in that battery that fought them that day. He told me that those boys came back to Knoxville and told the Colonel of the 4th Indiana Cavalry if they ever captured a rebel surgeon by the name of Cole to do all they could for him as he had saved their lives.

I am living at Jackson, Tenn., and moved here from Walker county, Ga., in 1866. My old home is on Duck Creek at the Burnt Mill school house. Marsh station on the Chattanooga Southern is on the old place. I have never found a better neighborhood than was in our valley, although I have a host of friends in Jackson, Tenn. We have a fine Confederate Camp and all are uniformed.

Please excuse my letter as I have but little time as I am in the railroad office. Having seen that you mention White's Battery I could not help writing these lines.

**Your comrade,
Dr. W. R. Cole**

FOR PRIVATE SHAW THE WAR had just become real. He contemplated shooting another human being for the first time. It's clear that the nature of combat shook him. But he swallowed his nerves with his first shot and proceeded to follow what Sergeant McCracken and his fellow soldiers were doing. He had been a solider for just over a year; though he had seen skirmishes, this was the first one in which he looked down the end of his rifle at another human being. Perhaps he thought it best not to think so much about the significance of what he was doing, but rather to form a battle line with his unit and focus on the job at hand. The metaphor of the era was known as "Seeing the Elephant," witnessing something exotic and experiencing the bigger world beyond the small one of day-to-day life, sometimes at great cost.

James Alfred (Jim) McCracken (1825-1910) was a thirty-eight-year-old sergeant in Arba's Company F from Tilton, Georgia. He served through the end of the Civil War and survived unscathed. He married Mary Ann Edwards in 1853. Before the war they had three children; the youngest child, Mary Georgiana, was born in January 1861 just a year and a half before her father enlisted. After the war Sergeant McCracken returned to farming in Central Georgia, southwest of Macon. He and his wife had two more children, and he lived to the age of eight-four years, dying in January 1910 in Parrott, Georgia.[110]

After the Battle of Shiloh in 1862, Private Augustus

---

[110] James Alfred McCracken. Compiled Service Records and family genealogy.

Harvey Mecklin (1834-1913) of the 15th Mississippi Infantry wrote in his diary: "I thought of the hundreds, perhaps thousands that this day must pass into eternity. I thought of the many widows & of those that must this day be made. I thought of weeping mothers & sisters & anguish river hearts of lovers & minds. I thought of my own liability to fall a victim,—perhaps in one more hour—then came up the momentous questions. Am I prepared."

Mecklin was injured at Shiloh and discharged for his resulting disability. In 1863, a year after being discharged, he became a Presbyterian minister.[111]

IN MID-JANUARY 1864 General Longstreet had his sights on reengaging in Knoxville, Tennessee. He rounded up his cavalry, which included Alba's regiment, and made a move on Union forces around Dandridge, Tennessee.

On January 19, 1864, Brigadier General Samuel Perry "Powhatan" Carter (1819-1891) reported to the Union command in Knoxville, Tennessee: "Learned that skirmishing was going on at Hudson's Branch, 8 miles below Dandridge, on the north side of the French Broad, yesterday evening about 3 or 4 o'clock, between some of our own and the enemy's cavalry forces and that our force engaged at that point were falling back toward Strawberry Plains, being greatly outnumbered by the rebels."[112]

The next day—January 20, 1864—Lieutenant General James Longstreet reported to General Samuel Cooper (1798-1876): "The enemy is still on the retreat; our cavalry is in pursuit." Then on January 22, 1864, he wrote: "The cavalry is now in pursuit of the enemy, who seems to be making his way to Knoxville."[113]

The engagement that forced the Union to retreat back to

---

[111] Augustus Henry Mecklin Papers, Mississippi Department of Archives and History, Jackson, Mississippi.
[112] Charles F. Bryan, Jr., *A Gathering of Tories: The East Tennessee Convention of 1861*, (Tennessee Historical Quarterly, Spring, 1980).
[113] *OR*, sr. 1, vol. xxxii, pt2, 579.

Knoxville had implications for Captain White's Horse Artillery Battery, which was almost lost, as we learn in the letter from Dr. William R. Cole that Arba requested be printed in the *Walker County Messenger* in 1902. Cole witnessed Colonel Isaac W. Avery charging his cavalry to prevent Captain White's Battery from being taken. Found hidden in the records of Dr. Cole's past is a common family story of tragedy often found in the Civil War.

DR. WILLIAM R. COLE WAS BORN in 1837 in Chatham County, North Carolina. He graduated from the University of Nashville Medical School and was certified as a physician right before the start of the war in 1861. He enlisted in Company G of the 9th Georgia Volunteer Infantry in June 1861 at LaFayette, Georgia. Just over a month later, he found himself at the First Battle of Manassas on July 21, 1861. Soon after he became disabled as a result of typhoid fever, which required a lengthy convalescence, and was discharged from service in September 1861. By 1862 he began serving as a hospital steward and then assistant surgeon for the rest of the war.[114]

Dr. Cole's brother 3rd Sergeant Thomas T. Cole (1842-1863) enlisted in Company E of the 39th Georgia Infantry at LaFayette, Georgia, in spring 1861. He was captured along with most of his company at Vicksburg, Mississippi, on July 3, 1863, where he took the Oath of Allegiance five days later and was furloughed on July 22, 1863. He most likely was wounded at Vicksburg and died on November 23, 1863, while recovering in Rome, Georgia.

Cole's sixty-one-year-old father, Harbert Cole (1803-1864), enlisted as a Private in Company B of Culbertson's Battalion Cavalry, Georgia State Guards, in August 1863. His military records list him as "Old and unable for service." A few months later in December 1863, Union forces arrested Harbert Cole as a citizen in Lafayette, Georgia, perhaps for

---

[114] Dr. William R. Cole, Compiled Service Records.

aiding the Confederate Army. He died at Camp Chase prison in May 1864 of anemia and is buried in grave 148 with the inscription: H. A. Cole – Citizen.

As a practicing Rebel surgeon in a time of war, Dr. William R. Cole operated on two soldiers from the Union's 4th Indiana Cavalry. Military hospitals often provided first aid to the wounded on both sides; in some cases they released the POWs back to their own side for recovery from their wounds. Dr. Cole never fully recovered from his bout with typhoid fever. After the war he farmed and practiced medicine for a short time. He later took a job as a bookkeeper for the Illinois Central Railroad and died in Jackson, Tennessee, in June 1906.[115]

Dr. Cole's mention of his time serving in Captain White's Horse Artillery Battery brings to mention two men named Nelson with a similar story of family tragedy.

Seventeen-year-old Noah D. Nelson (1846-1864) from Murray County, Georgia, was serving in Captain White's Battery along with his older brothers, forty-one-year-old William Shannon Nelson (1822-1900) and nineteen-year-old Isaac M. Nelson (1844-1864). Also serving was William Shannon Nelson's twenty-two-year-old son Andrew McDuffy "Mack" Nelson (1841-1931).

All four had originally enlisted in Company F of the Third Confederate Cavalry in May 1862 in Spring Place, Georgia, and in May 1863 all four had transferred to Captain White's Battery. It was common for fathers, sons, and siblings to try to stay together during what must have been very confusing times traveling to unfamiliar places. It offered a bit of familiarity and allowed family members to look out for each other. But it could also set the stage for painful emotional distress if things went bad.

The military records show that on January 27, 1864, Noah D. Nelson was killed in action. In the account written by Arba and Dr. William R. Cole, the event with White's

---

[115] Cole family genealogy.

Battery seems to tie in with the Battle of Dandridge, which occurred on January 17, 1864. The discrepancy could be in that the records were written months after the fact, and the dates were sometimes not precisely recorded.[116] Noah's brother Isaac was captured during the same battle that almost resulted in the loss of Captain White's Battery. He was sent to Rock Island, Illinois, where he died of typhoid fever on March 19, 1864.[117]

William Shannon Nelson and his son Andrew McDuffy "Mack" Nelson had witnessed the loss of two family members on the same day. They both survived the war and returned to farming in northwest Georgia. William Shannon Nelson died at age eighty-three years in 1907. Andrew later worked in a cotton mill in the twentieth century, living to the age of ninety before dying in 1930.[118]

Now, across the divide, the Johnny Rebs and the Billy Yanks stopped fighting for a few moments, contemplating their individual situations and sizing each other up as a cold wind whistled through the trees.

July 3, 1902
MY EXPERIENCES
In the War of 1860 Briefly Told.

We all quit but one yank, who would not quit when all the rest did. When both sides agreed to the cessation, we all came from our hiding and were walking about in plain view of each other, but the man that would not give up could be easily seen behind a fence through the cracks. He kept shooting —reckon he wanted to kill one Johnny and it soon developed that he was picking at this one. The first time he shot after the rest quit and came out, he shot and the ball passed me and hit a chicken in the barn lot and Jake Hale, of Co. K., said, "Hey there, consarn you, quit killing the

---

[116] Noah D. Nelson, Compiled Service Records.
[117] Isaac M. Nelson, Compiled Service Records.
[118] Nelson family genealogy.

chickens' He shot again and killed a pig that was in bed with its mother in a straw pile. Then I said to him, "Don't shoot the pigs and chickens; shoot me." So he kept shooting and I kept telling how much he missed and how high or low and on which side until he shot seven times and that was such a close call I stepped behind a shed post of the barn and said, "Now try me." He shot again and hit my post. Then I said, "Lookout Yank, you are getting too close to me" and I went into the barn and in a crack between two logs I got a lying-down rest and shot. He never moved for it. I reloaded and raised my sight for 200 yards and, with all the pains I could take in drawing a bead on him, I fired and he fell. Then some of his comrades ran to him and the officer who I supposed was in charge rode up and I took a pull at him. About that time White's battery had come to the front and began shooting and the yanks got, and us after them and soon we were all relieved and fresh men took our places and on toward Knoxville all that and the next day. There was a continual running skirmish both days and late in the second evening we found in front of us a high ridge where a field ran up near the top on our right. There their skirmishers were stubborn and it took ours a good while to move them and when they did General Martin at the head of the command marched up to the top of the ridge and was met with a volley waiting in ambush.

The General turned back down the road saying, "Steady, men! Steady, men!" and the yanks kept shooting, and Jake Hale of Co. K, was shot through the left knee, After he was shot and our leader was gone we all with one accord disappeared in a moment into the dense forest that was on our left and east of the road. Not withstanding we were in the road by fours and well closed up and the yanks had a good view of that sort of a line for perhaps a half mile, the front being in their grasp, they never shot anyone but Jake Hale that I know of or got a prisoner. General Martin's object was to go back a piece and form a line—don't remember whether it was formed or not. We who went into the woods kept under cover until we were at a safe distance, then nightfall was on us and we put out pickets and rested on our arms through the night. Then we went back over the same ground through Dandridge.

That country was well stripped of anything to live on. It seemed to the observer that every nook and corner had been searched and all that was there had been taken away and used by the two armies. We had to hunt new grounds so went through Rogersville and Bull's Gap. Then we were in Green county. I remember a few of the 4th were detailed for some thing, (I believe it was to scour the country off the main road to see if we could find any cattle). As I remember we drove in three and as we drove up to a quaint old farm house the command had gone on and, as was the general rule, there were stragglers in search of something to eat and feed on. Three were hemmed in the near-by log barn by the old lady of the place and while they were searching in the shacks for corn, she with board in hand, was telling them to come out.

A. F. Shaw

BY LATE JANUARY 1864 THE RESULT of thousands of men from both sides trying to survive in the harsh winter had stripped the land bare in a large thirty-mile wide swath from Knoxville, Tennessee, sixty-five miles east to Rogersville, Tennessee. Both armies had been running each other all over the Holston River valley. Now that the Union Army had retreated for the time being back to Knoxville, it allowed the 4th Georgia Cavalry to head south over the Broad River into Greene County, Tennessee, and areas that had not yet been picked clean.

The process of foraging for food for both the soldiers and their horses by now must have become intolerable for the starving citizens of East Tennessee. This part of East Tennessee at the north edge of the Great Smokey Mountains was made up of subsistence farmers deep in the middle of winter, living off the foods they had preserved from their farming efforts the prior year. These were the food stocks they needed to survive winter. Even as they tried to defend their property by any means, they were no match for armed soldiers.

The last of the skirmishes resulted in Sergeant Jacob K. Hale of Company K being wounded with a shot to his left knee. His injury resulted in him never being able to return to the 4th Georgia; for him a frozen battleground in East Tennessee would mark the end of his war.

The thirty-seven-year-old Hale was born in Wythe County, Virginia, but later moved to Walker County, Georgia, around 1849 where he married his first wife Permilia Elvira Gilbert (1833-1876); they had eleven children. After the war Hale and his family moved to Sebastian County, Arkansas. When Permilia died in 1876, Hale married her younger sister Nancy Elizabeth Gilbert (1837-1899) the next year. Jakob K. Hale would farm in Arkansas until his death in 1895.[119]

ON JANUARY 31, 1864, CREWS' BRIGADE listed the total men both present and absent at 3,453 troops. Not counting those absent, there were just 1,043 men "aggregate present" with only 730 men and 63 officers actually "present for duty." The ranks had been greatly depleted after the Knoxville siege and the impact of winter.[120]

On February 6, 1864, Major William W. Wheeler of the Union's 23rd Michigan Infantry Volunteers serving under the XXIII Corps under Brigadier General Mahlon D. Manson (1820-1895) reported: "Longstreet's Headquarters is a Morristown... It is reported that on the 17th ultimo Longstreet was at Dandridge with 20,000 men and twenty pieces of artillery, hoping to force a general engagement. Strips of rawhide were issued to his

---

[119] Jacob K. Hale, Compiled Service Records and family genealogy.
[120] *OR*, sr. 1, vol. xxxii, pt2, 640.

men to bind up and protect their feet."[121]
July 10, 1902
MY EXPERIENCES
In the War of 1860 Briefly Told.

The men in the barn saw they had to do something and there was no way of escape only through a window where one log had been cut out. One man went out it. She ran to board him and the others got out at the door. What a laugh! He was not long getting out.

We went on and stayed in Bull's Gap that night and it rained before day and until noon, but when day came we went on and overtook the command. It had passed through the gap and camped. When we caught up, it was in the saddle and moving southeast or some what south to Price's ford on the Nolachuckee river. The Price that lived there was an old man and was a bachelor. He and his negroes were all of that household. We camped and again I was detailed with others to guard the wagons over the river and help pull and load them with corn. The river was rising fast from the morning rain and some of the wagons crossed with the corn all right and, as I now remember, two washed down and no more would take the risk and turned up the river seven miles to a bridge and never got in until about twelve the next day. I was one of the lucky ones and was sent over in front of the first wagon. All could have come over if they had had day light and had driven above the deep water. It was dark when the first wagon crossed.

Do not remember how long we stayed at Price's but I remember about being on a scout one day over the river and it rained and got the river on a big swell the time and our crew had to go to the same bridge to cross. I believe it was called Latspeach's bridge. Any way, we stayed all night at the widow by that name. She was a true southern right's woman and fed us and seemed glad to do so. She said that

---
[121] Ibid.

southern right's people had to be careful about what they said. She was real intelligent. I well remember how she looked and how she talked. She was a lady much after the form and make up and speech and expression of the mother of J. D. Fricks.

We camped at so many places that I am all tangled up about their rotation, but I believe my time is almost out in East Tennessee. The last place we camped at before left was on a plat of nice red oak and hickory land very slightly rolling and facing south. That was where I left my rundown horse and mounted a young U. S. mule that had been captured. He was a dandy—a regular cracker jack, and he could beat more than half of the horses running.

I remember we stayed at that place some time and we foraged east of the camp along the valley at the west foot of the great Smokey Mountain and adjacent to the starting up of the fine road that crossed over to Webster and Asheville, N. C. One day the forage detail went out in that valley after corn and twenty-two men of the 2nd. Ga., regiment of the Cruse brigade decided to cross the mountain and come back to Georgia and that night Colonel Cruse called for a detail of a hundred men and three commissioned officers to be in the hundred to go after them. The orderly woke me up at midnight and said: "Shaw, you are detailed to report at Colonel Cruse's headquarters at once." How bad I hated to get up, but the decree had gone forth and I had to go. At the headquarters Cruse told the Sr. Lieutenant—Reese—to take these men and go after the twenty-two that deserted that day. We started by the star light and daylight found us at the foot of the Smokey Mountain, where we scattered out and fed and ate breakfast preparatory to a long march. On the mountain we found deep snow and but few little huts and the finest bodies of very large spruce or hemlock trees and lots of them felled across the road to blockade. The horses had to jump over them, they were so large.

A. F. Shaw

NOW MOVING CLOSER TO THE Smokey Mountains in Greene County, the heart of the Union sympathizers in East Tennessee, Arba crosses the Nolachuckee River at Price's Ford. He then crosses Latspeach's [sic] bridge and mentions a widow he and his fellow soldiers stayed with by the same name. This would most likely have been Mary Ann Earnest Lotspeich (1789-1878), whose family history records her and her husband, John W. Lotspeich (1772-1845), as living next to a bridge named after them.[122] The German Lotspiech and Swiss Earnests (Ernsts) families were some of the earliest settlers in Greene County, living around the towns of Newport, Sweetwater, and Chuckey.

In the military records for the 2nd Georgia Cavalry a significant number of soldiers are listed as AWOL around February 9 and 10, 1864.

At the same time, under the orders of Colonel Charles Constantine Crews, Arba and a hundred other soldiers are detailed, along with Lieutenant Redmon Thomas Reese of the 3rd Georgia Cavalry and two other officers to go in pursuit of the twenty-two men from the 2nd Georgia Cavalry.

Reese was born in January 1831 in Warren County, Georgia, to Martha Patsy Mims and Redmon Reese, Sr.; Redmon was a slaveholder and a veteran of the War of 1812. Reese's father died a few months later in July 1831 when Redmon, Jr. was still an infant. Reese married Sarah Ann Waters in 1852. By the time his small band of soldiers reached Ellijay in late February 1864, Reese was in a hurry. Sarah was pregnant with their seventh child, Elizabeth Louise, who would be born on April 24, 1864. But Lieutenant Reese's furlough at home would be short-lived. Less than a month after his daughter's birth on May 20, 1864, he was captured shortly after the Battle of Resaca and sent to the prison at Johnson Island, Ohio, and then forwarded to

---

[122] Earnest/Ernst and Lotspeich family genealogy.

Fortress Monroe, Virginia. He suffered from the terrible conditions of a POW and ended up in General Hospital No. 4 at Richmond, Virginia, on September 23, 1864, with chronic diarrhea and emaciation before being permanently furloughed on October 7. For Reese, it marked the end to his war. He returned to Gordon County, Georgia, to recover and went back to farming. He served as Justice of the Peace and County School Commissioner for over twenty years. He and Sarah had ten more children in the years after the war, making it a grand total of seventeen children. He died in June 1908 in Gordon County, Georgia.[123]

NOW A LARGE GROUP OF REBEL soldiers began to head southwest through the snow in pursuit of a group fellow soldiers who had gone AWOL. They must have decided they had had enough of winter in East Tennessee so started to trudge through the mountains and snow heading back home to Georgia. It would prove to be Arba's early ticket back home as well.

Union Winter Camp

Sketch by Edwin Forbes
1863 – Library of Congress

[123] Lieutenant Redmon Thomas Reese, Compiled Service Records and family genealogy.

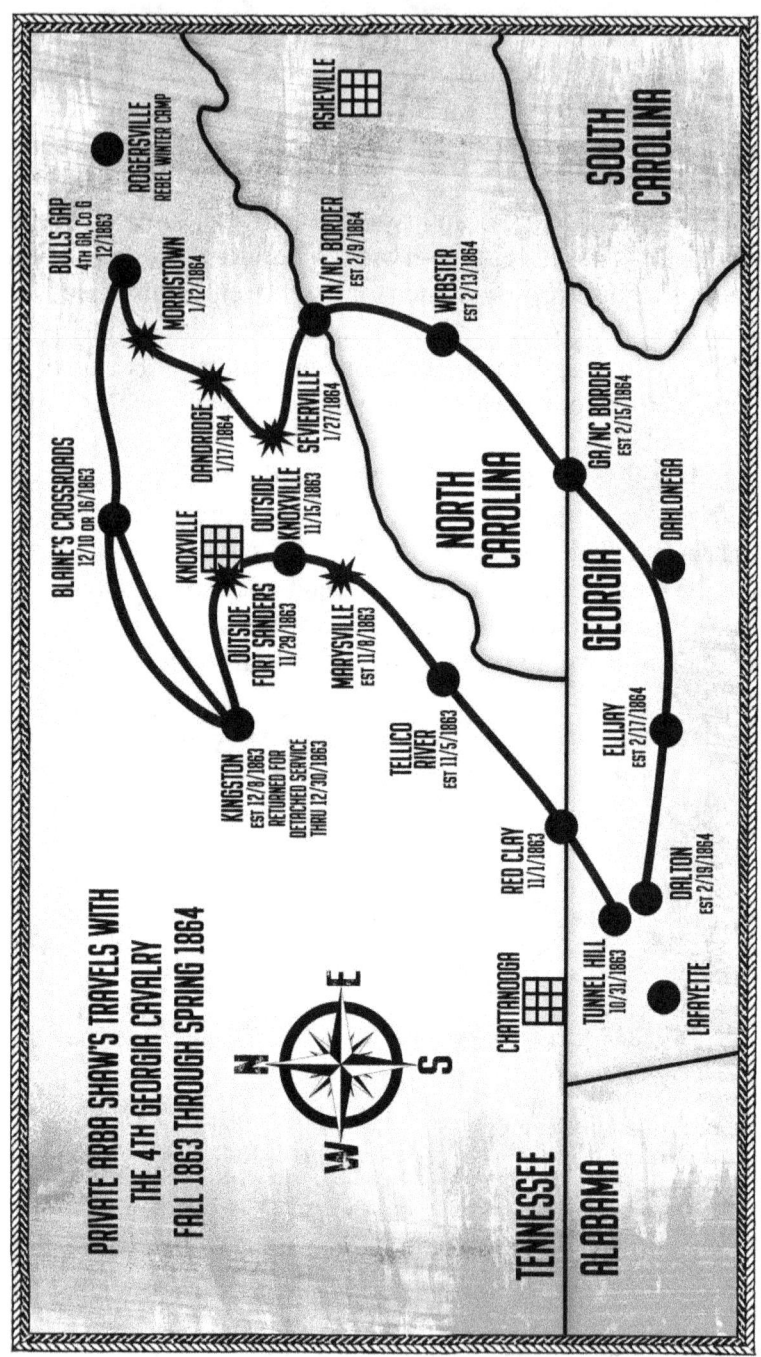

CHAPTER SEVEN
THE REALITIES OF WAR

July 17, 1902
MY EXPERIENCES
In the War of 1860 Briefly Told.

Two items of note I failed to mention at the west foot of the Smokey Mountain. After my mule was done eating I had failed to get any breakfast, and I mounted Jack and rode to another nearby house to see if there was anything to be had to eat. There were others with me on the same business, and, as usual, we met a refusal. We did not feel like tackling that mountain and snow without breakfast, and we knocked a bee gum in the head and helped ourselves. We ate a square meal, then we went to the foot of the mountain where we were all to meet after our repast. We all met at a house and saw an old man. He said he was 124 years old. He was blind. He said his eyes went out because of age.

All ready and off together, we got across and went in camp; about ten o'clock in the night at Boyd's, and late as it was, some thieves stole four of our best horses that night. The officers thinking it a safe place allowed us all to sleep without a camp guard. We were on hot trail of the men, and the bulk of our crew went before day the next morning and trapped for them, and got all but three and had them back in our camp about sunrise. As I remember, they turned up a right hand lane about two hundred yards to a farm house to camp, and our men were deployed on each side and at the mouth so the men, when they rode in, could close in on them.

That much so well done, now to find the stolen horses. There was a man came to us who proved to be a friend indeed, and gave us to understand that he knew who it was that got the horses, and he thought he could find them, and a posse lit out and did find them, but the men implicated could not be found while we stayed, and the second morning the horses were all at their stake and ready for action. Lieutenant Reece in command, sent the nineteen prisoners in charge of eighty-six of one crew, one of them a lieutenant, back across that snow capped mountain, which took all day and half of the without any stops in any ordinary gait.

When the prisoners were disposed of, Lt. Reece, (I will say here belonged to the third Georgia) took the rest of us, including my lieutenant, F. G. Horn, A. T. Shaw, Ben Holman, and a third Georgia man,—Coffey, are all I now can name, (there were thirteen of us,) and after the escaped three. Reckon they thought they would not be pursued any further after the first catch and they would travel at ease. Our detention by the stolen horses gave them a day ahead of us. We went on and could hear of them often, and by the time they had left the different places, we could know we were gaining on them, and as I remember, we caught up with them in two days. We stopped at a house at sundown to inquire and they had just left. They asked to stay all night there, the man said. We turned in to a nearby school house for the night, and after dark, Lieut. Reece not being in charge (too much mountain dew) Lt. Horn took some of us and surrounded the house where the men were and got two of them. The other by some book, like the bird, had flown and avoided capture. Don't know what became of the two the next morning. They were turned over to the military authorities, and we went on after the other man, but he was too sharp for us. We could hear of him a day or two—after that lost him.

By this time we were in old Georgia. When we got into North Carolina and East Georgia they were free of the ravages of the army, and we found it easy to get supplies, and one man being lost, the Lieutenant decided it was so far back, and so risky, that it would be a good time to visit home ten days, and we struck for Elijay, crossing the Tennessee

river in Georgia where it was only an ordinary sized creek.
A. F. Shaw

THEY HAD ABOUT A DAY'S HEAD START. Twenty-two deserters from the 2nd Georgia Cavalry had decided to head home to Georgia while on foraging detail. Clearly, they had had enough of the miserable cold weather and the sometimes frosty reception they were getting from the East Tennessee locals. A detail of a hundred men, which included Arba, crossed the Smokey Mountains hot on their tails just to the east of the present-day national park. Winter was in full fury in early February 1864. The search party detail consisted of men from the 3rd and 4th Georgia Cavalry. They succeeded in quickly capturing nineteen of the twenty-two deserters—so quickly, in fact, that they sent them back to where they started: over the Smokeys to where the command was wintering in Tennessee along with eighty-six members of the search party. It is not recorded as to what punishment resulted in their scheme to head home.

The thirteen remaining search party soldiers continued to track the last three deserters further southwest in North Carolina. The 4th Georgia's Lieutenant Felix Grundy Horne and the 3rd Georgia's Lieutenant Redmon Thomas Reese led the small party. Finally, two more of the deserters were captured, leaving one last man who took them closer and closer to northern Georgia before slipping away. It is not clear what happened to the two men who were captured and turned over to military authorities. The 1861 Confederate Articles of War[124] states: "All officers and soldiers who have received pay, or have been duly enlisted in the services of the Confederate States, and shall be convicted of having deserted the same, shall suffer death, or such other punishment as, by sentence of a court-martial, shall be inflicted." The Confederate Army of Tennessee commanded

---
[124] 1861 Confederate Articles of War.

by General Braxton Bragg reportedly had deserters summarily shot with no trial.

Having made their way on horseback through seventy-five miles of mountainous terrain in search of the last remaining deserter, Lieutenants Horne and Reese concluded that it made no sense to retrace their steps back into East Tennessee. They were so close to Georgia. So by the luck of drawing this detail and not being sent back with the initial wave of captured deserters, Arba would get home to Georgia a full month before the return of the rest of the 4th Georgia Cavalry.

July 24, 1902
MY EXPERIENCES
In the War of 1860 Briefly Told.

At or near Ellijay, I believe it was, Lieut. Reece took the men that wanted to go his direction home and left the rest with Lient. Horn. We passed through the gold region where there were lots of pits dug promiscuously in the surface of the earth; passed through Ellijay and stayed one night with the father of two of the Cove's most prosperous citizens— Miss Martin and John Davis. At that time John was living in a house nearby. He was a refugee from his home at that time, it being too squally for him to stay at home in safety. The next night we stayed at Spring Place where Lient. Horn wrote ten days leave of absence for all of us.

We all stayed together till we got to Dalton, and there we disbanded to go, or try to go home. Some could go home but others could not. It was too far and snakey for me. I went to H.E. Hamilton's near Gordon Springs and from there to Chattooga Co., where some of my kin lived and stayed with them till the time was up for me to report at the stated place.

When I got to my kin's I met brother Jim, a 16 year old brother, and the first thing he said was, "I see you now and I am not going to let you get away from me any more." It was too squally for him to stay at home with mother and father, like many others, had left long before. I tried to prevail on Jim to stay, as he had a good home with Dr. Hamilton, but all to no avail. He was fixed in his purpose and would go. When my time was up for me to start to Cartersville, Ga., Jim saddled up old "Curley," that was a prime factor in rearing father's family, and away we went. I had papers, but he did not belong to the army and had none. The guards at Rome passed us all right, but when we got to Worley's bridge over the Etowah the guards disputed our right and they took us to the provost marshal at Kingston. He would not reason on the matter and consigned us to the guard house that night and the next day sent us to Dalton to go in the infantry.

There we were carried to provost quarters to be disposed of and there we found a man that had reasoning sense. I asked him to let me go and talk to General Johnston about this paper and he said it would be no use, the general would not talk to me. I said, "General Johnston is a gentleman and I know he will talk to me" and he let a guard go with me. We found the general up stairs in his office and the guard gave him my paper. He read it and asked me what I wanted and I said, "That paper shows that I was on my line of duty and my being brought here under guard proves that the genuineness is disputed; that at the time it was written, the officer was acting under orders of his superiors and it was the best that could be done under the circumstances. And now, general, Lieut. Horn's home is in Tunnel Hill and he said he was going to try to run the blockade and see his family and come out and stay with your army in the day time and what I want you to do is to have Lieut. Horn hunted up and brought here to certify to this paper, and if he doesn't certify to what I say about it. I am willing to serve in the infantry." The General said, "All right, I will investigate the matter as soon as possible" and we went back to the provost offices and Jim and I were allowed to choose our company and regiment and we went to Co. E. thirty-ninth Georgia.

While we were there I went to work to locate father to prove what I told the authorities that Jim was not old enough to be subject to service in the army. I found him by the aid of a Mr. Malden who was acquainted and new the name of the post office where father was and be sent a certificate to General Johnston and Jim was released at the same time, he to go to father and I to my respective command. It took twenty-seven days to get things in form for our release and I had a spell of bilious fever while I was there.

A. F. Shaw.

The remaining detail of thirteen men passed close to Georgia's gold country near Dahlonega, Georgia. Dahlonega was the location of a United States branch mint that had

North Georgia College students are practicing military drills in front of the original Dahlonega Mint building circa 1877-1878.

Photograph by Julius Lindsay Schaub

turned the gold found in the Georgia mountains into coinage. The mint officially opened in 1838, primarily to mint gold coins of $1, $2.50, $3, and $5 denominations with the first distinctive "D" mint mark for coinage. The "D" mint mark would be used again to represent the Denver, Colorado, mint at the beginning of the twentieth century. At the start of the war in 1861, the Confederacy seized the mint, and for a few months gold coinage continued to be minted until the energy required to wage war took precedence over the need for minting coins. The mint would never make coins again, and soon after the war the building became part of North Agricultural Georgia College. The structure burned down in December 1878, and the present-day University of North Georgia's administration building was erected on the old mint's foundations in 1879.[125]

Lieutenant Redmon T. Reese (1831-1908) of the 3rd Georgia would split with some of his men from Arba's group around Ellijay, Georgia, heading toward his home in Sonaraville, Georgia. At this point in the war it was difficult for Arba to head home because the events that would lead to the fall of Atlanta were beginning to align themselves. The valley to the west of LaFayette, Georgia, was just too "snakey" [sic]. So he headed for relatives twenty-five miles to the south in Chattooga County, Georgia, where he was reunited with his sixteen-year-old brother Jim.

James (Jim) Benjamin Shaw
1848-1920

James (Jim) Benjamin Shaw was born in January 1848, four years after Arba. Jim had watched his brother turn eighteen years old and join up in the 4th Georgia Cavalry. Now he was set on following in his brother's boots, and it is obvious that Arba does not approve of this idea. In late February 1864, Jim was just sixteen years old but the

---

[125] "The Neighborhood Mint, Dahlonega in the age of Jackson," Sylvia Gailey Head, Elizabeth W. Etheridge; Gold Rush Gallery, 2000.

war had forced him from his home in McClemore Cove; he was now living with relatives.

After the war Jim Shaw came home to McClemore Cove and returned to his father's farm, but he had other ambitions than farming. In 1870 he married Jane Bradley, who was born in South Carolina in 1848 and whose family had moved to nearby Catoosa County, Georgia, just before the war. The couple had six children. During the 1870s Jim decided to pursue his interest in medicine and studied to be a physician. Perhaps it was a matter of his experiences during the war with its rudimentary medical techniques, combined with his brother Arba's own war-related injuries. He graduated from the University of Nashville Medical Department in 1882. In 1885 he moved his family west to a small town named Sheridan, just south of Little Rock, Arkansas. There he opened his practice as a physician where he was active for forty years. He was also the vice president of the Grant County bank. His wife Jane died in June 1889, and Jim remarried just over three months later to Martha Ann Holliman (1858-1941). They had one child together. Dr. James Benjamin Shaw continued to practice medicine until a year before his death in May 1920.[126]

Because Arba had arrived back in northwest Georgia a good month before the 4th Georgia Cavalry, he was presented with a dilemma. He did not know where his command was or whether it would show up any time soon. It's hard to imagine that Arba's Lieutenant, Felix G. Horne—who had decided to head home to Tunnel Hill, Georgia, and had provided Shaw with a ten-day leave—even knew where the 4th Georgia's command was himself. Arba could not just freely travel without drawing attention to himself and his brother. He was a soldier without a unit so they sent him to headquarters in Dalton, Georgia.

Following the failure at Knoxville and the disaster at Chattanooga in late 1863, the Confederate forces were

---

[126] Dr. James Benjamin Shaw, Compiled Service Records and family genealogy.

reshuffled in late December. Confederate General Braxton Bragg was out, and General Joseph Eggleston Johnston was in, taking command of the Army of the Tennessee. This included Major General Joseph Wheeler's cavalry corps, which was composed of four divisions that had upwards of 13,500 men. The 4th Georgia Cavalry was in Major General William T. Martin's Division as part of Brigadier General Alfred Iverson, Jr.'s Brigade.

It was pretty cheeky for nineteen-year-old Private Arba F. Shaw to demand a meeting at the headquarters of General Johnston. The fact he was able to actually get some of the General's time to plead his case is remarkable. General Johnston would have been a very busy man. At this time in the war he was less than two months from the opening move of the chess game that would become known as the Atlanta Campaign with Union General William Tecumseh Sherman.

The result was that he and his brother Jim became members of Company E of the 39th Georgia Volunteers, also known as the "Walker County Light Guards" under Captain John F. Bentley of Nashville, Tennessee. In searching the records of this company, Arba and Jim's names do not appear as they were with the unit for just a short period of time. Clearly, the reason for choosing this company was that it was composed of people they knew from back home, including a couple of Shaw cousins. Jim's (Arba's brother) first taste of army life would be short-lived as he was just sixteen years old—though his time would surely come at some point in the future when the Confederacy would take all the young and old able-bodied men they could get.

July 31, 1902
MY EXPERIENCES
In the War of 1860 Briefly Told.

It was the 1st day of March, 1864, when Jim and I went to the 39th and we got away on the 27th which was Sunday. The provost marshal fixed the passport for us to go on the W.&A. train to Kingston, also a requisition for our stock. When we got to Kingston the provost man there said he did not know anything about our stock, but he said to hunt around and see if we can find them, but he said he thought they had been sent to Cedartown. We went to hunting and found our saddles all right in the corral where the stock were first put up. The keeper said the one that Jim rode had died of blind staggers so that fixed that part. "But where is my good mule?" He said he didn't know. I kept hunting in the various camps and at last I was rewarded. Jack was found with five other mules hitched with the halter chains to a wagon tongue. He had on the same halter— his own—and I looked around and found his bridle and Jack and I were soon on our way.

By this time some of the wagoners noticed me and said, "Hold on there. What are you going to do with that mule?" I said, 'He is my mule," but one said, "Let's see about it." An officer came up. I showed him the papers and explained to him how they came in possession of the mule and he said all right and let me go on my way rejoicing. I felt that I was backed up by the proper authority and was not afraid to act.

I went back to where Jim was taking care of our saddles and other belongings and in a very short time Jack was under the same saddle and the same old boy was in the saddle. He had not been hurt. He had the same go ahead in him. and when I would touch him with the spur he always would kick the foot that spurred him.

Now we are on our way to Stilesboro in Bartow county and we can get there by dark and we will see father too when we get there. We got there at sundown. Father met us and of course we all enjoyed the meeting. The next day we boys went to the farm with father and he decided to keep Jim with him as he was too young to go in the army. Father was superintending the farm for cousin Darel Wingard, while Wingard kept his store.

While I was at my wits end and studying about where to go and who to report to, not knowing but what my command was still in East Tennessee, where we left it, or possibly gone into Virginia, as it was nearing there when we left, and I was 28 days behind my time to meet Lieut Reece at Cartersville, my command came up to the gate and Wingard's store, it was late in the evening and by permit I stayed with father that night and went on the next morning and overtook the boys as they left the camp. We went on to Blue Mountain, Ala., where we camped a few days, and it was there that Judge Hugh P. Lumpkin joined us. Then we went to Oxford, Ala., where we stayed some weeks to get a much needed rest.

Meantime, the campaign from Dalton to Atlanta opened up. When we came up to help the boys, as I remember, the first thing we did was to dismount and march down just above the water's edge to oppose the crossing of the yankees. Why we were not allowed to be on top of the bank I never could understand, and according to my memory, while we were there in that seemingly awkward place there came an order to Co. F. for a detail and it fell on me. I did not know what was wanted but I was willing to risk the next assignment being more desirable than that. When out, there were others detailed from other companies for the same duty. The order was to report to Gen. Iverson's headquarters in Calhoun. That was the first time I ever heard of, or saw, Iverson. He had been appointed our Brigadier General. When we got to his office he put us on "that dangerous courier duty. Then I heartily wished the other fellow had been sent instead of me, but however mote it be.

A. F. Shaw

ARBA AND HIS BROTHER JIM were in the 39th Georgia Infantry for just over three weeks through most of March 1864 until they could finally secure traveling papers, allowing them to catch a train from Dalton and head sixty-five miles southwest to Cedar Town, Georgia, in search of a certain horse and mule.

"Cedar Town," as it was known during the Civil War, had but seven more months of existence remaining when Arba and Jim rode into town. Union General Hugh Judson Kilpatrick (1836-1881) completely burned the town to the ground in his pursuit of Confederate General John Bell Hood after the fall of Atlanta in October 1864. When the town emerged from the ashes after the war, it would wisely drop the "space" in its name and be known as just "Cedartown." But there the Shaw brothers went one for two in their search; like a needle in a haystack, they did find Arba's mule, Jack, though it took a little arguing to settle the matter. From Cedar Town they headed twenty-five miles east to Stilesboro, Georgia, where their relatives lived.

THIRTY-NINE-YEAR-OLD DERRILL LEMEUL WINGARD (1825-1907) had married Arba's father, William M. Shaw's, first cousin Louisa Rebecca Shaw (1826-1863) in January 1853 in Bartow County, Georgia. He became a mercantile store owner and had tried to balance his responsibilities as an entrepreneur with the Confederate Army's need for men. Derrill eventually mustered into service as a Private in Company E of the 10th Georgia Cavalry State Guards on August 1, 1863.

The couple had five children, three of whom survived childhood. The latest arrival to the family was Edward Lamar Wingard who was born in November 1862. In 1863 Derrill's wife Louisa died. The exact date of her death is not recorded, but it must have occurred in the six weeks after he mustered into the 10th Georgia Cavalry State Guards. Perhaps coinciding with Derrill's sudden discharge from the unit by order of Adjutant General H. L. Wayne on

September 14, 1863. It was surely a painful time to have just left for the unknowns of war, dealing with thoughts of your own mortality, only to be shocked by the death of your spouse at home. With Louisa gone, Wingard was left with caring for his three children, and Arba's father, William, who could no longer stay in McClemore Cove due to the advancing Union forces, had come to help on the farm.

After the war Derrill moved to Kentucky and married Margaret Ann Newkirk in 1868. He and his second wife had three children together; they were part of the great post-war western migration moving to Kansas in 1872 and then to California, where they settled in Long Beach around 1887. He was a grocery merchant in each of the places he went, retiring in Long Beach, California, two years before he died in 1907.[127]

In what must have felt like an amazing coincidence to Arba, his 4th Georgia Cavalry brothers marched up to Wingard's General Store just when he happened to be there. This would have been over three months after he had left them in the mountains of East Tennessee. He was clearly running out of options and probably would have ended up in an infantry unit if the 4th Georgia had not so conveniently shown up. Finally reunited with the boys from Company F, they all made their way into eastern Alabama to rest.

IN EARLY APRIL 1864 CAPTAIN WILLIAM J. Rodgers and the 4th Georgia Cavalry's Company D was on "detached service" in East Tennessee. Rodgers is the Captain accused of killing Fannin County's William Clayton Fain, mentioned in the introduction to this book.

Captain Rodgers was born around 1820 in a small town called Harrison, Tennessee, upriver from Chattanooga. He was a captain in the Mexican War, fighting in Company H of the 4th Tennessee Infantry. In the Civil War, unable to get command of a company in a Tennessee regiment, he joined

---

[127] Derrill Lemeul Wingard, Compiled Service Records and family genealogy.

and became the Captain of Company D of the 4th Georgia Cavalry. His Company D was one of eleven companies in the 4th Cavalry. Normally, a Cavalry Regiment is made up of ten companies. Soon Company D would prove to be a slightly peculiar company, always away from the rest of the regiment on "detached service."

One of Company D's Lieutenants, William H. White, was personally brought up on charges for court martial by Captain Rodgers. White was tried before a Confederate military court for telling some of Company D's men to desert to the enemy near Chattanooga. Lieutenant White was found guilty and court-martialed on August 20, 1863; he was scheduled to be executed two days later on August 22, 1863. However, official military records do not record that the actual execution took place. Soon after that date there was a wave of desertions in Company D—perhaps the "D" stood for dysfunctional.

IN 1905 THE *CHATTANOOGA DAILY TIMES* published a series of articles in July 1905 titled "Story of the Great War of Secession." One of the articles reported that White was indeed executed and that "men that knew him well say that he was not guilty of the charge on which he was tried." Company D's Orderly Sergeant William J. Gillespie actually went on the record in the newspaper regarding the outcome of Lieutenant White's court martial as "denouncing the act in the severest terms," though Gillespie stayed with his unit through September of 1864 when his record of service comes to an end. The newspaper article further stated that Captain Rodgers' Company D once numbered 100 men but by April 1865 the company had been reduced to less than two dozen troops. However, the article doesn't mention the forty-plus men who are shown in the military records as deserting from the company during its history.

This is the dilemma of records from the Civil War on both the Confederate and Union sides. There are no clear official military records of what happened on a day-to-day basis, let alone month by month within a lot of the individual regiments, companies, or for single soldiers. For Avery's 4th Georgia Cavalry you will find very sparse information. The only records pertaining to the movements of Company D through the entire Civil War are from November to December 1863 in which it is recorded that they were "Near Dalton, Ga." That's it. Nothing more of where they were before or afterwards.

AT THE START OF MAY 1864, GENERAL WILLIAM Tecumseh Sherman began his push into Georgia, and the 4th Georgia moved back into northwestern Georgia near Calhoun. Sherman's strategy was to destroy the Confederate Army of Tennessee, and he had three Union armies amassed to accomplish this objective. The Atlanta Campaign had begun.

Back to the east in Virginia, on May 5 through 7 the first clash between Robert E. Lee and Ulysses S. Grant was taking place at the Battle of the Wilderness. With Lee's forces on the verge of collapse, General James Longstreet's (1821-1904) troops arrived to fend off disaster. Caught in the battle's crossfire, Longstreet, who was at West Point for three years together with Grant in the early 1840s, was seriously wounded when he was struck by a bullet that passed through his neck and right shoulder.[128] He would never regain the full use of his right arm, and the wound must have damaged his larynx as his voice would remain whispery for the rest of his life. Lee's horse was felled by his own troops. The Rebels would be pushed to Spotsylvania, Virginia, to battle on May 8.[129]

Meanwhile, in northwest Georgia on May 7, Sherman took Tunnel Hill, which was a critical resource of the

---

[128] Robert M. Steckler and Jon D. Blachley, "The Cervical Wound of General James Longstreet" (*Archives of Otolaryngology – Head & Neck Surgery* 2000), vol. 126, 353-359.

[129] James Longstreet, *From Manassas to Appomattox: Memoirs of the Civil War in America*, (Philadelphia: J.B. Lippincott Company, 1896), 565-571.

Western & Atlantic Railway. Sherman's army began pushing the Rebels south along the route of the railroad through each small town. The 4th Georgia Cavalry had moved to an area southwest of Calhoun, Georgia, in advance of the Battle of Resaca.

August 7, 1902
MY EXPERIENCES
In the War of 1860 Briefly Told.

The place we were guarding on the Oostanaulah when I was detailed to report to Gen. Iverson, was the Mike Frick's Ferry, three miles south of Calhoun, Ga., which I expect to say something of more importance about at the proper time.

Headquarters again. The couriers were subjected to company rule, their names being enrolled and were detailed in the order of their names. The battle at Resaca was on and at its highest pitch and we cavalry had all we could do to oppose the enemy crossing the river on the flanks. The general kept his adjutant busy writing all through the days and part of the nights and ever once in a while the general would say, "Courier." The man pointed out would mount his horse and report to the general and he would tell us where to go to and go quick. Then he would give us the document folded and sometimes sealed, with the inscription on the outside to present to guards to pass courier and all the soldiers would soon know the couriers and they would pass on unmolested. Don't know where the other boys went and I don't now remember where all I went, but I worked from Resaca to Frick's Ferry.

One day my work was assigned me as courier from headquarters to the ferry at the west side of the town where one of our batteries was engaged in a duel all day and when I was told by the captain of the battery I would have to wait awhile, I would hitch Jack and run in and help the boys fight. When the cannons fired they would kick back several yards and we would roll them back in position and load while the gunner took his aim. All ready, the man with the friction primer would put it in the touch hole and then that unnerving report would come. The primers were about the size of a slate pencil and about two inches long, made of metal and hollow and the hollow was filled with an explosive and a small wire was doubled and twisted and the tube was made on the twisted wire, the wire passing through the upper end of the cap or primer, leaving an eye in the middle of the wire. The man that fired had a strong cord tied to a small strong hook and with the hook in the eye and the cap in the touch and by a vigorous jerk the wire was pulled out and away would go the missle. Some cannon balls were solid and others were made hollow and full of grape and canister shot, all round. The grape was about one inch in diameter and the canister looked much like the size of our tame grapes. It always seemed to me that the larger shot ought to have been called canister because the lesser ones resembled the grape so much. Powder was poured in the shells among the grape and canister and a larger primer, to stop the hole in the shell, was made of pasteboard and primed with an explosive that would burn as a fuse. By estimating the number of seconds it would take a shell to go to where it was wanted to burst, the gunner was enabled to know how many seconds to prime with and the firing of the cannon would ignite the fuse and away it would go smoking and frying to its mission and when the fuse burned through the powder in the shell would explode it and scatter the shot and shell in all directions.

I would not get to stay at the battery long but would have to go back with an answer and in a few minutes was called to go again. Several times during that day a yank would come in to a field just over the river and when he would get out from the fence a piece the boys would shoot at him and he would run back every time and in the evening a crew was sent undercover of the river bank and woods to watch and when he came in again to come in behind him and bring him in.

A. F. Shaw

THE ARMY OF THE TENNESSEE under General Joseph E.

Johnston included three Infantry Corps: Hardee's Corps under Lieutenant General William J. Hardee, Hoods Corps under Lieutenant General John B. Hood, and Polk's Corps (Army of the Mississippi) under Lieutenant General Leonidas Polk, who was killed in action on June 14, 1864, after which command was taken by Major General William W. Loring and Lieutenant General Alexander P. Stewart. The artillery reserve was under the command of Brigadier General Francis A. Shoup.

The Cavalry Corps under Joseph Wheeler included four divisions and the Artillery Reserve: Martins' Division under Major General William T. Martin, Kelly's Division under Brigadier General John H. Kelly; Humes' Division under Brigadier General William Y.C. Humes, and Jackson's Division under Brigadier General William Hicks Jackson.

When Arba became a courier for Brigadier General Iverson, Iverson's brigade was composed of the 1st Georgia Cavalry under Colonel Samuel W. Davitte (1831-1898), 2nd Georgia Cavalry under Colonel Charles C. Crews, 3rd Georgia Cavalry under Colonel Robert Thompson, 4th Georgia Cavalry under Colonel Isaac W. Avery, and 6th Georgia Cavalry under Colonel John R. Hart.

From spring through early August 1864, Colonel Crews relinquished the Brigade's command to Iverson and returned to the command of the 2nd Georgia Cavalry.[130] For Colonel Crews, who had performed so well as brigade commander for over a year, receiving the accolades from his commanding officers must have been a surprising turn of events.

IN SPRING 1864 BRIGADIER GENERAL Alfred Holt Iverson, Jr. (1829-1911) was a man looking to repair his tattered reputation. It was within Martin's Division as part of Iverson's Brigade that the Colonel Avery's 4th Georgia Cavalry found itself for the Atlanta Campaign.

---

[130] *OR*, sr. 1, vol. XXXVIII, pt3, 642.

The son of Alfred Iverson, Sr. (1798-1873) served as a U. S. Congressman from 1847 to 1851 and then as a U. S. Senator from Georgia from 1855 to 1861. Alfred, Sr. had helped his son gain a commission as second lieutenant as a volunteer in Company D of the Georgia Battalion of Mounted Infantry during the Mexican War. Alfred, Jr. was described as "first and last a soldier," a strict disciplinarian, and a stickler for military protocol. After the Mexican War, he was stationed in Kansas. When the Civil War began, he resigned from the U. S. Army. He was soon a Captain in the 20th North Carolina, distinguished himself early on in Virginia, and by November 1862 had been quickly promoted to Brigadier General.

Brigadier General Alfred Holt Iverson, Jr
1829-1911

It was Gettysburg in the summer of 1863 that became Brigadier General Iverson's undoing. His 1,400-man brigade advanced into an unseen line of Union troops, and it soon became a slaughter. To make matters worse, Iverson was not with his men as the brigade suffered casualties of more than two thirds of its men and the capture of most of the remaining survivors. Rumors swirled regarding where he was when the calamity took place, and he soon lost the support of his troops. General Robert E. Lee removed him

Martin's Division Cavalry Corps

(Atlanta Campaign) Major General William T. Martin

Morgan's Brigade Brigadier General John T. Morgan followed by Brigadier General William Allen	1st Alabama - BG William W. Allen 3rd Alabama - Col James Hagan 4th Alabama - Col Alfred Russell 7th Alabama - Col James C. Malone Jr. 51st Alabama - Col Milton L. Kirkpatrick 12 Alabama Cavalry Battalion
Iverson's Brigade Brigadier General Alfred Iverson Jr.	1st Georgia - Col Samuel W. Davitte 2nd Georgia - Col Charles C. Crews 3rd Georgia - Col Robert Thompson 4th Georgia (Avery's) - Col Isaac Avery followed by Lt. Col. William C. Cook 6th Georgia - Col John R. Hart
Wheeler's Horse Artillery	Wiggins' (Arkansas) Battery Lt. J. P. Bryant Ferrell's (Georgia) Battery Huggin's (Tennessee) Battery Huwal's (Tennessee) Battery White's (Tennessee) Battery

first from combat command and then from the Army of Northern Virginia, sending him back to Rome, Georgia, in October 1863.

MIKE FRIX FERRY, AS DESCRIBED BY SHAW, was actually known as Lay's Ferry or sometimes Tanner's Ferry, which was located on the Oostanaula River west of Calhoun, Georgia. Arba's confusion came from the fact that there was a large brick house on the south side of the ferry that was owned by the Frix family, who lived in nearby Calhoun. The "Frick's House" is shown on a couple of maps dating from the 1860s. The maps also show the Lay family had a home on the north side of the ferry.

The Frix family, who also regularly switched the spelling of their surname to "Fricks," were landowners with at least 480 acres in Gordon County on the north and south side of the Oostanaula River. Michael Treece Frix (1804-1872) is shown as owning lot numbers 150 and 137 in the 1852 Gordon County Property Tax digests. A hand-drawn 1864 map shows lot 150 right where Lay's Ferry was, and lot 137 is where the Frix homestead stood. His son George Washington Frix was born in 1829 in Rabun Gap, Georgia. In the 1850 census, twenty-one-year-old George's occupation was listed as a railroad conductor. He married Josephine Reid in January 1854 in Monroe, Georgia, and worked the family property including building the large two-story brick house on the south side of the Oostanaula River at Lay's Ferry.[131] In some accounts the building was listed as having a horse lot on the site, which would have been a place to buy and sell horses and mules.

---

[131] *Atlas to Accompany the Official Records of the Union and Confederate Armies*; (Washington, Government Printing Office, 1891) Plate 61, No 12.

On November 20, 1856, Josephine Reid Frix died in childbirth. George Frix then married Georgia E. Nucknolls in April 1858, and they had a son, Alexander Washington, in

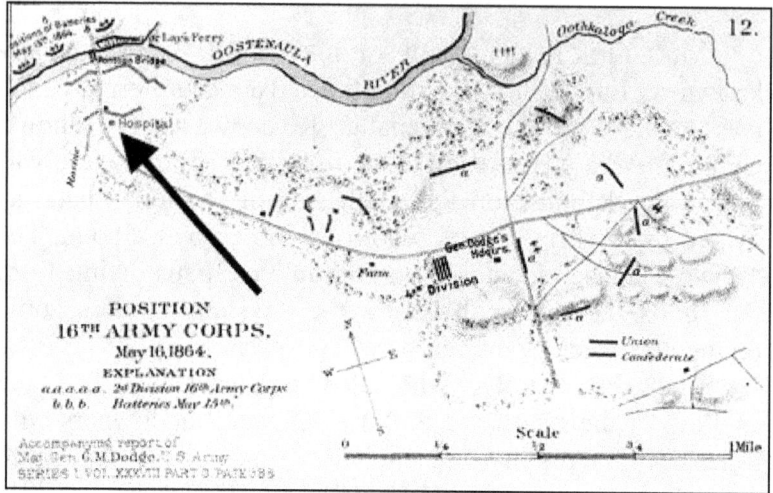

Battle of Lay's Ferry
The Frix two-story brick house is in the upper left of the illustration.
*1880 illustration published in
"Joseph M. Brown's Mountain Campaigns of Georgia"*

June 1859. Tragically, their marriage would be a short one. George Frix died of tuberculosis on January 31, 1860. George's large two-story brick building sat unoccupied, having become the property of his father, Michael, after George's death.[132]

In the 1860 census, which was conducted in June of that year, fifty-five-year-old Michael "Frix" is recorded as a farmer with a rather large personal estate valued at $10,000. He lived in Calhoun with his fifty-six-year-old wife Sarah, four of his own children, and his first grandson, the late George Frick's six-year-old son Alfred. George's second wife, Georgia Nucknolls Frix, returned to her father's home in Forsyth, Georgia, after her husband's death with her infant son Alex.

---

[132] Frix family genealogy.

Rebel Correspondent

As the Civil War began, the medical director of the Army of the Tennessee built his hospital network using all kinds of buildings throughout the South as they became needed. It seems like the vacant two-story brick "Frix" house fit the bill and became a Confederate Hospital. Today most of the Frix relatives are buried in a family cemetery off Herrington Bend Road, just across from where the old Civil War hospital was located.

August 14, 1902
MY EXPERIENCES
In the War of 1860 Briefly Told.

When the boys got over there they watched for the yank to come in the field again and this time he, not being shot at, came on apparently unconcerned and the boys when they saw him in the field got over the fence and brought him in across the river. He said he wanted to quit fighting and would rather be a prisoner than to fight any longer and he was quizzed a great deal and treated as a prisoner.

After that day I don't remember what came next, but will say that in a day or two before the artillery duel above mentioned, Gen. Iverson sent a scout across at that same ferry and me with it to go as far as we could in the direction of Snake Creek Gap. We went to the furnace and a scout went farther and returned reporting that the gap was full of yanks coming on. The gap is a deep gorge that cuts a large mountain in two and wide enough that there are several good farms in the Gap. The Gap is six miles long. We went back and the yanks were close on our heels when we got back. Then was when the duel began at Calhoun. One day the General took some of his staff up on the high hill east of Calhoun and through his long spy glass was looking for their position and they had a long glass, too, and they saw us and began shooting cannons at us. The first shot struck in the street, the second went about half way up the hill and the third went through our squad and went in the ground about

10 feet behind us, but before they had time to load again we were done gone back to our quarters. About that time Lient. Logan was wounded in his thigh. It was amputated, but in a day or so he died. He was a 4th Ga. man.

I was sent one day down to a cross-roads, where the road that came out from Frick's ferry crossed the Calhoun and Borne road, with a dispatch to Gen. John T. Morgan and when I got there his Alabama brigade was down resting, awaiting orders. As soon as he read the dispatch he said, "Courier, you will have to go with me a while," and of course I had to obey orders then he had the mounting call sounded and in a minute we were all in our saddles and going into the struggle at the Fricks' ferry. When we got in sight of the yanks in a long straight level place in the road just southeast of his house the yanks sent a solid shot at us and it came so close to us we could feel the wind of it and if it had been three or four feet lower it would have killed many men. Its course was almost parallel with the road but was on angle enough to leave the road and go through a red oak tree by the roadside about as high as we could reach from the saddle. In a minute or two more the head of the column was at the Fricks horse lot where General Morgan stopped and, as I remember, he made that his headquarters, and White's battery was playing its part on the eminence that the brick dwelling stood on. While I was waiting I saw cannon balls dismount two of the guns of White's battery and saw the brick fall when the yanks shot a hole through the house. It was a close call for the boys, but as I remember there were none of them hurt, but after it was over some of them said they were the worst scared they had ever been, even to their brave Lieut. Pembroke down. At the same time the clash was heavy at the river with the small arms and Morgan was sent there with his brigade to reinforce. The yanks were trying to clear the way so they could put in a pontoon bridge and come over. In a a day or two I believe they crossed below and it was then the feature of things changed. All the cars began to be pulled south on the W.&A. R.R. Soon one morning I saw long trains of freight cars going down from Resaca and in a few minutes I was started to the general wagon master and when he read the dispatch it was not long till the wagons were all rolling in retreat. The yanks were across below and on the flank move.

A. F. Shaw

June 4, 1864, *Harper's Weekly* – Engagement at Snake Creek Gap
Sketch by Theodore R. Davis

THE OOSTANAULA RIVER, WHICH snakes from northeast to southwest, was the natural barrier between Resaca and Calhoun, Georgia. In 1864 only a couple of ferries were allowed passage over the river from north to south. The undefended Rebel left flank at Snake Creek Gap to the northwest of Lay's Ferry was the place where a group of scouts, including Arba, were sent early in the morning on either Sunday or Monday, May 8-9, taking the road that followed Snake Creek up through Sugar Valley. What they saw must have come as a shock. They skirmished a little, then hastily turned and ran upon what they saw. It was the Army of the Tennessee and around 25,000 men, who probably were equally surprised that the Rebels' left flank offered no resistance. Clearly, it was a strategic mistake by Confederate General Johnston. Arba and his scouts would quickly retrace their route southeast back to Rebel lines at Lay's Ferry.

On Monday, May 9, under the command of General James Birdseye McPherson with Brigadier General Thomas "Fighting Tom" William Sweeny (1820-1892) commanding the lead division, they flooded through the gap, turning east toward Resaca and occupying Bald Hill just to the west of town. Their goal was to cut the critical Western & Atlantic Railroad supply lines by taking out a bridge over the Oostanaula River at Resaca.

But General McPherson made his own strategic mistake when he hesitated and overestimated the strength of the Confederate forces at Resaca, much to the consternation of General Sherman, and retreated back to Snake Creek Gap.[133] At that moment McPherson had but two months left to live. As things escalated in Atlanta in July 1864, he would become the second-highest ranked Union officer killed in action. Soon two other Union armies under General Sherman—the Army of the Cumberland and the Army of the Ohio—moved into Snake Creek Gap on a cold, rainy Wednesday, May 11, as heavy artillery was heard rumbling for the next two days in the north toward Dalton. On Friday, May 13, the Union forces began to flood out of Snake Creek Gap aimed for Resaca. By Saturday, May 14, the Battle of Resaca was underway.

THIRTY-YEAR-OLD CAPTAIN WILLIAM Reuben Logan (1832-1876) of Company G was born near Cleveland, Tennessee, but moved to Union County, Georgia, near Blairsville after he married his wife, Martha Jane Hughes (1828-1881), in November 1860. He had worked there in the Ordinary's office in the Union County courthouse prior to the war. Logan had been promoted to Captain in November

---

[133] Benjamin LaBree, *The Confederate Soldier in the Civil War, 1861-1865*, (Louisville, Ky., Prentice Press, 1897), 222.

1863 so Arba misidentified his rank. He was wounded on that Saturday during the Battle of Resaca, and Confederate Surgeon J.B. Edlin amputated his right leg on Sunday. But the Captain did not die, as Arba reports. In fact, he would write a letter from Forsyth, Georgia, to Dr. William A. Carrington on November 2, 1864: "I respectfully ask to be furnished with an order on the Company of which you are corresponding secretary for an artificial limb."

Captain Logan remained on the company muster rolls through 1865 and would survive the war, returning to his duties in the Ordinary's office in Union County afterwards. The remaining stump above the knee never healed properly; soon he began suffering from mental health problems, which today would most likely be recognized as posttraumatic stress disorder (PTSD). His delusions were described as paranoia, reckless conduct, and threatening acts of violence, which ultimately required him to be admitted to the Psychiatric Hospital in Milledgeville, Georgia, where he died and was buried in April 1876.[134]

While the Battle of Resaca raged, the 4th Georgia Cavalry was engaged with Brigadier General Sweeny's 2nd Division, 16th Corps of Union forces, who late in the afternoon of Saturday, May 14,[135] had managed to ford to the east side of the Oostanaula River in canvas boats launched into Snake Creek at Lay's Ferry. A fierce battle erupted, and White's Battery was positioned on the east side of the river close to the Frick's old two-story brick home, which was now the Confederate hospital. After dark Sweeny retreated across the river, allowing the Rebels to evacuate the hospital.

In 1890 Union Major William Henry Chamberlin (1833-1912) of the 81st Ohio Infantry wrote an account of the events of that Saturday afternoon that

---

[134] William Reuben Logan, Compiled Service Records and family genealogy.

[135] Lewis Franklin Roe and John P. Wilson, *From Western Deserts to Carolina Swamps: A Civil War Soldiers Journals and Letters Home,* (University of New Mexico Press, 2012), Chapter 6.

on the 14th of May, while the main contest at Resaca was in progress, the division to which I belonged–the Second Division, Sixteenth Corps–was sent far to the right to effect a crossing of the Oostanaula River, at Lay's Ferry. That point was so strongly defended that at a lower point was chosen, where Snake Creek empties into the Oostanaula. Canvas boats, capable of bearing twenty men each, were launched in Snake Creek, under cover of heavy fire by a brigade, and then a skirmish line was called upon to cross the river in these boats and clear away the force occupying the opposite bank, which was covered with trees and afforded excellent protection to the enemy.[136]

On Sunday, May 15, as Captain Logan was likely experiencing the unimaginable trauma of battleground surgery, the 58th Indiana regiment and a company of pontoniers constructed a pontoon bridge over the Oostanaula River at Lay's Ferry. By noon the Yanks poured over in skirmishing with the Rebel forces,[137] including the 4th Georgia Cavalry.

Corporal Charles A. Wright (1833-1902), also of the 81st Ohio Volunteer Infantry, published an eyewitness account from his point of view in 1887: "The next day a pontoon-bridge was laid at the ferry, two or three hundred yards above the mouth of Snake Creek, and the troops crossed in considerable numbers. Several regiments crossed and moved to the right into the timber. The 81st crossed and, turning to the left, took position along the riverbank, its right resting near the road. The rebels, principally Wheeler's cavalry, were fortified about one-fourth of a mile from the river; a large brick house in our front was filled with their sharpshooters. They were dislodged by a single shot from Walker's [sic] battery, stationed on the other side of the

---

[136] W. H. Chamberlin, Edited by Robert Hunter, *The Skirmish Line in the Atlanta Campaign; Sketches of War History 1861-1865; Volume III,* (Robert Clarke & Co., 1890), 185.
[137] John J. Hight, *Hight's History of the 58th Indiana Volunteer Regiment,* (Princeton Press of Clarion, 1895), 296.

river."[138]

This account appears to be in sync with Arba's account as he accompanies General John Tyler Morgan (1824-1907)

Lay's Ferry was the location of the "hospital building west of Calhoun, Georgia."
The building was originally owned by the Frix family.

and his brigade of Alabama cavalry regiments to Lay's Ferry, witnessing a cannon shot passing right through the walls of the hospital and the loss of a couple of White battery cannons. The artillery fire came from the west side of the Oostanaula by way of Captain Frederick Welker's (1834-1914) batteries twelve-pound Napoleon cannons at 800 t 1,100 yards range. This detail was reported by Lieutenant Andrew T. Blodgett (1841-1864), who commanded Battery H of the 1st Missouri Light Artillery.[139]

---

[138] Charles Wright, *A Corporal's Story: Experiences in the ranks of Company C, 81st Ohio Volunteer Infantry during the war for the maintenance of the union, 1861-1864*, (Philadelphia, Penn., James Beale, 1887), 102.
[139] *OR*, sr. 1, vol. XXXVIII, pt3, 468.

The Confederate forces were now retreating to the South. By Monday, May 16, Union forces under General Sherman entered Resaca. "The feature of things" had indeed changed.

General Morgan's life after the war exposed his extreme racist beliefs in becoming a firebrand opponent of Reconstruction. As a lawyer, he returned to practice law in Selma, Alabama, where he would become the Grand Dragon of the Ku Klux Klan in 1872.[140] With his Klan influence, he was elected to the United States Senate six times, serving in Washington, D. C., from 1876 until his death in office in June 1907. As a senator, Morgan was notorious in championing bills that helped set the course of white supremacy and the era of Jim Crow, which included introducing legislation as a Senator that attempted to legalize racist vigilante murder or lynching as a means of preserving white supremacy in the Deep South. His fellow senator from Alabama at the time of his death was another Confederate Brigadier General war veteran, Edmund W. Pettus, who had a bridge over the Alabama River at Selma infamously named after him. Pettus became the Grand Dragon of the Ku Klux Klan in 1877, five years after Morgan. He also died in office forty-six days after Morgan, leaving Alabama with two empty senatorial seats in the summer of 1907.

August 21, 1902
MY EXPERIENCES
In the War of 1860 Briefly Told.

Don't remember what day we left Calhoun. When we did leave the retreat was slow, rather of a contesting nature for a time till we got to Adairsville where Johnston's army was thrown in line one evening and had a considerable little brush. There we couriers did some active service and had many close calls. We had no time to spend out of the saddle

---

[140] Susan Lawrence Davis, *Authentic History, Ku Klux Klan, 1865-1877*, (New York, American Library Service,1924), 59.

and no time for regular turn; just any of us was sent that was present when one was wanted.

The General's headquarters and the doctor's were together behind a hill and the wounded were brought in so fast that the doctors could not give them prompt attention. Some could walk alone, some by a man holding them, and some were toted on the litters. Litters were made of two poles about eight feet long and a width of strong cloth two yards long sowed to the poles. The man was placed on the cloth and two men would get between the handles and walk away with the man. The doctors would cut off legs and arms when it was necessary and the cut-off limbs were buried when it could be done.

While that fight was going on Anderson Bryant and I had just got back off of an errand at the same time and had rode up and stopped and he was a little farther along than I was and to my right when he heard something pop behind him. He looked at me and said, "What was that" and I said, "Look there at your horse. It was a minney ball. It tipped my nose and went through your horse and into that pond." The ball had come from a yank's gun over that hill and done that work as it was on its decent. It only graised the skin on my nose and went through the hindmost quarters of the horse. We retreated that night and the horse had to be left.

As I remember after we left Adairsville all that our army done was to defend itself until it got across the Oostanaulah river and it was about that time the old couriers were relieved and fresh men took our places. The yankeys had crossed the river below us and were trying to cut us off, but Gen. Johnston sent his army south to meet them, and a short time after we got across and the yanks had crossed, I reckon Gen. Wheeler thought he wanted to disturb the yanks play house a little and to do that he sent a part of the Fourth Georgia up the Oostanaulah river to cross on a bridge and fall in on their rear. We went and ran into a wagon train near Cassville at a point where our road crossed the W. & A. R. R. and intersected the main road from Cassville toward

Atlanta. After a little spat with the wagon guards the concern surrendered but don't remember what we did with the wagons but I believe we burned them and tore up some of the R. R. and the telegraph.

It was all done in a few minutes and we were on our way with the prisoners and mules to that covered bridge we had crossed on in the morning. We got there at dark and there began to fall one of the hardest rains I ever felt and all that was in it was soaked to the bone. The guards and the prisoners stayed in the bridge house all night and kept dry but the main bulk of us had went through and as we went up the hill it was so dark we could not see only when it lightened. All the way we could know we were together was to call the man in front of us, for we couldn't see the white horses. It didn't take many minutes of that sort to do us so we camped and after the severe part of the squall was over we made up fires and dried the best we could and at daybreak the men in charge of the prisoners were ordered up. They were all dry and went on back to Acworth where we met the balance of the command and just at that moment a courier ordered us to New Hope church and we went the quickest I ever saw a command go that distance. Don't know how far but it must be four or five miles and in the road at the west end of the church house about three companies of the Fourth Georgia were cut off and sent out west to meet the yankeys while the others could form and dismount. There was not a moment to spare. Colonel Avery lead the way.

A. F. Shaw

August 28, 1902
MY EXPERIENCES
In the War of 1860 Briefly Told.

It has taken me a long time to get to New Hope. When I did get there I was being carried away. In about 20 minutes the Colonel led us along the road until the yanks began to shoot at us from a pine thicket above an old field where he *deployed us to skirmish. He soon saw that would not do—the yanks had all the advantage of us and we could not see one of them and they were giving us some close calls at a short range and we mounted. The Colonel at once desired to draw us back and reform and did so and as soon as we were reformed we heard their bugle sound a charge and the yank yell rise and here they came mounted. It was a head of column charge. Our boys were ready for them. Our wet guns would not shoot, but the pistols were brought into action and men were shot on both sides. I saw a yank run up to Colonel Avery and shoot him through and Henry Stafford shot the same yank off of his horse on the spot and among all the noise I heard him say. "There I killed one." By this time some of the yanks were away past our skirmish line and we all fell back. The road was so full of yanks that we had to fall back through the woods on one side and a cut-off new ground on the other and in that new ground was where so many of Co. F. were captured. They went to northern prisons and stayed until it was all over. Those captured were Asa Massey, John Warren, Clayton Smallwood, J. H. Odum, R. F. Shaw and A. F. Shaw who got away. He was riding Jack and in the gully in the bottom of the ravine brush was piled and Jack fell down on my right leg. I put my left foot in the saddle and as he made efforts to get up I would push and keep drawing til I got out. The yank was there waiting for me. When I got up he said, "Surrender!" I said, "You see my condition." He sat there and waited for me to go around to Jack's feet and pull out a brush or two. Then Jack came to his feet. I thought I would mount and run out, but as soon as Jack was on foot he hit the grit and I grabbed the cross bar at the lower end of the levers of the bit with my left hand and tried to stop him but he went on all the same. My gun was in my right hand and with the ends of my fingers over-reaching the gun I caught the front of the saddle tree on the opposite side from me, my arm resting in the seat of the saddle and in that position Jack took me up that hill at about the rate of 15 miles per hour my captor hollering, shooting and saying,*

"Halt! Halt, you damned reb." I had a blanket rolled and tied on the back of my saddle and he shot one ball through it and it made 16 holes and then he shot my left thigh and lacerated it 10 inches but at that moment Lieut. Wash Hill shot the yank dead on the spot. I hung on to the mule and he carried me back to freedom. Lieut Hill belonged to Co. A. 4th Georgia. As Jack was still dragging me on we met M.C. Alexander and he caught the mule and helped me upon him and went down the Burnt Hickory road to where Dr. Eadlen was and in a few minutes we saw the prisoners our boys caught. Even unto their Brigadier-General they were hitting the grit afoot.

The boys stayed there several days and built fortifications and did some hard fighting there. I had not been with the Doctor but a few minutes until Col. Avery was brought down with four others in the ambulance and as soon as all their wounds were dressed we were all put in the ambulance and driven to Marietta.

As I remember I was the only one who could not walk with a support, my wound being in the thigh and the ball still in there. It hurt so bad I was unnerved. The nurse toted me on a litter. At last after an all night drive on the rough roads and every jolt almost giving me lock jaw we got to Marietta up in the next day.

We were put out of the ambulance on to the train bound for Atlanta.

A. F. Shaw

A close "by a nose" call for Arba as a mini ball grazed him near Adairsville, Georgia, was to be a forewarning. The tension was rising as the Confederate Army of Tennessee slowly retreated southward toward Atlanta. They were on their heels with each push by the Yankee forces, who used the iron rails of the Western & Atlantic Railroad as their guide. Atlanta would put Johnnie Reb's back to the wall; surely, they all knew it. Resaca fell, quickly pushing them

REBEL CORRESPONDENT

back through Calhoun on Monday, May 16. On Wednesday, May 18, they are pushed back again through Adairsville, which led next through Kingston and Cassville on Thursday, May 19. Each skirmish was like battling a hard, strong kick to the chest, causing a stumble backward with each blow.

After Kingston, General Joseph Johnston retreated into Allatoona Pass. Both armies rested for a couple of days, then on the night Monday, May 23, Sherman ordered his armies in another flanking maneuver to the west, moving toward Dallas, Georgia. Johnston anticipated the move and moved his forces to block the Yankees at New Hope Church. They dug in. Sixteen cannon were placed near the church under the command of Confederate General Hood's chief of artillery Colonel Robert F. Beckham. The bloody battle started on Wednesday, May 25, during a driving rainstorm late in the afternoon. The next afternoon, as Sherman moved toward Johnston's east flank, the 4th Georgia Cavalry quickly moved to counter.

Arba was eyewitness to the 4th Georgia's leader Colonel Isaac W. Avery being shot through the stomach. At the time it happened, the wound was considered to be fatal. He would walk with the help of crutches for the rest of his life. In his 1889 pension application affidavit, he states, "Shot through the body, the ball entering the left-side at the stomach and passing out grazing the spine. Wound declared mortal at the time. Suffered constantly. Eleven months ago taken down with the inability to walk without aid, that continues, losing use of both legs, and also all balance in my body, and requiring constant support and

Col. Isaac W. Avery, Jr. Later in Life
(1836-1897)

falling over without support. Also, stomach vitality gone, with loss of relish for food and paralysis of digestion. No use of either leg."

The Union forces attempted to get to the east of the Confederate forces during the battle, the details of which were recorded by Colonel Isaac W. Avery himself when he quotes General Johnston for his book, *The History of the State of Georgia,* published in 1881:

Here was a desperate bout, furious and bloody, in which Sherman was frightfully punished. Early he made an effort to turn our right and get between Johnston and the railroad. This was the afternoon of the 26th of May, 1864. Col. Avery was thrown at the double quick with a part of the 4th Georgia Cavalry to check the movement until troops could get up to thwart it." Gen Johnston says of this perilous attempt upon his flank, *"Although desperately wounded in the onset, Col. Avery, supported in his saddle by a soldier, continued the command and maintained the contest until the arrival of forces capable of holding the ground.*[141]

In Arba's account, he mentions Henry Stafford immediately killing the Union soldier who had wounded Colonel Avery. There is no Henry Stafford in the 4th Georgia Cavalry at the time of the Battle of New Hope Church. There were two soldiers by that name at one time in the 4th, but they were both killed in action in 1863. There was a Robert Henry Stanfield (1835-1903) in the same Company F as Arba, who may have been the soldier who killed the man who wounded Colonel Avery.

As the 4th Georgia Cavalry charged forward to check the flanking move, five soldiers in Company F were captured at New Hope Church; while Arba managed to get away, his luck wouldn't last long.

Thirty-nine-year-old Private William A. "Asa" Massey

---

[141] Isaac W. Avery, *The History of The State of Georgia from 1850 to 1881, Tracing the Three Important Epochs: The Decade Before the War of 1861-5; The War; The Period of Reconstruction,* (New York, Brown & Derby Publishers, 1881), 277.

(1825-1899), one of Arba's neighbors at Pond Spring, Georgia, was sent to the POW Camp at Rock Island, Illinois, where he remained until the war's end.[142]

Thirty-seven-year-old Private John T. Warren (1826-1915) was also sent to Rock Island, Illinois, as a POW for the remainder of the war, though the records show him as captured during the Battle of Resaca. His first wife, Mary Jane Russell, died 1862 while Warren was away at war, leaving five small children to live with their maternal grandmother until the war's end. After the war Warren returned to his home at Sugar Valley in Gordon County, Georgia, where he married his second wife, Sarah Ann Turner. They would have four children together. Warren was the entrepreneurial sort. Prior to the war he owned a mercantile store. After the war he erected a cotton gin in the valley but soon after suffered a serious injury while operating the cotton gin and lost his right hand. He was elected to the office of the Gordon County Tax Collector, serving one term from 1883 to 1885. Warren's second wife died in the 1890s, and he married a third time late in life. He died in 1915.[143]

Thirty-six-year-old Private Clayton S. Smallwood (1828-1865) lived with his wife, Mary Kelley, and eight children near Arba at Cane Creek in Walker County, Georgia. Records show him captured at LaFayette, Georgia, on July 13, 1864, where he was sent to Camp Chase, Ohio. Smallwood succumbed to pneumonia on April 4, 1865, and is buried just south of the camp in grave number 1814.[144]

Nineteen-year-old Private John H. Oldam's records show that he was captured near Alatoona, Georgia, on the same day as the Battle of New Hope Church and transferred north. He died of typhoid fever just 23 days after he was captured at the military prison in Louisville, Kentucky. The hospital at the time of his death would most likely have been

---

[142] William A. Massey, Compiled Service Records.
[143] John T. Warren, Compiled Service Records and family genealogy.
[144] Clayton S. Smallwood, Compiled Service Records.

Brown General Hospital. This hospital was erected by the Union Army and operated until 1866. He is buried in grave number 89 at Cave Hill Cemetery.[145]

Forty-year-old Private Robert Franklin Shaw (1824-1902) was a cousin of Arba's through one of his grandfather's brothers; he served alongside of him in Company F and lived near Arba in LaFayette, Georgia. He married Mary Frances McWhorter in 1849, and prior to the war the couple had eight children. Records show him captured on the same day as the Battle of New Hope Church, and he was transferred as a POW north to Rock Island, Illinois, where he remained until he was released on June 20, 1865. After the war he returned to Fricks Gap, Georgia, where he returned to farming and had three more children. He died in 1902 in Walker County, Georgia.[146]

When Arba falls into a ravine during a rush of the Yankees and his mule, Jack, stumbles, Arba is shot from behind and wounded in the leg. At that moment it could have gone either way if not for Lieutenant James Washington Hill of Company A who returned fire, killing the soldier who shot Arba. Lieutenant Hill himself at that moment had less than two months to live. He was killed in action on July 21, 1864, during the engagement at Bald Hill located about three miles from present-day Emory University.

Private Melville C. Alexander (1840-1912), who was twenty-three years old at the time and also of Company F, helped Arba back to the field hospital where the 4th Georgia's Surgeon Dr. James B. Edelen was already at work on the wounded in a medical tent along Burnt Hickory Road. Alexander remained a lifelong bachelor after the war and returned to farming in Walker County. He died in 1912.[147]

Dr. James B. Edelen, who carried the rank of Major, was

---

[145] John H. Oldam, Compiled Service Records.
[146] Robert Franklin Shaw, Compiled Service Records and family genealogy.
[147] Melville C. Alexander, Compiled Service Records and family genealogy.

from Jefferson County, Kentucky. Edelen had a checkered history during his time in the Confederate Army. In July of 1863 the Provost Marshall arrested him for drunkenness and tried this offense in Richmond, Virginia, which resulted in Edelen being relieved of his duties as Medical Purveyor of Major General Wheeler's Cavalry Corps. But less than a year later, on Thursday, May 26, 1864, he was serving as Surgeon for the 4th Georgia Cavalry in Brigadier General Alfred Holt Iverson, Jr.'s Brigade.[148] At this point in the war surgeons were in short supply.

Arba was taken south along Burnt Hickory Road to a medical tent close to New Hope Church. Shortly after, he is witness to the arrival of a badly wounded Colonel Avery. It is likely that Dr. Edelen was the first doctor to closely examine Avery's wound and deem it fatal. He was, of course, wrong.

NEW HOPE CHURCH WAS A VICTORY for the Confederacy, despite being outnumbered by almost four to one. The overwhelming artillery barrage against Union forces lead by Colonel Beckham was the deciding factor. The Union Army lost 1,664 men while the Confederate Army lost around 475 men. But victory was short-lived, and skirmishes with Union forces pushing the Rebels backwards toward Atlanta continued almost immediately in the days that followed.

However, for Arba and his commanding officer Colonel Avery, their fighting was finished. Army ambulances took them and the other wounded soldiers away from the Battle of New Hope Church to hospitals in Atlanta.

---

[148] Dr. James B. Edelen, Compiled Service Records and family genealogy.

CHAPTER EIGHT
HOSPITALIZATION AND RECOVERY

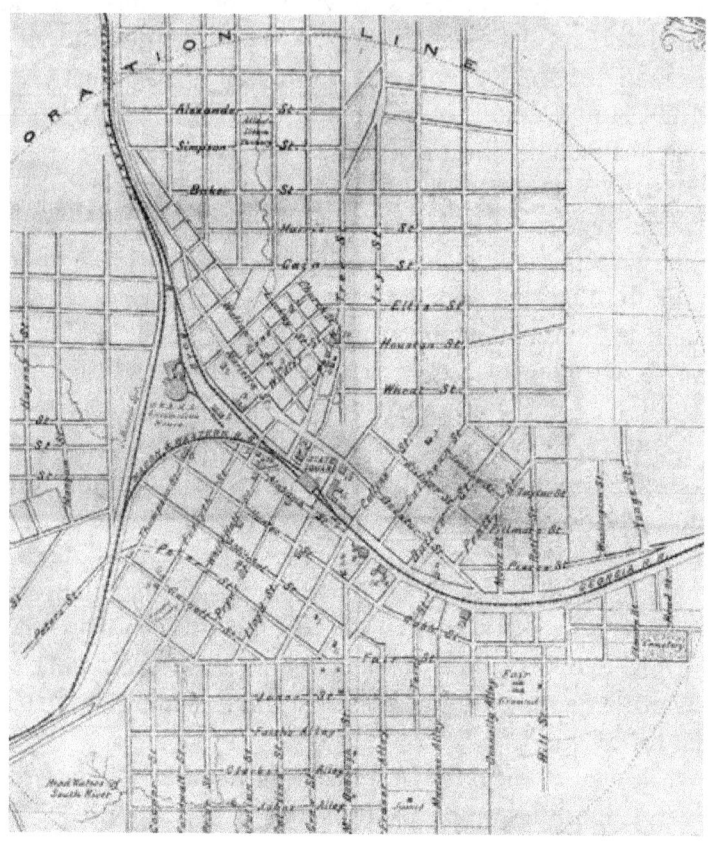

**1864 Atlanta, Georgia - At the center of the map is
"State Square" where the Union Depot was located,
The Fair Ground site where the hospitals were located are in
the bottom right at Hill and Fair Street.**

Fair Street is present-day Memorial Drive. Oakland Cemetery
is located in the bottom right and is labeled as "Cemetery."

*Library of Congress, Geography and Map Division;
Hand-drawn map on canvas*

Rebel Correspondent

September 4, 1902
MY EXPERIENCES
In the War of 1860 Briefly Told.

The train did not stand long until it sped away for Atlanta and we, with a lot of others that had been put on at other stations, were put in a distributing hospital where wounded and sick men were unloaded every day from the trains. The bunks in that hospital, like the soldiers, were bloody, dirty and lousy, but that place was only fixed to take care of us until the ambulances could get us away to the regular hospitals of which there were two in the city—the Medical College and Fair Ground. I stayed at the Fair Ground and when I got there the first thing was to doff my field raiment and don a bright clean shirt and slips and my own clothes went to the laundry house and when I wanted them they were clean. Every thing had to be done decently in that hospital.

When I was cleaned up I was still suffering so I didn't feel like life was worth living. I got up and sat on the side of my bunk and found where the ball was. It had made a little black rising looking place, the width of my hand above my left knee and I called a nurse and asked him to go and get the doctor to come and cut it out. It was not long until he was there with a narrow crooked lance and a pair of forceps. He cut into the top and pushed the forceps in and tore it out, at which I never flinched and hardly frowned. The nurse said I stood it the best he ever saw. The truth is it was already hurting about as bad as anything could hurt and from that minute I felt relieved as one does when an aching tooth is pulled.

Then I soon began to look around and see the surroundings. The nurses would come around and dress our wounds twice a day and feed us twice a day. They all, that is the Doctors, Matrons and nurses, were kind to us and lots of ladies would visit us every day and bring in something nice to eat and drop a cheering word, but some of the boys were suffering too bad to want anything but death to relieve them of their agony.

In there, was one man of French descent—I believe his name was Lefterandler—with both of his arms broken in two above the elbows, he having been shot with small arms. There was another named Vincent. He was from Cherokee county, Ala., and was an old time gunsmith. He was brought in the next day after I was and when the steward called on him for his name he could not speak but made motion for pencil to write. Thus he gave his name. He was shot in one cheek just below the eye. It was a minney ball. It went down and stopped inside of his collar bone and the doctors took it with forceps out where it went in. They chloroformed him and they were not long at the work Vincent was relieved and in a few days he could speak audibly, but the worst case I saw was that of a young man—Gibs, of Ala. He lost a leg. It was cut off about midway of his thigh and the flesh closed over and stitched as usual and it had got to the painful stage and he was complaining with it and a doctor cut the stitches and it soon spread open and drawed back and left the end of the bone exposed. Then he began to holler and pray and not a bit could he sleep, day or night and when I left his thigh bone was exposed two inches and he was getting weak. I never did know whether he got well or died.

Some of the wounded had gangrene in their wounds and when the sores were washed the doctor would put a solution on. They called it Darby's fluid. They put it in large black bottles and sprinkled it on through a small hole through the middle of the cork. That treatment did the work. As the patients improved all that on examination were not going to be able to do service in 30 days were furloughed for 60 days and let go to their homes to get well.

A. F. Shaw

THE TRAIN THAT TOOK ARBA from Marietta to Atlanta was the Western & Atlantic Railroad, coming from the northwest. Arba was transferred to what was known as a "Receiving and Distributing Hospital," which functioned as a triage unit in sorting the injured to determine who needed care first and what facilities were best suited to handle their injuries. This would have been very rudimentary at best during the Civil War. In Arba's case, on Friday, May 27, 1864, he was routed to the Medical College and Fair Ground Hospitals, which was in close proximity to the Georgia Railroad.

The Medical College and Fairground Hospitals[149] consisted of two facilities known as Fairground Hospital No. 1 or No. 2. The hospitals were made up of some forty buildings, which were repurposed at the site in 1862. They were located south of present-day Memorial Drive near Hill Street and just west of Oakland Cemetery in Atlanta. Oakland Cemetery at the time was known as the Atlanta Graveyard or City Burial Place and was expanded from the original six acres to forty-eight acres because of the Civil War. The cemetery is the resting place for approximately 7,000 Confederate soldiers, many of whom are unknown.[150] A large quantity of these soldiers likely came from the Fairground Hospitals.

IN MAY 1864 TWENTY-SEVEN-YEAR-OLD DR. ALBERT Harris Snead (1837-1901) of Richmond, Virginia, was in charge of Fairground Hospital No. 1. Thirty-nine-year-old Dr. David A. Maxwell (1825-1885) of Paducah, Kentucky, headed Fairground Hospital No. 2.

The other soldiers mentioned—Lefterandler, Vincent, and Gibs—do not show up in any of the sparse records of the time. Nor do they show up in the records for the Oakland

---

[149] Jack D. Welsh, *Two Confederate Hospitals and Their Patients, Atlanta to Opelika*, (Macon, Mercer University Press, 2005), 12.
[150] *Historic Oakland Foundation,* Atlanta, Georgia.

Cemetery Book of Confederate Burials, February 1862 to July 5, 1864.

Darby's Fluid was an early antiseptic made from manganese oxide ore and potassium hydroxide, which was deep purple in color. It was developed around 1857 by John Darby, a professor of natural science and chemistry at East Alabama Male College, which later became Auburn University. Used widely during the Civil War, as Arba indicates, the doctors likely did not understand why or even how it worked; the medical profession of the time had no clear idea of the concept of infection and its cause. Soldiers became experimental subjects as doctors looked for ways to save their lives under battlefield conditions. Arba's wound to the left thigh was quickly dealt with, the minnie ball "torn out" much to his relief, like "when an aching tooth is pulled." Perhaps he got a dose of the magical elixir called Darby's Fluid as well; if not, it was pure chance that he did not develop an infection.

At the start of June when Arba was released, Fairground Hospital No. 1 had 400 beds and Fairground Hospital No. 2 had 500 beds. As the Atlanta Campaign heated up, hospital beds became increasingly short in supply so additional hospitals were put in tents near the railroad depot. At the beginning of July 1864 as Union forces pressed south and the threat to the City of Atlanta increased, the order was given for the hospitals to be evacuated further south to Macon. But it was early June 1864, and Arba was released from the hospital and got away from the rising crisis in Atlanta with a sixty-day furlough just in time.

1864 Atlanta, Georgia – The Macon and Western Railroad tracks in the foreground were used in the route taken by Arba as he headed west to LaGrange, Georgia.

The Western and Atlantic's Locomotive House is the round structure in the distance. The structure was destroyed by Sherman's forces in November 1864.

Barnard, George N. (1819-1902) photographer
Glass stereograph, wet collodion. Library of Congress

Steve Procko

September 11, 1902
MY EXPERIENCES
In the War of 1860 Briefly Told.

With our sixty days furlough in our pockets, the ambulance came up to the door of the hospital and all that needed it were assisted to get in and soon we were driven to the car shed and unloaded. Some of the boys were off in a little bit, but others had to wait for trains going out the way they wanted to go. It was in the early p.m. when we were left there and my train—the West Point—never pulled out until about the middle of the night, but the Confederate Government had fixed a Soldier's Home by the car shed for such fellows as we were where we could eat and rest free of charge. I was at a loss, didn't know how I was to make it. I could not walk a step but provision had been made to meet such emergencies. There were crutches already made for the maimed and they gave me a pair. Then I could walk. They were not padded and how they did hurt under my arms.

The West Point train steamed in the shed at the appointed time and the nurses put me on the train and gave my saddle pockets and crutches to me and I was "allaboard" for LaGrange.

The porters set me off at LaGrange a while before day and no one to tell me which way to go. It was dark and the first time I was ever there and I had not the remotest idea what direction I wanted to go. When the sun rose that morning it seemed to be in the west and was that way all the 60 days. No matter where I was, the sun rose in the west and set in the east and south was north to me.

The train went on and I went on after it to the first crossing and turned left and upon got to where the road forked and I turned right aiming to stop at the first house for help and in about half a mile I found the house and in it a good samaritan. He was Col. Miller, commanding a regiment of state troops at West Point. By that time it was day break. I hollered at the gate and got no response (it *being Sunday morning they were taking the world easy.) I went in and rapped on the door and no answer. Then I went to a window and raised it. Then I could make noise enough to wake the Colonel. He asked me what I wanted. I said I was a wounded soldier and wanted to get to the widow Holoways, He said, "All right, come in." I went in and he roused up the negroes and after breakfast he had his horse and buggy rigged up and sent me to Aunt Susan's by his son. It was 8 miles and when I got there to my surprise I met father and brother Jim. Aunt Sou was father's sister; she had four sons in the army and one had died and a few days after I got there one lost his left arm in battle in Virginia and another was killed about New Hope battle and the other, the youngest, was yet at home—had just become subject and the bitter thought of what had happened to his three brothers— two already dead and the other less an arm brought on him a burden that for many days unmanned him. Finally he overcame it all and went to his calling, abiding all the time in sincere prayer. He filled his place faithfully and when it was all over he was spared to his mother unharmed.*

These things made me think the more of my mother's praying, bleeding heart away far behind the enemy's front and she had a husband and two sons that were forced away and she not knowing whether she would ever see or hear of us any more. It impressed me the more to observe the right but in spite of all I could do the evil one would and does yet, at times, make me err. Oh, that it did not so be.

Father and brother were both spared and we were all at home together when the war was over.

A. F. Shaw

When Arba arrived at LaGrange, Georgia, roughly eighty-seven miles from Atlanta, he readily admits he was all turned around with his sense of direction. Getting shot tends to do that to a soldier.

He disembarked the train onto the LaGrange railroad

platform with a haversack containing all his worldly possessions and breakfast on his mind. One can imagine how difficult it would have been, with his unpadded crutches, to hobble down an empty Depot Street, slowly taking a left onto an equally vacant Bull Street, then walking away from LaGrange's town center.[151] He hobbled another block. Where was everybody? He clearly had no idea where he was going as he gingerly limped along, taking the next path he came to, which pointed south. It was called Whitesville Road, and he soon found himself standing in front of a house located on the right side of the street. The home was owned by Colonel Thomas Compton Miller (1814-1876).[152] He called out, but no answer. Then he had the nerve to slide open a front window and yell inside. Luckily, this was not followed by the answer of a gunshot aimed in his general direction. Hunger was definitely calling, and Arba was calling back.

The Colonel was a former Judge of the Inferior Court and Sheriff of Troup County up until the Civil War began. Miller was born in Belfast, Ireland, and came to the United States at age fourteen years in 1828. With the war underway, he led the local home guards or state troops as their Colonel, though no actual military record exists for him. Arba had certainly picked the right house.

The Miller household in the 1860 Census included his wife, Elizabeth, and seven children, with two sons, Frank and Palmon, being old enough to serve in the Confederate Army. In fact, at that particular moment in time, one of his sons had less than five weeks to live. Twenty-two-year-old Francis V. (Frank) Miller perished just weeks later at the Battle of Cool Spring in the Shenandoah Valley of Virginia on July 18, 1864.

Colonel Miller was also an owner of a total of eight enslaved individuals—three adult women, two adult men,

---

[151] Troup County Archives – *Survey of 1860 Buildings and Roads conducted in 1923.*

[152] Thomas Compton Miller family genealogy.

and three male children between the ages of 1 year and 13 years, as noted in the 1860 slave census.

After a much-needed breakfast, Arba hitched himself and his belongings, including his crutches, into a buggy provided by Colonel Miller. He was soon traveling to a small settlement known as Long Cane where his Aunt Sou lived. Long Cane was southeast of LaGrange, almost halfway to the next train station in West Point, Georgia.

This was to be a bittersweet reunion with his aunt, along with the surprise that his father and his brother James were also at the farmstead. It's serendipitous that Arba's father seems to turn up each time at the place where Arba is headed, but he was also a refugee from his own homestead. Living with family members in safer areas of Georgia would have made sense. At this point Arba's father and brother were living a gypsy-like existence, moving from relative to relative further and further away from the onslaught of dangerous war conditions that permeated northwestern Georgia almost all the way to Atlanta.

Arba's Aunt Sou, or the "Widow Holloway," was Susan Ann Shaw Holloway (1818-1883),[153] Arba's father's sister. Her husband, James Holloway (1814-1847), had died long before the war in 1847, leaving Aunt Sou to raise six children, ranging in age from infant Anthony born on September 20, 1847, to age eleven years. Anthony, then sixteen years of age, may have been born after his father's death.

Aunt Sou's family had certainly suffered through the war. When Arba arrived the family was mourning the loss of twenty-eight-year-old Henry Holloway (1836-1864),[154] who had been killed in action a few days before Arba was wounded at the Battle of New Hope Church. Henry had been lost at the Battle of Cassville, Georgia, around May 17, 1864, (aka the Battle of Adairsville) and was at that moment resting in a mass grave of 300 "unknown" Confederate

---

[153] Susan Ann Shaw Holloway family genealogy.
[154] Henry Holloway, Compiled Service Records and family genealogy.

soldiers near the site of the battle in Bartow County. They knew he was one of the dead; however, no one was there who could identify his remains so he and his brother-in-arms were buried in a mass grave. The idea of soldiers wearing dog tags for identification wasn't suggested until the end of the Spanish-American War in 1899, and not officially adopted until 1906. Many a soldier in the Civil War would handwrite some kind of identification in their clothes in the event of their demise. But with no standard for this, it became pure chance if the identification was ever found.

Military records do not explain why Henry Holloway was in and around Cassville, Georgia, on that fateful date. They show him to have been a Private in Company H of Colonel James Henry Fannin's (1836-1909)[155] 1st Georgia Reserves. Fannin was also a Troup County resident. Henry is shown to have enlisted in Atlanta on May 2, 1864. The 1st Georgia Reserves were stationed at the notorious Andersonville Prison starting around May 9, 1864, as prison guards. After the war Colonel Fannin would testify for the prosecution in the trial of Andersonville commandant Henry Wirz (1823-1865),[156] noting that day in his testimony. Wirz would be convicted and executed for the war crimes committed at Andersonville in November 1865 at Old Capitol Prison in Washington, D. C. This was the same prison where the four convicted conspirators in the assassination of President Abraham Lincoln had been hung four months at the Washington Arsenal, now the site of Fort McNair.

So we are left with the curious question of why Private Henry Holloway wasn't guarding Union prisoners at Andersonville on May 17, 1864. Instead, he was in Cassville, Georgia, where he was killed in action. He was the third Holloway in two years to be a casualty of the Civil War.

---

[155] James Henry Fannin, Compiled Service Records and family genealogy.
[156] Summary of the Trial of Henry Wirz, (40th Congress, Snd Session; Ex Doc No 23. – December 7, 1867), 148.

Henry's brother Cephus H. Holloway (1841-1862) was a Private in Captain Curtright's Company E, Georgia 41st Infantry. He was just twenty-one years old at a camp at Tupelo, Mississippi, on June 21, 1862, when he died of the number one killer of soldiers in the Civil War—disease.

Another one of Aunt Sou's sons, twenty-six-year-old Rufus B. Holloway (1838-1900), a Private in Company C of the 9th Georgia Infantry, was at the Battle of Gettysburg on July 3, 1863. At this famous conflict he was shot in the arm and captured by Union forces. He underwent a battlefield amputation at the shoulder as a POW two days later on July 5, 1863, and was transferred to the large Union hospital in Chester, Pennsylvania, where he spent the next two months. On September 7, 1863, he was sent to City Point, Virginia, which was a prisoner exchange swap point. He would be furloughed on October 3, 1863.

ARBA'S FATHER AND BROTHER WERE no doubt helping his Aunt Sou deal with her grief and manage her farmstead. They were also sheltering from all of the fighting going on up, in, and around their own farmstead in Walker County.

It is interesting to speculate as to Arba's father, Reverend William Shaw's, status regarding Confederate conscription laws. The First Conscription Act of April 26, 1862, had set the first age standard, making any white male between the ages of 18 to 35 years liable to serve. Five months later, on September 27, 1862, the age was raised to forty-five years. At that point Reverend Shaw was a forty-two-year-old who, under this new age designation, would have been required to enlist—but he didn't. On February 17, 1864, the ages required to serve changed again as the South began to run out of capable men to "all white men between the ages of 17-50." Within this group, men between seventeen and eighteen years old and forty-five and fifty years old could serve in the reserves of the states they lived in. No record shows Arba's father as enlisting, but Arba does mention that his father was suffering from "white swelling," a term of the time for tuberculosis of the bone or a chronic swelling of the knee joint, which made him lame and exempt from service.

Arba's sixteen-year-old cousin Anthony was facing his own potentially bleak future, having witnessed the war's effects on his three brothers. Arba would join them all to recuperate from his own wounds—wounds that for his entire family were no doubt both physical and mental.

September 18, 1902
MY EXPERIENCES
In the War of 1860 Briefly Told.

I stayed at Aunt Susan's my 60 days and everything was moving along in that part of the country as if there was no war, only the ablest men were gone to the army. The old men, the boys and the negroes were running the farms and the year I was there wheat was fine. Threshing was done in the gin barns. A feeder, a hand to untie bands, one to tote the wheat, one to push back the straw, one to measure and two little boys to drive the two spans of mules was all it took to ran a plant of that kind.

The threshers were made of two pieces of timber, say four feet long, placed cross like winding blades and worked on an axle in the cross and a pulley on one end of the axle. A frame was built for that to work in and boxed in and through a feed slot, the wheat resting on a table, it was fed, the feeder holding the straw till the grain was threshed off. The winding blades were run in a vertical position. The average out put was 50 bushels per day.

I came in handy for Aunt Susan and her two daughters, Roeny and Catherine. Their nearest store and post office was LaGrange and they would send me in a buggy about three times a week.

While I was there a young Doctor Dennis that was brought up in that neighborhood was killed by an exploding locomotive. He ran on the train to take care of the sick and wounded. At the explosion he was on the cab and he and another man were blown high and one went each way and when they fell they were 500 feet apart. One was 200 feet from the engine on this side, the other 300 on the other.

There are many things that I could write about here but it is too tedious.

I would attend church service at every opportunity.

While I was there an enrolling officer got after Jim to join the home guards. As he was 16 he wanted to go with me in the regular service when I went back but the officer would not wait and I told him to join the state troops stationed at West Point and I thought I could get him transferred when I was ready to go but Colonel Miller, on being asked for a transfer said: "No, I tried to get him in the notion to stay, telling him he would have an easier time but he would not be put off."

I went every week to West Point to see Jim and take him clean clothes and take the dirty ones to be washed and two days before time for me to go back I went after him. I took the same old carpet bag—a large one, empty that time—and left it in his tent and Jim got permission to go over the river with me into the town of West Point to bruise around a while and late about sun down we returned to camps.

Now I am going to tell you how I stole Jim. I told him to put his wraps in the carpet bag and he did so. By this time it was getting dark and he gave me the bag and I said, "Boys, I must go. Good night," and I went out, got in the buggy and lit out and stopped when I had driven a half mile away to wait for Jim. That was a cut and dried plan. Jim did about as usual a while and he walked out and was soon at the buggy and we were cutting the sand. It was ten miles to Aunt Sou's and we were soon there.

The next morning I had him by day in the office of the post commandant at LaGrange and sworn in to Co. F. 4th. Ga., and had him given papers to pass all guards and on he went. He had not been gone but a few minutes when Col. Miller, the same one that had helped me so kindly two *months before, came in to the office, I said, "Good morning, Colonel." "Good morning, Shaw. Where is that brother of yours?" "Ah, he is gone to the front. He was mustered into my company here and has just left." The Colonel said, "That is all right, I was hunting him."*

A. F. Shaw

THE SIXTY-DAY FURLOUGH MUST have brought a return to normalcy for Private Shaw. He was back on the farm, and the wheat was being harvested. The daily routine would have been a welcome diversion from the chaotic life he had been leading, surely calming the nerves of a soldier recuperating from the shock of his first gunshot wound.

Also at Aunt Sou's were two additional Hollaway cousins: twenty-four-year-old Rowena (Roeny) (1840-1916) and nineteen-year-old Catherine (1844-1920).[157] The two young women had grown up barely knowing their father, who had died when Roeny was seven years old and Catherine was three years old. This tragic event would have no doubt resulted in a difficult childhood for both of them. Yet somehow the seven Hollaways had survived and pulled together, only to be torn apart by events caused by the Civil War.

Roeny would marry William Cason Knighten (1830-1879) in 1873, and they would have two children. Catherine would marry Oliver Asbury Kelly (1846-1923) in 1868, and they would have ten children. Both sisters moved to Louisiana after they were married, living the rest of their lives about thirty miles from each other near Shreveport.

The train accident that Arba mentions occurred on July 18, 1864.[158] The Macon and Western Railroad's locomotive named "Sunshine" was traveling near Lovejoy Station about four miles south of Jonesboro, Georgia, when it exploded.

---

[157] Holloway family genealogy.
[158] *The Daily Chattanooga Rebel*, (Griffin, Ga.; July 20, 1864).

The engine and five cars were totally wrecked. The cause of the explosion was lack of water in the boiler. Killed instantly were the engineer James Huskieth, an unnamed fireman, and an unnamed slave owned by the railroad. Also killed were several other people including the same Dr. Dennis Arba mentions and Dr. S. A. Harris, a surgeon in Company A, 47th Tennessee Volunteer Infantry. Several passengers were badly injured including Private J. R. Tanner of Company A, 35th Tennessee Volunteer Infantry.

ON JULY 21, 1864, ARBA'S ELEVEN-YEAR-OLD brother Patrick died of an unrecorded illness at home with his mother in McLemore's Cove. His mother would have to bare the grief alone as all the Shaw men were refugees from their own home.

At the end of Arba's sixty-day furlough, his brother Jim, who had turned sixteen years old in January 1864, felt obliged to get in the action as well, joining the local home guards no doubt due to the prodding of Colonel Miller. Though technically Jim was exempt until he turned seventeen years old, the pressure for the sixteen-year-old to join up must have been great. But Arba had other plans. He wanted to have his brother's safety under his own watchful eye when he returned to service with the 4th Georgia Cavalry. So the two brothers worked out a scheme: The military records show that on July 29, 1864, a "Captain Barnum" successfully registered James B. Shaw in Arba's same unit, Company F, at LaGrange, Georgia.[159] Colonel Miller's reaction to the incident shows the difference in attitude toward a soldier's enlistment than we have today. When Colonel Miller learns of Jim's defection, he good-naturedly accepts the poaching of his soldier, saying to Arba, "That is all right." It was quite common for family members to join the same regiment and company so they could watch each other's back. It was also quite common for

---

[159] James B. Shaw, Compiled Service Records.

family members to be a witness to the maiming or killing of their kin in the heat of battle. By enlisting, James was owed a prerequisite fifty-dollar bounty in Confederate currency. It is unclear if the bounty was ever paid; even if it was, in less than a year that Confederate money would be worthless.

CHAPTER NINE
Rejoining the Fight

September 25, 1902
MY EXPERIENCES
In the War of 1860 Briefly Told.

After Jim got off, I went back to Aunt Sous and packed my duds preparatory to starting early to catch the train the next morning Aug. 4, 1864, and I believe father took me to LaGrange.

While I was at Aunt's I formed the acquaintance of Nath McCally. He was a bachelor of 35 years, was about 5 feet tall and weighed 335 pounds. His body looked to be as large as a 50 gallon barrel and his thighs as large as 10 gallon kegs, and his arms as large as a 3 gallon churn jar. He was a man of means and had a strong, double seated hack and when he went he took the back seat and it was full, and when he went some one or more of the young men of the settlement could go if they wished, and if not, he would take a black boy to drive the mules.

One more thing I want to mention, and then I will quit writing of things in these parts for the present, and that is that there was a Hospital at LaGrange and the head man tried to get me to take a horse and wagon and drive over that country and buy up poultry, eggs, butter and vegetables for the hospital but I would not. It would have been a nice bomb proof position but I preferred to go back and fill my place in the ranks.

Now, to the 4th of August, 1864. I boarded the train and in a few hours was at East Point, Ga. There I got off and found some convalescents of the 4th. Georgia in camp and found Jack with a new dress on. It was the first time I had ever seen him sheared off and he had not been roached since I left. Tom Price was taking care of him for me. I had not been at the camp long when Tom came in riding his horse and leading Jack. He had been in a field to let him browse. Tom said, "Hello Shaw, have you come back? "Yes, I'm here," and we parsed a few compliments. Then I said, "Whose mule is that?" He said, "Yours," but for my life I could not see a single trace that would lead me to believe it was Jack but when I put the saddle on him and touched him with the spur be kicked my foot. Then I said, "This is Jack." He was all right yet, and a plum good one.

As I remember it was the next day some of us were in Atlanta and we saw forts and an immense amount of breastworks made of two bushel sacks filled with sand. There were more sacks than I ever saw since, all put together. The next day we left for Covington, Ga., where we were to meet our command as it was coming back from capturing Stoneman. I believe our convalescent crew got to Covington the 7th, in the evening and later in the evening here came the old 4th, and I was real glad to see the boys. They had gone through the rub in the 75 days I had been gone; had been in hard-fought battles and their ranks were somewhat thinned out and I greatly missed the absentees.

Our good Captain, C. D. McCutchen, lived then at Covington. His family had refuged from Dalton. We all loved Capt. McCutchen. He was kind to us.

On the 9th of Aug. 1864 Wheeler started on that tiresome raid around through Tennessee. When we started from Covington the corn was ripe and ready for fodder to be pulled and some were pulling fodder and when we struck Tennessee the earliest corn was getting in roasting ear.

We went through Monroe in Walton county, where mother was born; then through Gwinnet. We passed Pine Log and Possum Trot, then on to the Cohutta Mountains where we were molested by bush whackers. First at the east base one fired into the advance guard and they pursued him and shot him, the ball going in at the back of his head and *raised the skin in the center of his forehead. When the 4th. Georgia came along and was opposite him, Major Steward had Co. F to dismount, form line of battle and march to where he was lying in an unconscious condition and gasping. I was one of four that toted him to the nearest house —About a quarter. It was a heavy turn for us by the time we got to the house. He had a parole in his pocket. He was in the siege of Vicksburg and belonged to the 41st Georgia. I will say I was told he was a bushwhacker and the ones that shot him wrote a note and dropped it by him and in it stated "This man is a bush whacker."*

A. F. Shaw

HIS SIXTY DAYS OF FURLOUGH WERE UP, his brother Jim had left LaGrange on August 4, 1864, headed to Atlanta to join up with the 4th Georgia Cavalry, and Arba was packing his haversack to head back east as well. He gives a very detailed description of a portly friend, Nath McCally, a man he had befriended on his short say with Aunt Sou. Nathan Calvin McCallay was born in 1825 and would have been a thirty-nine-year old farmer when Arba met him. There were several McCallay families living in LaGrange at the time, and Nath had seven brothers and sisters. His brother William Thomas McCallay had died at age twenty-one years in August 1862 in Lynchburg, Virginia, and was brought back to be buried at the family cemetery in Troup County. Nath would live with his mother after the war. He died on December 21, 1885.[160]

IN THE SIXTY DAYS HE HAD BEEN AWAY, the 4th Georgia Cavalry still had Colonel Isaac W. Avery unofficially listed as their leader. But Colonel Avery had been seriously

---

[160] McCallay family genealogy.

wounded, shot through the stomach and spine[161] at the same time as Arba's thigh wound at New Hope Church. Though he miraculously recovered, he had been relegated to desk work and further recuperation at his mother Mary Parson's home in Sandersville, Georgia, near the state capitol of Milledgeville.

General Joseph E. Johnston's army had continued to be pushed back from New Hope Church to Dallas, Georgia, and then to Kennasaw Mountain. Each battle represented another step backward toward Atlanta. On July 18, 1864, President Jefferson Davis had seen enough and replaced Johnston with Lieutenant General John Bell Hood.

Riding the train east from West Point, Georgia, to Atlanta on August 4, 1864, would have been precarious. That was the day the Battle of Utoy Creek began. Union forces under Sherman attempted a flanking move around the southwest side of Atlanta to take control of the supply lines coming into the city from the west on the Atlanta and West Point Railroad and East Point station. This was the very train line Arba was traveling on.

Arba arrived in Atlanta on the day this skirmish started; his train traveled close to the site of battle. The conflict began the next day, August 5, 1864, and soon turned into a siege lasting almost three weeks. He made it back just in time to be greeted by his mule, Jack, who had been cared for by Tom Price while Arba was on medical furlough.

Private Thomas B. Price, age twenty-nine years, was also a member of Arba's Company F. He had joined Avery's 23rd Battalion Georgia Dragoons a year earlier than Arba so he was a full-fledged veteran. Price had been with the Georgia Dragoons at the Battle of Shiloh. About a month from the day when he handed back Jack's reins to Arba, the 4th Georgia would be in Maury County near Campbellsville, Tennessee. Tom Price came down with some unnamed illness and had to be left behind; he was subsequently

---

[161] *Confederate Military History Vol. VII*, (Atlanta, Ga., Confederate Pub. Co., 1899), 477.

captured by Union forces. He was transferred up to Camp Chase, Ohio, where he would succumb to smallpox on November 19, 1864. He was buried in grave 490 at the Camp Chase Confederate Cemetery.[162]

THE FUTURE GOVERNOR OF CALIFORNIA, Army of the Ohio Cavalry commander Major General George Stoneman, was heading southwest from Atlanta with the mission to reach Andersonville prison and free the Union POWs being held there. On July 31, 1864, as they approached Clinton, Georgia, near Macon, Stoneman would become a POW himself. Along with his aide Major Myles Keogh and more than 1,000 of his men,[163] he was captured by Colonel Charles C. Crews, who was then commanding the 2nd Georgia Cavalry. Stoneman personally surrendered to Crews. The Major General became the highest ranked officer captured by the Confederates through the entire Civil War conflict. Stoneman would be swapped in a prisoner exchange in October 1864 for Confederate Brigadier General Daniel C. Govan—and at that particular moment the Rebels were badly losing the war.

Stoneman's aide, Major Keogh, would later be one of the casualties at Little Big Horn under Lieutenant Colonel George A. Custer.

The capture of Major General Stoneman must have been a big deal for Colonel Crews, who was back as the commanding officer of the 2nd Georgia Cavalry, having relinquished command of the brigade he had commanded from 1863 into early 1864 to Brigadier General Iverson. This would change within less than two weeks as Colonel Crews regained command of the brigade for Wheeler's raid into Tennessee.

BY AUGUST 7, 1864, ARBA WAS finally reunited with the

---

[162] Private Thomas B. Price, Compiled Service Records and family genealogy.
[163] OR, sr. I, Vol. XXXVIII, pt2-Reports, p925

4th Georgia Cavalry near Covington, Georgia. The 4th's numbers had been thinned in the preceding seventy-five days of battle, in which Arba had not been present, and the battle for Atlanta was raging fiercely to the west. But Wheeler's Cavalry was massing near Covington, like thousands of knights preparing for the next move in the chess game that was playing out all around Atlanta.

In a strategy that is questioned to this day, General John B. Hood was to take his knights and send them away from Atlanta. Hood ordered his cavalry, which by now numbered 4,000 troops strong under Major General Joseph Wheeler, on a raid northward to Dalton, Georgia, and then onward into Tennessee in an attempt to cut off Union Major General Sherman's supply lines. The disastrous result: General Hood was left to defend Atlanta without his cavalry. Soon Atlanta would fall.

Checkmate.

Thus began what Arba called Wheeler's "tiresome raid around through Tennessee." General Wheeler wrote in his report dated October 9, 1894, at the conclusion of his raid through Tennessee: "I was ordered by General Hood to move upon the enemy's line of communications, destroy them at various points between Marietta and Chattanooga; then cross the Tennessee River, break the line of communication on the two roads running from Nashville to the army; to then leave 1,200 men to continue their operations on those road; to then return again striking the railroad south of Chattanooga, and join the main army."[164]

Having been forced to flee Dalton and now residing near Covington was Company F's former Captain Cicero Decatur McCutchen (1824-1898). McCutchen had resigned his commission on April 17, 1864, when he was elected in November 1863 to the 43rd District of the Georgia State Senate. He had been promoted to Captain upon the loss of Company F's Captain Joseph E. Helvenston, who was killed

---

[164] *OR*, sr. 1, vol. XXXVIII, pt3, 957.

in action at Catlett's Gap in September 1863. After the war the Senator would return to Dalton, Georgia, where he led a distinguished career as a Circuit Court judge until his death in 1898.[165]

Now heading around the north side of Atlanta, Wheeler began to move between the routes of the north–south railroad and the Cohutta Mountains. The force would encounter bushwhackers who fired on the advancing cavalry. It's hard to know what a couple of bushwhackers could have been thinking when firing into a very large group of cavalry soldiers, but they pretty much guaranteed that soon they wouldn't be thinking of anything.

Major Augustus R. Stewart (1838-1909) must not have been too happy to have his men dismount and form a line of battle moving toward a man dying in the road. Bushwhackers in the North Georgia mountains in 1864 had become a growing problem in the chaos of the war. They preyed on the local citizenry by using the war as an excuse to pillage and rob indiscriminately. Many of the bushwhackers were deserters, pledging their allegiance to one side or the other and sometimes claiming sympathy to one side to disguise their true intentions. The result was a war within a war. Rebel bushwhackers would fight "Tory" or northern bushwhackers, and most of northern Georgia became dangerously engulfed in lawlessness. Average mountain citizens found themselves caught in the middle with no help to be found. But this time, the law won—sort of.

October 2, 1902
MY EXPERIENCES
In the War of 1860 Briefly Told.

I now remember that Captain Jeff Johnson of Co. C. was in the yard with us when we took the gasping man. The Captain said he had a brother in the 41st Ga. It strikes me

---

[165] Captain Cicero Decatur McCutchen, Compiled Service Records and family genealogy.

that he said his brother was the Colonel of his regiment, the 41st. We left the man there and went on up the mountain and we soon found a brother of the man we toted in. He was lying by the road dead. He was shot for the like offense of the first. They were Covingtons. A little farther up the mountain we saw a lad of about 16 lying by the road, riddled, and as I remember it was just over the turn a bullet passed through Gen. Wheeler's coat bosom and he ordered the shooter brought in and he too was surrounded and brought in this time. It was an old man—looked to be 60 or more. His hair and beard were all white, I saw the man lying by the road full of bullet holes. He shot with a squirrel rifle, of course. I was not at the capturing or killing. I helped tote the first man in.

At the west base of the Cohutta is where the Captain of Co. A. 4th Ga., Reuben Keith, lived. Lieut. Horn, of Co. F. was sent to the house to arrest the Captain and bring him in because he had quit the service of the army. When they found him at home Lieut. Horn said the Captain in his own house opened his bosom and begged Horn to shoot him, but Horn would not, but took him on, as he was ordered to do, as a prisoner and on the evening we left Spring Place we heard guns fire and after that—the next day—the report was circulated that the shooting was at Captain Keith; that he became desperate and undertook to take a gun from one of the guards and failing he broke off for freedom and was shot and killed. Lieutenant Horn was my author. It was all told to me. I never saw Captain Keith on that occasion and with out a doubt he was killed then. I have talked with some his friends and relations since the war and they say he was lost at that time and that about a year later the bones of a man were found in a briar thicket in the vicinity of that shooting.

After the capture of Captain Keith, and while he was a prisoner, the command went to Dalton, Ga., and after we crossed the Cohutta it fell my turn to go on detail again to scout the country for crowbars and hammers to tear up the railroad about Dalton and as we were going to the front with our tools, we rode past thousands of men fast asleep in their saddles and the horses were keeping their pace in the ranks. We had not stopped day or night to sleep, as best I remember, any at all from Covington to Dalton. The head of the command was about Dalton and did its fighting and tearing up before we had time to get there and we met an order to "about face" a little before dark and the command was soon down by the sides of the road fast asleep, me, too. I suppose the waiting was for our leader—General Wheeler—to get to what was the front.

After we "about faced," when the command mounted, I, in a sound sleep, not knowing anything about it, mounted and rode. I never will know how far or whether in my right place or not. The first thing I remember was like a dream. I was going back toward Dalton and had got back behind all of the command but the provost guard and Jack would stop and bray which would rouse me enough to shake him up with my spurs and start him on in a lope. Then I would go to sleep again and several times he waked me by braying and I would spur him up. Finally I come to a semi-conscious state and I thought I was on picket duty and occasionally a straggling man would come along and ask me if I was on picket. I would say "yes" and he would pass on and I sat at that place till the provost guard came along. I knew all the boys that were on that guard, but can't name any now but Sam Baker of Co. F. He said: "Hello, Shaw, are you on picket?" I said: "Yes," and he being well acquainted it woke me up. Then I said I was asleep and not on picket. Then I turned Jack about and he was soon a hitting the high laces and in about three miles we were in our place. This all took place in the night on the road between Dalton and Spring Place and where I went to sleep was in the flat east of the Oostananla river, about half way between the two towns. We, for the first time after leaving Covington, went into camp.

A. F. Shaw

CAPTAIN JEFFERSON JOHNSON OF COMPANY C had been in the original 23rd Battalion Georgia Dragoons and was a seasoned veteran. His brother Colonel Abda Johnson commanded the 40th Georgia Infantry; Arba had mistaken Abda for the leader of the 41st Georgia Infantry in his recollections thirty-eight years after the fact.

The Covington brothers in Private Shaw's account were from Ball Ground, Georgia.[166] At the start of the war the family of eleven (six boys and five girls) had supplied four sons of age to the Confederate cause. All four brothers had been in the Vicksburg Campaign in two different units. David Covington (1835-1864) and Ananias Covington (1842-1864) were both Privates in Company D of the 40th Georgia Infantry. Lewis Thomas Covington (1844-1864) and John Howell Covington (1833-1910) were both Privates in Company I of the 52nd Georgia Infantry.

John H. Covington was captured and wounded at the Battle of Champion Hill in Mississippi on May 16, 1863, which was an early part of the Vicksburg Campaign.

The other three Covingtons were captured at the end of the Vicksburg Campaign on July 4, 1863. The 40th Georgia's commanding officer, Colonel Abda Johnson (1826-1881), was captured on that day as well. The Colonel would sign an Oath of Allegiance to the United States witnessed by Major John C. Fry, the Paroling Officer, with the 20th Ohio Volunteers on July 5, 1863. Colonel Johnson would return to his command, ignoring the terms of the Oath of Allegiance he had signed, and would be with the 40th Georgia until the end of the war. He would later become the first mayor of Cartersville, Georgia.[167]

The three Covingtons would also sign Oaths of

---

[166] Covington family, Compiled Service Records and family genealogy.
[167] Colonel Abda Johnson, Compiled Service Records and family genealogy.

Allegiance to the United States, witnessed by the same Major John C. Fry between July 7 and 16, 1863. No record of John H. Covington exists showing whether he, too, signed the Oath, but it is very likely he did. Then all four Covington brothers must have skedaddled back to Ball Ground to hide—having had enough of the real war, it was bushwhacker time.

Lewis Thomas Covington, age twenty years old, would die under unknown circumstances on May 20, 1864, likely related to guerrilla activities in his county.

Then twenty-nine-year-old David and twenty-two-year-old Ananias would make the mistake of firing on Wheeler and his cavalry force of upwards to 4,000 men; both would lose their lives on the same day: August 13, 1864. Arba and his fellow soldiers would drag one of the Covingtons a quarter mile to where Captain Johnson would identify them as bushwhackers. One remaining soldier-brother, thirty-one-year-old John Howell Covington (1833-1910), would survive the war.

Private Shaw's account of the deaths of David and Ananias is corroborated by a Southern Claims Commission Settlement[168] by Catherine Moore Howell (1849-1913). Catherine was a teenager when this event occurred. Her family was from Plymouth, England, and had immigrated to the United States in November 1850. During the war the family were loyal Unionists living in Cherokee County, Georgia, harassed by Rebel soldiers and home guard. The claim was filed in 1878, specifically asking for reimbursement for two mules the Union Army had foraged, But in her testimony she told a similar story to Arba in relating to the Covington's demise, saying that Wheeler's Cavalry was part of it.

Mrs. Howell's account states that the Covingtons were Unionists and that one of the brothers had been hung during

---

[168] March 4, 1879; Southern Claims Commission Case #55019; Catherine Howell successor of Ann Moore of Cherokee County; State of Georgia; Settlement #8218.

this event: "Rebel scouts came and camp on us one night some 8 or 10 in number, of cavalry, ordered mother to cook supper & breakfast for them. They also fed their horses, these scouts belonged to Wheeler's command," she testified before the Claims Commission. "This same crowd of rebels killed two Union men, shot dead by the names of David Covington and Ananias Covington, brothers on about a half mile from the house, the other was about 3 or 4 miles off. The first was shot and the second hung and shot to pieces. I saw the rope on the man when he had been cut down."

In other accounts of the killings, the trigger finger is pointed at a group known as McCollum's Scouts, headed by Benjamin Franklin McCollum (1843-1880). McCollum, at the time of the killings, was listed as a Private in Company C of Phillip's Legion, a Cavalry Battalion of Georgia Volunteers started by Colonel William Phillips (1830-1908) of Marietta, Georgia. The records show McCollum as AWOL from this battalion on August 16, 1864. He was also known as the leader of a Rebel bushwhacker gang in Pickens County, Georgia, known as McCollum's Scouts. But to confuse matters even more, in early September 1864 McCollum would be commissioned as a Captain by Governor Joseph E. Brown in the Blackhorse Cavalry of the Georgia Militia. Apparently, at times he acted in an official military capacity, and at other times he operated as a Rebel bushwhacker.

These alternate accounts were offered in *History of Cherokee County* by Reverend Lloyd G. Marlin in 1932, which claimed that the Covington brothers were captured by McCollum's Scouts in Dawson County and brought back to Pickens County: "One of them was hanged; the other, attempting to get away, was shot and killed in the yard of a resident at Four Mile, on the Old Federal Road. The location of this double slaying is still known as "Covington Hang."[169]

So this is a whodunit, as well as another example of how

---

[169] Reverend Lloyd G. Martin, *The History of Cherokee County*, (Walter W. Brown Publishing Co. 1935, First Edition), 211.

the facts of an event get blurred over time. It seems the earlier accounts of 1878 and 1901 are closer to the facts, coming from two completely independent sources. Of special note: When the Covingtons signed their Oath of Allegiance in 1863 at Vicksburg, they meant it. On that day they became Unionists.

CAPTAIN REUBEN ROPER KEITH, AGE FORTY-ONE YEARS (1823-1864), was five-foot-nine-and-a-half-inches tall with dark hair and blue eyes. Keith was born in Greenville, South Carolina, and later moved to Whitfield County, Georgia, in the late-1840s to marry Mary Ann Loughridge (1828-1909). Mary Ann was the daughter of former Georgia Senator and pro-Unionist Colonel Benjamin Loughridge (1800-1877). Colonel Loughridge had achieved his rank in the local militia in the 1830s and lived east of Dalton in an area called Pleasant Valley in Murray County. The Loughridge plantation was on the west side of the Old Federal Road that led to Cleveland, Tennessee. He was also a slave owner in possession of nineteen human beings (seven adult males, three adult females, and nine children) in the 1860 slave census. Captain Keith in the 1860 Census lived with his wife and family about nine miles to the west of his father-in-law in a community known as Rural Vale. But since his furlough with typhoid fever in 1863, he likely lived in a home on property owned by his father-in-law with his wife and at least five children.

Colonel
Benjamin Loughridge
1800-1877

When the Civil War broke out, Loughridge's two oldest sons William and James, along with three sons-in-law including Reuben Keith, join the Confederate side. Another son-in-law was a staunch abolitionist and would join the Union cavalry. The Loughridge family must have had very interesting dinner table conversations. Surely, all weapons had to be left at the door.

Captain Keith had enlisted in the 4th Georgia Cavalry as the Captain of Company A on September 20, 1862, in Dalton, Georgia. In August 1863 Captain Keith contracted typhoid and was furloughed home to recover.[170] Typhoid was a common disease during the Civil War; if a soldier didn't die from the disease, it took him a long time to recover. Soldiers with typhoid would develop skin lesions known as "rose spots," with additional symptoms of fever, diarrhea or constipation, fatigue, respiratory distress, and general malaise. Civil War doctors had no idea that typhoid was caused by poor sanitary conditions in the water they were eating or drinking. By 1864 the fatality rates from typhoid fever were as high as sixty percent.[171]

ON TUESDAY, APRIL 5, 1864, while the 4th Georgia was at camp near Oxford, Alabama, its commander, Colonel Isaac W. Avery, sat in his tent and penned a letter to Major Arthur Pendleton Mason (1835-1893), then the Assistant Adjutant General of the Army of the Tennessee who was headquartered in Dalton. This was the calm before the storm as in one month the Atlanta Campaign would begin right at Major Mason's doorstep.

I have to report the following facts in regard to Capt. Reuben R. Keith, Co "A" 4th Geo Cav. The last August 1863 Captain Keith was taken down with Typhoid Fever, He has never been to his Regiment since, nor has any official notice been received from any Hospital as regard to him. He has been hence ordered to his command by me in the last month by letter. He is a resident of Murray Co., GA, and is outside

---

[170] Captain Reuben Roper Keith, Compiled service records.
[171] Alfred Jay Bollet, *Civil War Medicine: Challenges and Triumphs*, (Tuscon, Ariz., Galen Press, 2002), 273-274.

the army lines and rumored to be paying suit to the enemy. On account of him having been a good officer I have waited on him for an explanation of his conduct. It is also rumored that he is Deputy Sheriff of Murray Co, appointed lately for the purpose of getting out of the army. His father-in-law is a bitter Union man & his defection under such influence probable. He deserves to be dropped from the rolls.[172]

Avery must have been clairvoyant. Reuben had indeed changed his loyalties, having signed an Oath of Allegiance in Chattanooga just ten days earlier on Sunday, March 27, 1864. He was dropped from the rolls of the 4th Georgia Cavalry on June 7, 1864.

The story passed down from the Keith family was that Captain Keith was seriously ill at home convalescing. Soon after Wheeler's Cavalry had retaken Dalton, they showed up at the Loughridge farm and stole all the livestock and destroyed the crops and fences. When they found out that Captain Keith was nearby at his home, they went there and took him from his bed, tied him to a horse, and led him away. His death was recorded as August 15, 1864, which coincides with the Second Battle of Dalton. The family later found his body and buried him in Loughridge cemetery in Eton, Georgia.

James George Alexander Loughridge
1844-1918

Two weeks later his brother-in-law James George Alexander Loughridge (1844-1918) had seen enough. James would travel to Cleveland, Tennessee, and join the Union

---

[172] Letter to Major Arthur Pendleton Mason by Isaac W. Avery, April 5, 1864.

side in the 5th Tennessee Mounted Infantry.[173]

What Arba would not have known was that his future great-granddaughter Anna Ruth Pryor (1925-2010) would in the middle of the twentieth century marry Jesse Clarence Keith (1923-2011). Captain Reuben Roper Keith was Jesse Clarence Keith's 3x great-uncle.[174]

IT HAD BEEN A FAST-PACED AND EXHAUSTING five days for the Wheeler raid to get from Covington to Dalton, skirmishing as they went. They were so exhausted; the soldiers were now asleep in the saddle while their horses followed the horse in front of them in an endless stream of catatonic cavalry.

Arba's recollection of his encounter with Company F's thirty-seven-year-old Private Samuel Baker (1826-1864) could not have taken place, however. Baker had died in a hospital in Griffin, Georgia, on May 30, 1864, leaving a wife and three young children. But, then again, Private Shaw was not immune to the effects of exhaustion himself—both in 1864 and in 1901 when he put these recollections in writing.

---

[173] James George Alexander Loughridge, Compiled Service Records.
[174] Shaw and Keith family genealogy.

CHAPTER TEN
BACK TO TENNESSEE

October 9, 1902
MY EXPERIENCES
In the War of 1860 Briefly Told.

After we went into camp north of Spring Place I was sent out on a forage detail and when we got back I saddled Jack and fed him and made me a pallet. It was midnight, and I was just turning in when Sargant McWhorter said: "Shaw, it is time for you to go on picket," and how bad it did hurt me. I grumbled that time. I had been on detail duty all day and toted a long heavy crowbar on my shoulder for miles and I felt that I had done enough for one day, but argument was worthless. I had to go, and stayed the rest of the night and to 1 o'clock the next day, before I was relieved. I sat there on Jack twelve long hours without relief, water or food. Jack could stand, pick and sleep, but oh, me, I had to fight sleep and it was a hard fight, it was the military order to put men to death if they were found asleep on picket, and when I was relieved and got to the command, it was in the saddle again and marching toward Cleveland, Tenn. Older men than I could possibly tell about the happenings of the raid a great deal better, as I was only a wayward lad of 19 years, but what they would tell would be their part. They can't write up my experiences nor me their's.

The command would tear up all the railroad it could. Cleveland was garrisoned, as were several other towns we found on our way and Wheeler would tackle the Yank, in the towns, and if he did not want to take it he would fight them until we had done all the dirt we could to the railroad and then he would go around and pass on. We got to be expert in the art of tearing up railroads. We would form a line and a man would get hold of each tie and where they were wide enough apart a man would go between and lift under the track. "All ready, up you come," and over would go miles of railroad in half a minute. Then we would pile up the ties and fire them and lay the track across the burning ties so they would bend when they got hot, and when there was enough wood in easy reach suitable, all bands would go to building fires on the track and in a few minutes the track would get hot enough to expand and sometimes the pressure was sufficient to make the track shoot up in a bow as high as our heads.

We went on till we got considerably above Knoxville. At Sweetwater we had a little spat soon one morning. Companies A. and F., were all that were in it on our side and Lieutenant Bill Hancock was in command of the squadron. We were dismounted and marched north of the town until the Yanks began to shoot at us when we stopped and took shelter by the shade trees of a yard around a house. There was not much shooting done. The Yankees soon disappeared from our sight and took the advantage of a thicket to the north side of the house and a patch of Balsam weeds that were very tall between the woods and us and the next we saw of them they were in 25 feet of us and wholly unexpected. Jim Whittle was the first man to see them. He threw up his revolver and said: "Will you surrender?" and then shot, and about the same time a Yank shot and scalped John Bigerstaff and he, we all thought, was killed. The ball struck about the center and the lower part of his roach and glanced up. When he fell Lient. Hancock in place of saying: "Give them Hail Columbia," said "retreat" and all the boys ran but me at the first command, and I would have ran too, but I wanted some of them to help take John out. I could see that the Yanks had disappeared, surprised as well as we were, but nobody staid to help me with John and as the last one cleared the fence into a nearby corn field I thought I had better go too and soon I was in that field of corn and the boys were so far *ahead of me they were all out of sight.*

When we got back in town we went in the upper story of a brick house and gouged out brick to make port holes. We stayed there a while and no Yanks came. From that house, through the port holes we could see Bigerstaff as he lay, as we thought, dead. He was one of Co. F. When we decided we were more scared than hurt we went back. Bigerstaff was not dead and could sit up on the ground and talk rational. He said that a piece of his skull had come out. He was taken to a citizen's house, and left. We all thought he would be sure to die but be got well and is living yet, I believe, in Whitfield county, Ga.

After this, we went on to Louden and ran on the Yanks again and routed them. Then we took in the town.

Now there is a space from Louden to the extreme northern part of our raid that has gone behind a mist from me. Don't remember how much railroad we destroyed or whether we fought any or not. We went north of Knoxville but don't know to what point. We left the East Tennessee railway. But one thing I do remember, we lived principally on apples and roasting ears. We would raid orchards and fill our haversacks.

A. F. Shaw

The main objective of the Wheeler raid into Tennessee was to try and disrupt the railroad supply lines to the Union forces who were laying siege on Atlanta. As Private Shaw and his company moved north toward Cleveland, Tennessee, their goal was to do just that all the way to Knoxville, becoming experts "in the art of tearing up railroads." They first focused on the East Tennessee and Georgia Railroad, which had been built in the 1850s providing service between Dalton, Georgia, and Knoxville, Tennessee, through Cleveland and Loudon, Tennessee, along the way. Now that they had reached the area around Knoxville and torn up all the rails they could, the plan was to turn west toward

Nashville.

The Union side had the same expertise tearing up railroads around Atlanta. Later in November 1864, when Sherman and his troops marched to the sea, the destruction of the railroad infrastructure was one of the reasons for his actions. One technique became known as "Sherman's neckties" in which rails were heated and wrapped around a tree, making them unsalvageable.

The example of the impact of the Civil War on individual families is clearly evident in the personal stories

An example of the Union rail bending technique became known as "Sherman's neckties."
December 31, 1864 – Harper's Weekly

of Sergeant McWhorter, First Lieutenant Hancock, Corporal Whittle, and Private Biggerstaff.

First Sergeant James Hamilton McWhorter (1844-1908) was a week away from celebrating his twentieth birthday on August 24 as Company F made its way into Tennessee, following a path similar to the one they had traveled less than a year earlier to the Battle of Knoxville. McWhorter was an original member of Colonel Avery's Georgia Dragoons so he had experienced the Battle of Shiloh.

Much of the McWhorter family was fighting for the

Rebel cause. Patriarch Andrew Brown McWhorter (1815-1905) was a forty-nine-year old Private in Company A, 6th Battalion, Georgia State Troops. Brothers Warren Osborne McWhorter (1835-1885) and Samuel Wightman McWhorter (1843-1910) were both first sergeants in Company G of the 9th Georgia Infantry. Private William Henry McWhorter (1840-1862) was in Company C of the 44th Georgia Infantry and had died at a CSA Hospital in Farmville, Virginia, due to chronic diarrhea on September 22, 1862.

After the war Sergeant McWhorter would marry Amelia Edwards (1837-1915) and farm in Walker and Chattooga Counties until his death in Walker County in 1908.[175]

The "little spat" at Sweetwater, Tennessee, saw Company A's thirty-six-year-old First Lieutenant William D. Hancock (1828-before 1900) commanding both Companies A and F. The death of Company A's Captain Keith just days earlier must have still reverberated in his mind as both companies began skirmishing with the Yankees. Lieutenant Hancock had been leading Company A since 1863 when its Captain Reuben R. Keith had left on furlough with typhoid. Hancock surely would have known Keith well, even if he was AWOL from Company A. An additional weight on his shoulders would have been the loss of his brother Captain Benjamin L. Hancock (1830-1863) of Company H, 2nd Georgia Infantry, who was killed in action at Gettysburg on July 2, 1863. Bill Hancock was born in South Carolina and moved to Georgia to marry his wife, Frances (1831-1920), in the late 1840s. The couple had four children—all girls—before the start of the war. After the war the family would live in Whitfield County, Georgia, with Lieutenant Hancock dying sometime before 1900.[176]

Company F's twenty-two-year-old Corporal James Campbell Whittle (1842-1917) was also dealing with the loss

---

[175] First Sergeant James Hamilton McWhorter, Compiled Service Records and family genealogy.
[176] Lieutenant William D. Hancock, Compiled Service Records and family genealogy.

of his father, Captain Albert Gallatin Whittle (1816-1864), as he fired his revolver at a Union soldier who appeared just twenty-five feet from him. His father was an enrolling officer for the CSA who was captured not too far from where his son was skirmishing in Sevier County, Tennessee, on January 20, 1864. The elder Whittle would be shipped to Camp Chase, Ohio, where he would die just over a month later on February 25, 1864. After the war Whittle moved to Texas and married Julia M. Micheaux (1845-1930). They would have four children together. He would die in a Confederate Home in Austin, Texas, in 1917.[177]

The remarkable survival story of Company F is Private John B. Biggerstaff (1834-1889), being struck in the forehead by a minnie ball, which exiting upward while incredibly not damaging his brain. Arba's account was supported in *History of Walker County* by James Alfred Sartain published in 1932:

At The Battle of Sweetwater - *The minnie balls were flying thick and fast, John Bickerstaff [sic] was struck in the forehead and fell to the ground. To all appearances he was dead and some of the boys began to dig a grave, when Gus McCutchen ran up and after an examination, said: "Boys, he is not dead, and we must get him away from here." The minnie ball had pierced his forehead, going upward and outward, leaving the lining membrane of his brain exposed, but not lacerated. They received orders to fall back and carried their wounded comrade to a cabin near by were two old ladies lived, in whose care they left him, with request that they do all they could to relieve his suffering. Kneeling down by his helpless mate Ben Chastain said, "John, I'm down town for a little while."*[178]

---

[177] Corporal James Campbell Whittle, Compiled Service Records and family genealogy.
[178] James Alfred Sartain, *History of Walker County, Georgia*, (The A. J. Showalter Company, Dalton, Ga., 1932), 229.

Rebel Correspondent

FIVE YEARS LATER, IN OCTOBER 1869, a mysterious man on horseback dressed in a black suit and wearing a large black hat rode up to Ben Chastain's little farm at Duck Creek Valley, south of LaFayette in Walker County, Georgia. George Chastian, Ben's eldest son, greeted the man.

"Buddie, hold my horse, I am an old war-mate of your father's and want to see if he will recognize me."

It was John Biggerstaff, having survived fate on August 20, 1864, at Sweetwater, Tennessee, surprising his old friend.

"You've been gone down town a long time," said Biggerstaff, who then spent the evening giving explanations of what happened. John Bickerstaff [sic] told his comrade that he could hear but could not see nor speak, and heard the sound of the spade as it was plied in the earth, and could hear the words spoken to him. The ladies tenderly nursed him till he was able to be moved, then conveyed him as far as they could toward his home; others did the same thing using one-horse wagons, or buggies, until he reached his home in Cobb county near Marietta.

John B. Biggerstaff would marry his first wife, Elizabeth Putnam (1835-1878), in 1868. They would have four children together. The family moved to Rutherford County, North Carolina, in 1875. After Lizzie's death in 1878, he would marry again in 1882 to Cynthia Baber Long (1834-1905). He died in 1889 and was laid to rest in Rutherford County, North Carolina.[179]

---

[179] Private John B. Biggerstaff, Compiled Service Records and family genealogy.

October 16, 1902
MY EXPERIENCES
In the War of 1860 Briefly Told.

And when we got corn for our horses we would get enough for ourselves, too, and if we could not make fires to roast it we would eat it raw. Wash Phillips said he could eat as much as Wolford, his horse—10 ears and a bundle of fodder.

One day we passed a farm where an old time thresher was running. It was like the second one I ever saw. It had a cog wheel around the track; it was called circle power.

I believe we went as far North as Newmarket on the East Tennessee Railroad. Any way about the middle of the day we headed for Middle Tennessee. The news reached us that our daring John H. Morgan had been killed and the report was that he stopped at a house to get dinner and there being several women there they managed to get some of them off to some near-by Yanks and tell where Morgan was and the Yankees went and killed Morgan at that house. Also, it was reported that the man's name that killed him was Andrew Campbell. Of course, this was all flying reports.

After we turned toward Middle Tennessee, like many other roads we had been on, we saw many places and things that we had seen the winter before and as we were marching south on the long bare ridge, made so by being cleared for a field, to the ford of the river, where we camped at the night the two bush whackers shot in our camps, and as we were going along through that field on this occasion the Yanks saw us from a height on the west side of the river and did their best to kill some of us with cannon balls and shells. Two of them passed across Co F, and went into the ground just to our left a few yards but we went on and were soon at the ford and were crossing where we saw again the quaint old battle scarred well dairy that I have told you about the day we captured the 2,200 beef cattle.

Up to this time, as I remember, we had camped but twice to take a night's rest since we left Covington, Ga , once at Spring Place and then at Sweetwater, Tennessee, and before we struck the Cumberland mountains, we camped two nights and a day at one place and the morning we left we drew our beef a few minutes before we left and I put a piece on the coals to broil and Lieutenant Colonel Cook came to my fire and cut a ration off of my piece and put it on the coals and I cut another and put it on and ate the first. Then the saddle call was sounded and we all saddled and the mount call was sounded in quick succession and the Colonel was not done saddling. I ran to the fire to get my steak and it was not done, but I had no time to wait I just stuck up the piece the Colonel had on the fire and mounted and left my own for him. It was all my beef any way. The Colonel had none and didn't ask for that.

There are some things I have passed that I had forgotten. As we were descending the western slope of the Cohutta mountain for some cause the command stopped a few minutes and Major Gus. Steward rode back the line to see a pistol that Lieutenant Pargerson had got from one of the dead bushwhackers of that day. It was a fine one, self-acting, and while the Major was looking at it he pressed on the trigger and it shot Lieutenant Pargerson thro' the left knee. Then the Major gave him back the revolver and said, "D—n the luck!" and went back. As I remember the Lieutenant was placed in the ambulance and a man was detailed to care for him and he went the round with us back to Dixie. He was one of the 4th Ga. Lieutenants and was a veteran of the Mexican war of 1846 and took an active part in the wide-famed Sarogorda Battle which, as I remember, was virtually the decisive blow between the United States and Mexico.

The other item was on one night in East Tennessee. I was one of a crew to guard the ordinance wagons and we came to the river. I believe it was the Tennessee and it had to be crossed and was swollen a little and I with two others was sent across to see if there were any Yankee pickets and to locate the going out on the other side. When we had satisfied *ourselves I believe two of us went back and the other stayed to kindle up a fire to guide the teamsters across. As we first went over we got in some swimming water. On the return we bore up more and when we got back and reported there were rails put on top of the wagon bodies and the ordinance went over dry. Here I will say for the benefit of the young readers that ordinance was minny-balls and powder cartridges, and caps put up in blocks and so many blocks put in water-proof boxes.*

I ate my beef as I went. We are now headed for Cumberland Mountain and one time this day, I believe it was Major Steward got hold of a newspaper and in it he read a piece that stated that General Wheeler was on a raid in East Tennessee but "we don't know where he is now" and the Major said, using a side-pocket word. "I know where we are at."

A. F. Shaw

Food was the problem as Wheeler's Cavalry moved through Tennessee. Their minimum rations had long run out so foraging for food for man and horse or mule alike was just another part of their daily routine. They were all living on corn, and the area corn fields served as what could be called the first "drive-thru" for the cavalry. The menu options were limited—roasted if they had the time, or raw if they didn't. There were no options to super-size their orders, though everything was free, all you can carry, taken as needed. The horses and mules didn't mind raw corn, but it must have been an acquired taste for a hungry soldier. From time to time the soldiers were lucky enough to get beef, though that was at a cost to the unlucky local subsistence farmers in Middle Tennessee. There were many who saw their livestock population wiped out by Wheeler's raid.

Company F's Private George Washington "Wash" Phillips (1844-1911) was born in Murray County, Georgia. Wash was slightly younger than Arba at was just seventeen years old when he enlisted in December 1862. Most of the really young soldiers were unmarried when they first mustered into service so when the war came to an end, they all soon got hitched. Similar booms in weddings would occur at the end of World War I and World War II in the twentieth century. Surely, their thinking must have been: "I have survived this insanity, I've seen countless death of friends and loved ones, so it's time to get on with living." Wash Phillips did just that; he married Sarah Ann "Sallie" Rodgers (1841-1911) in March of 1867 in Whitfield County, Georgia. The increase in weddings was followed by the inevitable baby boom. Wash and Sally would soon have eight children together.[180]

IN A SPECIAL DISPATCH TO THE *CINCINNATI Gazette* dated August 31, 1864:

A citizen of Athens, Tenn., gives the following details of Wheeler's raid in East Tennessee:
He says Wheeler's force is not less than five thousand, only a small portion of which is armed with anything but pistols. Wheeler's officers said he had no intention to attack our forces at any point, and declared the attack on Dalton was against his orders; where it is positively known that he made the demand for the surrender of the garrison. He had eight pieces of artillery when in Athens. He made thorough work in destroying the railroad between Charleston and Philadelphia, East Tennessee, being employed over a week at the work.
All the horses and mules in McMinn County were seized, and a large number of beef cattle. While in McMinn and Monroe Counties, Wheeler's men conducted themselves in a most unruly manner, robbing and stealing indiscriminately. Wheeler himself ordered them to pillage the stores, and afterward, private houses. Hundreds of women, white and

---

[180] Private George Washington Phillips, Compiled Service Records and family genealogy.

black, were ravished in the two counties, and the most horrible outrages committed by the desperadoes.

THE 4TH GEORGIA CAVALRY REACHED NEW MARKET, Tennessee, around August 23, 1864. They then began moving quickly to the west toward Nashville. Private Shaw's dates were a little off in his recall of events. The death of Morgan actually occurred slightly later in the timeline of his account of Wheeler's raid.

The "Thunderbolt of the Confederacy," Brigadier General John Hunt Morgan (1826-1864) was killed on September 4, 1864, in Greeneville, Tennessee. The incident occurred in the garden or near the stables of the Dickson-Williams Mansion where he was staying.

Federal Cavalry surprised Morgan's men, and Morgan tried to simply walk away from the chaos of the event until ordered to halt by Union Private Andrew J. Campbell (1832-1894). When Morgan failed to obey the order, Campbell shot and killed him. Three days later the Irish-born Campbell would be promoted to 2nd Lieutenant of Company G of the 13th Tennessee Cavalry (Union) as a reward for his quick thinking by his commanding officer, Lieutenant Colonel William H. Ingerton (1835-1864).

After Colonel Isaac W. Avery was seriously wounded at New Hope Church in May 1864, his right-hand man, the twenty-eight-year-old Lieutenant Colonel William L. Cook (1823-1907), took command of the 4th Georgia Cavalry. Cook had been born in Anderson County, South Carolina, in 1836. He married his wife, Mary, in South Carolina sometime around 1855; they would have three children together. In the 1860 Census, Cook was living in Jackson County, Georgia, with his family, making a living as a farmer. He enlisted in Avery's Georgia Mountain Dragoons as 1st Lieutenant in January 1862, quickly moving up the ranks and becoming a Lieutenant Colonel in January 1863 at the end of the Knoxville and Eastern Tennessee campaign.[181]

Second in command under Lieutenant Colonel Cook was twenty-five-year-old Major Augustus R. Stewart (1838-1909). Stewart was born in Jackson County, Alabama, and had moved to Walker County, Georgia, as a boy. By 1860 he was living in Ringgold, Georgia, and working as a grocer. He married his wife, Julia (1845-1886), around 1860, and the couple had two children during the beginning of the war. At five feet, ten inches with a fair complexion, light hair, and blue eyes, Stewart enlisted as a 1st Lieutenant to the Ringgold Rangers in the summer of 1862. The independent cavalry unit became Company K of the 4th Georgia Cavalry soon afterwards. Stewart was promoted to Major in February 1864, replacing Major D. Jackson Owen who was forced to resign his commission after being seriously injured.[182] Major Stewart's brother Captain Peter W. Stewart (1835-1913) succeeded him in heading up Company K.

It was Major Stewart who mishandled the pistol that wounded Company G's Lieutenant William C. Parkison (1825-1883) in the left knee. For Lieutenant Parkison, the Civil War was his second rodeo. At nineteen years old, he joined Company G of the 2nd Tennessee Infantry as a Private at Chattanooga, Tennessee, for the Mexican War. In April 1847 his unit saw action at the Battle of Cerro Gordo under the command of General Winfield Scott. He mustered out eleven months later at New Orleans, Louisiana, in May 1847. It is unclear if he was injured during the Mexican War from sparse military records; however, he began receiving an eight-dollars-a-month invalid pension from 1851 through 1857.

On Parkison's return from the Mexican War, he married Mary Ann Boyd (1822-1883); they would settle in Hamilton County, Tennessee, and had five children, three of which

---

[181] Lieutenant Colonel William L. Cook, Compiled Service Records and family genealogy.
[182] Major Augustus R. Stewart, Compiled Service Records and family genealogy.

survived into adulthood.

Parkison began his Civil War military service as a 2nd Sergeant and was promoted to 3rd Lieutenant during the Knoxville/East Tennessee campaign in November 1863. In the Cohutta Mountains Major Stewart was inspecting the pistol Parkison had recovered from one of the Covington brothers when it accidentally discharged; the round passed through his left knee. Parkison would limp along for a few weeks while Wheeler continued the Tennessee raid into early September. A promotion to 2nd Lieutenant followed in November 1864. Military records for him end with the recording of this promotion so it is likely he did not return to action after his "friendly fire" wounding—though surely a promotional jump to Captain should have been more in order for having your own Major accidentally shoot you in the knee. After the war the Parkison family moved to Yell County, Arkansas, where he farmed until his death in 1883.[183]

October 23, 1902
MY EXPERIENCES
In the War of 1860 Briefly Told.

The paper that the Major was reading was a northern paper.

Don't know how long it took us to get to the mountain but we crossed Powell's river near the foot hills. It, like the Tilaco, was extremely clear and about the same size where we crossed it. Soon we struck the mountain. Don't remember the name of the road, but will call it the Grassy cove road. It seemed to me we started up the mountain about the middle of the day and entered the cove about sundown. The cove was like a large, well rounded sink hole and had no outlet for water only as it would sink. There were hundreds of acres of it looking to be all in cultivation. There were quite a number

---

[183] Lieutenant William C. Parkison, Compiled Service Records and family genealogy.

of settlements in the cove. The land did not look to be more than ordinary mountain land. It was very prolific in the production of crabgrass, hence its name.

When we got on the top of the mountain again we camped and by times the next morning we were in the saddle and moving on in the direction of Sparta, which was at the west base of the mountain. We had nothing to molest us and we jogged along all day. That part of the mountain was almost a total wilderness but we saw a number of places from the size of gardens to good sized little fields that were over layed with an even surfaced sand stone that was totally destitute of vegitation. There was not a crevice to be seen and it was as clear as the rains and winds could make them. There was not any dirt or trash on them. At dusk I got to the foot of the mountain and went in to camp and at the foot of the mountain we saw a red elm tree that looked to be as much as 6 feet through at the stump. As I remember it was close to the road near Sparta.

About midnight, as often, the order was, "Shaw, it is your time to go on detail." Accordingly I and all the other boys that were detailed, saddled up and reported to Gen. Wheeler's headquarter's and the General was called up. When we found him he told the officer in charge to go to the Sligo ford on the Kanyfork river and inquire along as we went if there was any of the enemy in the country that would be likely to molest the army as it followed us the next day.

We reached Sligo early the next evening and found the way clear and we were then as far as we had orders to go. The next thing to be considered was to find something to feed on and eat and accordingly we left the public road and went down the river in a settlement road and soon it led us in to a rich cove where there was a plenty. The cove was walled with high mountain-like hills, seeming to have no outlet, only the way we went in. The fields extended across the narrow cove and high upon the hills on either side and we saw stacks of old fodder high up on the steep hills and when we fed and ate to our hearts content we went back to Sligo and rejoined the command. Sligo was an old time stage stand. From there we were soon across the river and going in the direction of Smithville where we camped a few days in the spring of 1863 and near which place we saw the only pine trees that grew native in all of our varied rounds in middle Tennessee. They grew on a knoll, possibly of five acres. They were tall and slim and but few of them. We saw pine growing at Pulaski but they bad been planted by the hands of the curious.

After we passed the pines it was soon dark and the scenery was all hidden and by this time we were getting near enough to the Nashville and Chattanooga R. R. that it was necessary for us to dash and do what we did quick. We passed through a section where we had rambled over before and we were soon near enough to begin our work on the railroad about Murfreesborough. Some would make havoc of the railroad while the others were engaging the garrison. That day, the 4th Ga. went mounted in line of battle through a field of the finest cotton I ever saw. It was high and the best loaded with boles. It was in the last days of August and it had not begun to open. We were then advancing on Lavergne. We captured it and tore up all about there. There was a cooperage plant there in operation, It was working cedar.

We went on toward Nashville doing all the dirt we could and when we got in sight of Nashville the yanks made too bold a front to suit us and we stirred us up a little scrap with them and turned off to the St. Louis and N. V. R. R. and went about 15 miles to the southwest and camped for the night without unsaddling, I believe, and just parted off right and left.

A. F. Shaw

Rebel Correspondent

October 30, 1902
MY EXPERIENCES
In the War of 1860 Briefly Told.

We slept on our arms and again after dark when we all had got fixed for the night the Sargeant Major came around and said to the captains: "We want a man from your company to report to Gen. Wheeler." "All right," and it was my time again. We went—a hundred of us and a captain; the General said go to a point on the St. L. & Ne. V. R. R. and tear up some of it. The point we went to was said to be in four miles of Nashville.

Soon after we started the captain stopped at a house and pressed in a man to guide us through the nearest way. The guide was on a lame horse but we got there all right. When we got there all but the pickets dismounted and went to building fires on the railroad. The twilight had got sufficient that I saw as I was going to picket south of the crossing two men going down the hill south of the house as two of our men went up on the north side. They were going to tell Brownlow we were there. I went back and told the captain what I saw as the two went up on the north side. He sent some men back with me to build a high fence across the lane and by that time the two southbound men had got to their camp and the yanks were soon coming down the lane. As I remember, we gave them a volley to check them while the boys could get to their horses; then we took the north end of the big road and put down patty a while. We soon found a field of fine melons and made a raid on it but we only got a few when the yanks were in sight and shooting at us when the rear guard checked them again.

I speak for myself. I got a good sized rattle snake melon and divided it with some other comrade. Then it was gouge in dirty face and hands—no time to waste or use a knife. We ran on a piece and we had got through with the melons when a group of us went in a paled yard to beg something to eat and the yanks ran on us in the yard but one fellow spurred his horse and he breasted against a pannel and made away for our escape. They were checked again by a return fire and soon we all closed up, when we found the captain trying to swap horses with a citizen. He would have swapped but the horse he wanted was in the pasture with his head and tail high in the air and was hitting high places. About that time the Blues fired at us again. Then we went on and left them and kept going and were not molested by them any more and in the evening we found the command where we left it.

It was waiting for us and at the break of day Col. Brownlow ran a part of his regiment down the road between our sleeping boys. They roused up and took their arms and captured them. They had just got back in the service after they had been captured and exchanged the second time and the boys broke a long link out of their chain that morning. They were newly equipped out and out, horses and all.

It was not long after we got back until we all were in the saddles again and again we were in a portion of the country we had been in in '63. We were at Auburn again where we saw the same horse mill and we saw many other things familiar.

Now we are in a fine rich country. One day we saw a deformed horse; its front parts were ordinarily formed and its hindmost legs were so short that when he walked his back was almost as steep as the neck of the giraffe.

Now we are in September and I reckon it was on the 2nd day, early in the morning, a courier brought a dispatch to Lieutenant Horn ordering him to take 12 of his company that needed fresh horses and acting at once he started and I was in the bunch. We were ordered to scout the left advance and if we found any horses better than ours to leave ours and take them. Soon after we started we left the Franklin road to the right where we found a captain and 4 or 5 of his men at a horse lot in the act of taking off a fine horse. The Lieutenant stepped up and took hold of the bridle and said, "What authority have you got to take that horse and the captain said, "My men." Then he said to the Lieutenant, "What *authority have you to take this horse" and Horn said, "Gen. Wheeler is my authority." Then the captain mounted and he and his crew left saying they would be back in a few minutes. Horn said "All right, we can be found." Lieutenant Horn changed rigging on to the fine horse and took us back to meet the captain and his men. We took the advantage of them. We formed where a high banked creek ran from the east and made a curve, then ran north and across the big road we left. The road that left the public road was on the bank of the creek and a high fence was on the west side of the road. Lieut. Horn formed us in the spread made by the curve. It was 30 or 40 yds wide where we formed.*

A. F. Shaw

Union Colonel James Patton Brownlow (1842-1879)

WHEELER'S RAID HAD FINISHED ITS work of destroying the East Tennessee and Georgia Railroad around Knoxville, and now it made its way west to do the same to the Nashville railroads. For several days they were able to move relatively unscathed through a countryside that was familiar from their first campaign fighting in middle Tennessee. How long ago that must have seemed. When they reached the railroad near Murfreesboro at the end of August 1864, they began to encounter resistance from Colonel James Patton Brownlow's 1st Tennessee Cavalry Federal troops.

Colonel James Patton Brownlow, age twenty-two years (1842-1879), was the son of U. S. Senator William Gannaway Brownlow (1805-1877). The Senator was a

Unionist from Tennessee who had opposed secession. He was held in Knoxville as a POW in the early days of the war in 1861. He was released and escorted to Nashville in March 1862 which was then Union controlled. Besides being a politician, he had a career as a journalist and Methodist minister and was nicknamed "Parson Brownlow." "Senator Parson Brownlow" would serve as Governor of Tennessee in the Reconstruction era after the Civil War. This no doubt led to an impossibly long title on his calling cards.[184]

The Union 1st Tennessee Cavalry had experienced fighting against Wheeler's Cavalry in the months leading to the Siege of Atlanta. Having been given intelligence that Wheeler was moving from Knoxville toward Nashville, they had all been moved by train from Marietta to Nashville by way of Chattanooga in the last days of August 1864, on the Western & Atlantic Railroad. The Senator's son Colonel James Patton Brownlow and the 1st Tennessee Cavalry began skirmishing with Wheeler's Cavalry near the depot of the Nashville and Chattanooga Railroad at Laverne, Tennessee, on September 1, 1864.

Senator William Gannaway Brownlow 1805-1877

The skirmishing stretched into the morning of September 2. Wheeler moved due west through Nolensville to Franklin, Tennessee; Brownlow's 1st Tennessee followed. At that particular moment, 235 miles to the southeast, Atlanta fell to Sherman's armies.

THE BOOK *HISTORY OF THE FIRST REGIMENT of Tennessee Volunteer Cavalry in the Great War of Rebellion* was

---

[184] Senator William Gannaway Brownlow, Compiled Service Records and family genealogy.

published in 1902, the same year as Arba's writings were being serialized in the *Walker County Messenger*. Its author, Sergeant William Randolph Carter (1843-1919) of Company C, 1st Tennessee Cavalry, provided a highly detailed day-by-day account of his regiment's fight against Wheeler's Cavalry in early September 1864.

Wheeler had swung around Franklin and was approaching from the south. The two columns met on a high range of hills about one mile from town on the turnpike leading from Franklin to Columbia. The fighting was severe and began at close range, and in a few minutes the hill was completely enveloped in smoke. Almost at first fire, Colonel Brownlow, while gallantly leading his men into the very ranks of the enemy, fell severely wounded and was borne from the field amid a perfect tempest of bullets. A musket-ball passed through both legs, producing a very painful wound—a wound that almost proved fatal. He was immediately carried to the rear, where his wounds were dressed, but almost bled to death before the surgeons reached him.

Colonel James Patton Brownlow would survive the wounds through both thighs received near Franklin. Lieutenant Colonel C. M. Dyer would assume his command. Colonel Brownlow was transported to the Franklin home of Dr. Daniel Bonaparte Cliffe (1823-1913), which had been turned into a Union field infirmary. During his convalescence there, the twenty-two-year-old Brownlow fell in love with his nurse, Belle Cliffe

Belle Cliffe Brownlow
1850-1878

(1850-1878), the doctor's fourteen-year-old daughter. After the war, Brownlow was nominated by President Andrew Johnson and received a promotion to Honorary Brevet Brigadier General. He married Belle Cliffe in 1866, and the couple made their home in Franklin. They had two children, who did not survive infancy. Brownlow worked for the railroad and as a farmer and printer in Franklin. Belle died in 1878, and Brownlow followed in 1879, both most likely of tuberculosis. They are buried together in Franklin.[185]

November 6, 1902
MY EXPERIENCES
In the War of 1860 Briefly Told.

One end of our line was at the fence and the other at the creek. When the Captain came with his company, we halted them in the narrow way and told them to cut their patching, but they didn't cut. We all stood and jowered awhile, and the Captain said to the Lieutenant: "What is your name?" and he said, "Horn is my name." Then the Captain said: "I will report you to General Wheeler," and Horn replied: "Report and be d----- " and the Captain ordered his men, about 35 of them, to "about face" and we all went our way and changed off several of our horses that day.

We went on till we struck a high ridge and we had to file right and go through a squeeze at Franklin where the boys were in a little spat with the yanks and soon we were from under fire again and where me and Jack parted. Jack was footsore and his back was a sight. It was scaled by being wet so much. He couldn't travel on the pikes. I mounted my new horse—a good one—and the third day we got in the Campbellville fight (it was on the 5th of September 1864,) where I was shot twice and my horse killed while I shot four times.

We were marching south thro' the village and when

---

[185] Union Colonel James Patton Brownlow, Compiled Service Records and family genealogy.

south a little way we turned square west and on the turn I saw some yankees lying down on their horses about 200 yards south and were going east in a gallop. Soon they were onto our rear and shot one —Pink Lanum—in the back of his head. Then some of us rode up to the north lane fence, pushed it off so our horses could jump over and by that time we were face to face with the yanks. They stopped and what few there were of us that jumped over the fence did the best we could. The most of the horses stampeded but some of the boys came back when they could stop their horses. We all had us a man and more, too. I did my shooting at a man that had on a red sash. His horse stood still all the time and mine would jump and try to run off all the time, but the last time I shot I thought I hit him. The boys said somebody shot him. We were about thirty feet apart. When I shot the last time a spent cap fell off and lodged on the stock of my pistol and when I was taking it off was when I was shot and my horse killed. My horse walked a few steps before it fell. I have often been asked if I dropped my pistol. My fingers were wedged in the trigger guard so that when my arm fell it hung to them till I could reach down with my left hand and get it before it went to the ground, but it was as bloody all over as could be. John Dupree was ordered by Lieutenant Horn to take me out. He got off of "Tige" and put me on and walked on the bloody side to hold me on and we met Loss Thornton and he rode in the left side and held my left arm. I begged them to leave me, but they would not and they soon found Dr. Eadlen and he stopped the blood and turned me over to Uncle Ben Chastain.

The boys whipped in the fight and one of them brought my saddle from my dead horse, put it on a lead mule and put me up and we started on toward the Tennessee river and when nightfall came the command turned out right and left and camped with the saddles on and the bridle reins in our hands and our weapons fastened to us so that we could be ready for action in a moment.

That night the 4th Georgia slept in the fence corners of

a lane and in the corner opposite the one I was in Bill Edwards, of Company K, was sleeping and his horse lay down on his arm and broke it. I was suffering and was awake and heard Bill call his brother Jim up and tell him about it and Jim said, "the devil you say." I believe Jim went for the doctor or took him to the doctor, I am not sure which.

We stayed there all night and started on about sun up the next morning. The wounded were not required to march in ranks. We were sent to a ferry to cross with the wagons and the command went further down and crossed at Mussle Shoals, The wagons and the wounded crossed at a ferry a few miles above Florence, Ala., and when we got to the ferry we were crowded out Uncle Ben made me a pallet so I could rest under the bank and it was after dark when we got there and it was day in the morning when we got across. The boat was kept busy all night and when we got across Uncle Ben hunted up a doctor to dress my wounds. They had gone into the third day without attention. Then he took me to a citizen's house and managed to get my clothes changed and my dirty, bloody ones washed. When they were dry he took me to South Florence and left me in a hospital with the rest of the wounded and he went on to join the command. When he was fixing to leave me I broke down and wept like a little child. I wanted him to stay with me so bad, but I got along all right anyway. The wounded of our command soon all came in and we had a good time.

A. F. Shaw

AS THE FRANKLIN, TENNESSEE, skirmish with the Union 1st Tennessee Cavalry came to an end in the afternoon of September 2, 1864, the two enemies moved parallel to each other southeastward toward Campbellsville, Tennessee, and continued to challenge their positions with light skirmishes. Union light artillery was provided by Battery G of the Ohio 1st, lead by Captain Alexander Marshall. A unit was organized at Camp Dennison near Cincinnati with soldiers from Geauga and Lake Counties.

Arba's faithful mount's, Jack the mule, time in military service had come to an end. Jack had loyally transported Arba since January 1864 when he began his service in the CSA as a captured U. S. Mule on the Tennessee/North Carolina border. Now nine months later, the war-weary, footsore animal was traded for a new horse.

The skirmish at Campbellsville began with a member of the 4th Georgia Cavalry's Company C, Private Pink Lanum, being killed instantly with a shot to the back of the head. Lanum had enlisted on July 1, 1863, in Kingston, Tennessee.[186]

Shortly after Lanum's death, Captain Jefferson Johnson had his horse shot out from under him. Two months after the battle in November 1864, he would submit a requisition for Reimbursement of the horse: *"For 1 Horse killed in action at Campbellsville Tenn of 5th day of September 1864 valued at $1500.00."* The requisition was approved and certified by Major Augustus R. Stewart, "commanding regiment" and approved by Colonel C.C. Crews.[187] If Major Stewart was now commanding the regiment, what happened to Lieutenant Colonel William L. Cook?

For Arba, September 5, 1864, was a day that was burned into his memory for the rest of his life. He surely would dream about the incident in the years after the war. It marked the day he was seriously wounded after being shot twice—in his right arm and hand. The shooter was a Yankee on a horse that stood rigidly still. Arba's new mount was skittish and wouldn't stand still. The smell of burnt gunpowder and smoke from other soldiers' weapons in close proximity filled the air. They were just thirty feet apart. The Yankee was wearing a red sash. Arba got off four shots—he thought the last shot hit the Yankee. His fellow soldiers would later recall that someone got him. Arba's new horse

---

[186] Pinkney Lanum, Compiled Service Records.
[187] Captain Jefferson Johnson, Compiled Service Records.

fell dead in the field, and the wounds to Arba's right arm bled profusely. Red blood seeped all over his right side—deep red like the color of the Yankee's sash.

In his lifetime Arba never knew what became of his adversary. He never knew the man's name. He only knew: *"I did my shooting at a man that had on a red sash."*

Sergeant William Randolph Carter in *History of the First Regiment of Tennessee Volunteer Cavalry in the Great War of Rebellion* would later write:

The pursuit was resumed early on the morning of the 5th, and when near a small hamlet called Campbellsville, Croxton[188] overtook a portion of Wheeler's force, and a lively engagement ensued. Wheeler had taken up a strong position in an extensive beech forest, which afforded great protection to his men. The artillery was run up and opened a brisk fire on the enemy. Croxton ordered the First Tennessee, under Lieutenant-Colonel Dyer, to charge him with the saber. In the execution of this order the First Tennessee was compelled to charge across an open field under a brisk fire...soon Wheeler's troops were routed and flying southward.[189]

IN THE U. S. ARMY REGULATIONS OF 1861, red sashes were entitled only to senior non-commissioned officers.[190]

Sergeant Carter follows up his account of the events of September 5, 1864, at Campbellsville with a list of men of the 1st Tennessee killed or wounded:

---

[188] Union Brigadier General John T. Croxton (1836-1874).
[189] W. R. Carter, *History of the First Regiment of Tennessee Volunteer Cavalry in the Great War of Rebellion 1862-1865*, (Knoxville, Tenn., Gaut-Ogden Co. Printers and Binders,1902), 195.
[190] *Revised United States Army regulations of 1861, with an appendix containing the changed and laws affecting Army regulations and Articles of war to June 25, 1863*, (United States. War Dept. Washington: Govt. Print. Off., 1863), 468.

Rebel Correspondent

***Killed or Mortally Wounded**–*Company F, John H. Shaver; Company C, Sergeant L. Geasland, mortally wounded, died in hospital at Nashville, Sept 30; Company K, Harrison Key; Company L, John W. Pettit and W. H. Osmit.

***Wounded**–*Company A, James Harris; Company F, Geo W. Black, Peter Henry and Nathaniel Spencer; Company I, A. J. Kelly, severely wounded and captured; Company C, James R. Chambless; Company M, Harvey Bales.[191]

Unidentified Union Sergeant
is wearing a sash that would have been red
based on 1861 army uniform regulations.
Sixth-plate tintype, Library of Congress

---

[191] W. R. Carter, *History of the First Regiment of Tennessee Volunteer Cavalry in the Great War of Rebellion 1862-1865*, (Knoxville, Tenn., Gaut-Ogden Co. Printers and Binders,1902), 195.

The only senior non-commissioned officer either wounded or killed that day was J. L. Geasland. He would have been the only man wearing a red sash.

Sergeant Jackson L. Geasland (1844-1864) was 5' 6" tall with a fair complexion, light hair, and gray eyes. Born in Knoxville, Tennessee, Geasland had joined the army as a Private in a three-year enlistment at Flatlick, Kentucky, on April 1, 1862. He was promoted to sergeant in August 1862. After being wounded at Campbellsville, he was moved to U. S. General Hospital No. 14 in Nashville, Tennessee, where he clung to life for twenty-five days. The gunshot wound to the right lung would prove fatal on October 1, 1864. At the time of his death he was single. The inventory of his effects listed at the hospital were one blouse, one pair of trousers, one pair of boots, one pair of socks, and one blanket. He was owed a bounty of $100 but had received an advance of $46.98 into his clothing account. It was not reported if the money was sent to his next of kin, listed as his mother, Margaret Geasland, in the final inventory report. He was originally buried in grave number 9506. At some point after the war his remains were relocated. Today he lies in Nashville National Cemetery in Madison, Tennessee, in Section G, Site 8004.[192]

Sergeant Jackson L. Geasland's Grave in Nashville

Based on the evidence, it is highly likely that it was Sergeant Jackson L. Geasland who wounded Private Arba F.

---

[192] Union Sergeant Jackson L. Greasland, Compiled Service Records and family genealogy.

Shaw. They both fired upon each other from just thirty feet away at Campbellsville. That's closer than the dueling standard of twenty paces, more like just ten paces. On that day, Arba won the duel. Both soldiers were the same age, just twenty years old.

It took the quick thinking of Company F's Lieutenant Felix Grundy Horn (1838-1903) to get the wounded Private Shaw away from the battle. Two Company F Privates—John S. Du Pré (1835-1918) and Pleasant Lawson "Loss" Thorton (1831-1907)—moved Arba to the 4th Georgia's Surgeon Major James B. Edelen, who was able to stem the bleeding. This was the second time in just over three months that Dr. Edelen was treating Arba for a gunshot wound.

Private John S. Du Pré, age twenty-nine years, lived in Whitfield County, Georgia, at the start of the war. After the war he married Delara Martha Main (1846-1935) and raised a family of eight children together while faming near Dalton, Georgia, until his death in 1918.[193]

Private Pleasant Lawson "Loss" Thorton, age thirty-three years, was farming near Dalton in 1860. "Loss" had married Harriet Graham Vance (1829-1926) in 1853. As the war began they had four children; they would wait until after the war to add two more to their family. After the war the family moved to Bradley County, Tennessee, then to Boone, Arkansas, and finally to Grayson, Texas, where he lived until his death in 1907.[194]

AFTER THE BATTLE THE WOUNDED were spirited away, making a beeline for East Florence, Alabama, where the Confederate hospital was located. Sergeant Benjamin Lafayette Chastain, Arba's uncle, watched over him as they made the roughly sixty-mile trip in two days, arriving in East Florence on September 7, 1864.

---

[193] Private John S. Du Pré, Compiled Service Records and family genealogy.
[194] Private Pleasant Lawson Thorton, Compiled Service Records and family genealogy.

In Arba's regular column in the *Walker County Messenger* on August 16,1890, some twelve years before he would sit down and write his account based on his memories of the Civil War, he wrote more specifically about the details of being seriously wounded on September 5, 1864. He also lamented about being unable to attend a reunion of the 4th Georgia Cavalry that was being held that month in Dalton, Georgia. This earlier version parallels his later writings in recalling being wounded at Campbellsville and provides interesting context.

Walker County Messenger
Frick's Gap
August 16, 1890

Today is the pleasurable day at Dalton with the veterans of 4th Georgia Cavalry, and I am bowed down with affliction until I can't be there. It is thirty-eight days since I got hurt and then a spell of catarrhal fever followed, so I am as helpless as a small todler yet.

It would have been one of the most pleasurable events of my life to meet with the boys that went with me through thick and thin, some of whom were as a father to me, and others as devoted brothers. It was on General Wheeler's last raid from Covington, Georgia, around through Tennessee that the regiment left me in a pitched fight in Middle Tennessee near Campbellville, and west of Pulaski. I was shot through the right arm and hand and my horse killed at the same time, and don't know how many more shared the same fate but Pinkney Lanum was first on the list. He was shot before the line was formed, and Captain Jeff Johnson was shot and lost a horse in the same fight. When Lieutenant Felix Horne saw what had befallen me he sent John Dupree to take me out. My horse being dead, John dismounted and helped me upon Tige and Tige toted me out in the midst of the fight. It was not long until I became faint from the loss of blood and begged John to help me down and leave me. But about that time we met Loss Thornton, and he rode by my left and John on my right, the bloody side. In that way they got to Dr. Eaden's ambulance and the doctor dressed my wounds, and put me on a sled mule and gave me over the the care of the clever B. L. Chastain. We made the best of the situation we could.

The first night we camped in a lane, and Bill Edwards' horse lay down on him and broke one of his arms. That gave us another cripple. We got to the north bank of the Tennessee river in the early part of the next night, and because of the press we could not get the ferryman to put us over until the next morning. The wounded was gathered and left at South Florence, Ala. There Ben Chastain was ordered back to his command, and left me weeping most bitterly because I wanted him to stay with me. There I was put in a room with Bill Edwards, George Freeman and Lieutenant Pargerson, of company K. He was shot by accident through the knee by Major Gus Stewart as we were crossing the Cohutta Mountains, the day we killed so many bushwhackers. We went on through to Florence. I staid at Florence a few days and was furloughed and went to the regiment near Russellville, Ala. and stayed with them that night on Cedar Creek. This was my last sight of the 4th. It was there that I saw some prisoners under guard. The punishment was to mark time which they suited to the familiar hymn, "How firm a foundation." The next day Jim Whittle was given charge of me and left me at uncle William P. Shaw's on little Bear creek five miles above Pleasantsite, Alabama.

A. F. Shaw

JOSEPH WHEELER'S CAVALRY RAID into Tennessee was now over. Excerpted from his report dated October 9, 1864, Wheeler concluded his account with his final take on the success of his efforts:

The results of the expedition were as follows:

First. Causing the enemy to send to their rear to re-enforce their garrisons, troops several times as strong as my force.

Second. The destruction of the enemy's line of communication for a longer period than any cavalry expedition, however large, has done.

Third. The capture, destruction, or appropriation of stores

Fourth. Breaking up depots and fortified post in Tennessee and Georgia

Fifth. Capture of 1,000 horses and mules, 200 wagons, 600 prisoners, and 1700 head of beef-cattle.

Sixth. Capture and destruction of over 20 trains of cars loaded with supplies.

Seventh. Bringing into the service of the Confederate States over 3,000 recruits.

All this was accomplished behind the enemy's line with a loss of but 150 men killed, wounded, and missing. In every engagement with the enemy's cavalry we were in all respects victorious, capturing prisoners, colors. and arms.
During the time embraced in this report my command has averaged twenty-five miles a day in direct marching, either swam or forded twenty-seven rivers, and has captured, killed, or wounded three times the greatest effective strength it has ever been able to carry into action.

Respectfully, colonel, your obedient servant
JOS. WHEELER
Major-General[195]

---

[195] *OR*, sr. 1, vol. XXXVIII, pt3, 960-961.

Rebel Correspondent

Sergeant William Randolph Carter
1843-1919

SERGEANT WILLIAM RANDOLPH CARTER in *History of the First Regiment of Tennessee Volunteer Cavalry in the Great War of Rebellion* offered a slightly different historical assessment thirty-eight years later:

This was the last stand made by Wheeler. Finding himself closely pursued, he withdrew and moved rapidly through Pulaski, and after an exciting chase he succeeded in crossing the Tennessee River near Rodgersville, Alabama. The loss inflicted to our railroads was very light, and so closely was Wheeler pursued that not a single place of any importance was captured, and on the whole, his raid was not a success.[196]

---

[196] W. R. Carter, *History of the First Regiment of Tennessee Volunteer Cavalry in the Great War of Rebellion 1862-1865*, (Knoxville, Tenn., Gaut-Ogden Co. Printers and Binders, 1902), 195-196.

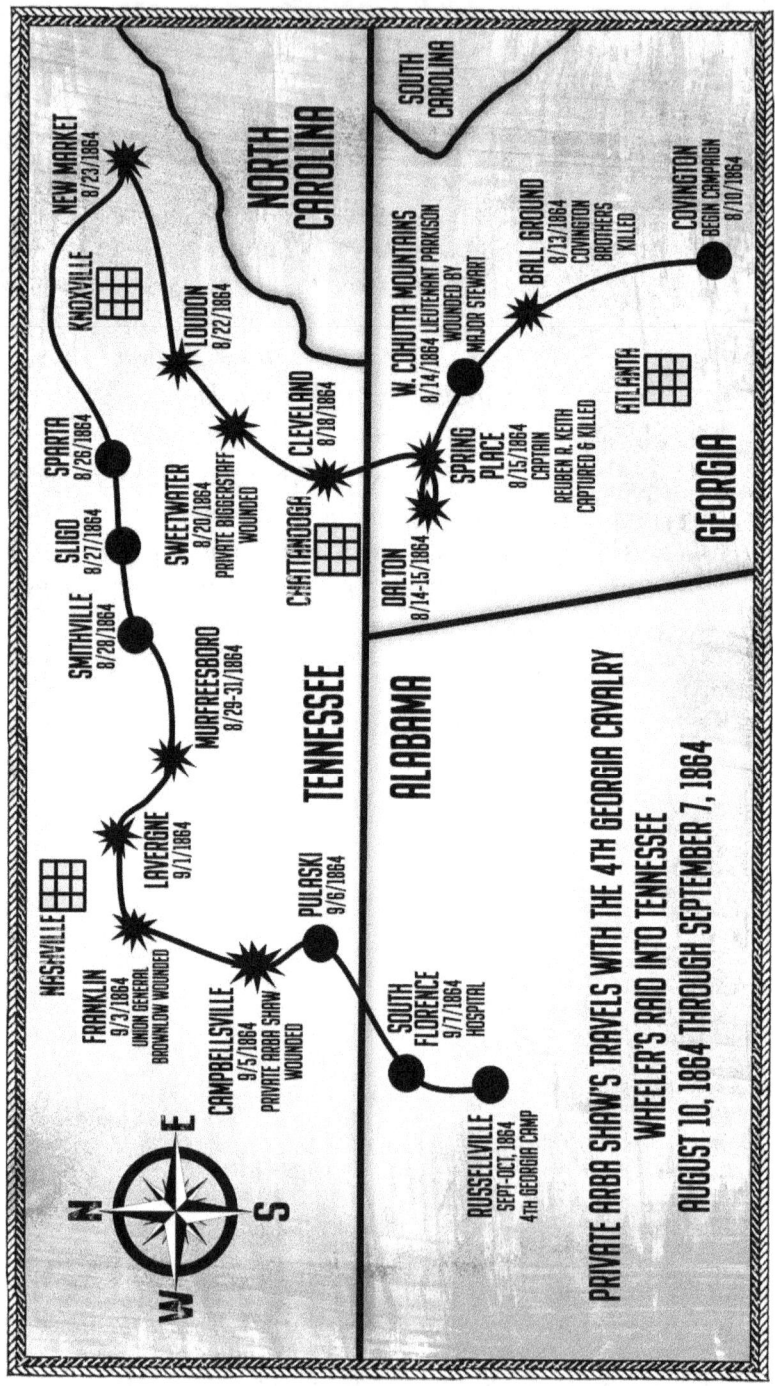

CHAPTER ELEVEN
LOSING THE 4TH

November 13, 1902
MY EXPERIENCES
In the War of 1860 Briefly Told.

The Florence Hospital was a hotel building and we stayed in the rooms up stairs. In the room I stayed in was George Freeman, Bill Edwards and Lient. Pargerson. the nurses were Jim Edwards and I can't remember the name of the other man—the one that brought Lient Pargerson through from the Cohutta.

There was one Lieutenant there of the 7th Alabama who was shot through his throat. The ball went through so as to cut his tongue off at the root but by some little threads it stayed and grew back. I saw another man of the 7th Alabama who had four thumbs. The extra thumbs were on top of his large one and came out at the joint, next to the band. They were about an inch long and were complete in form and looked like a little baby's thumb.

While we were there some ladies would visit us and bring in something nice to eat and one day they were all in the doctor's office next to the room I was in and we did not know it, and Jim Edwards, as he was gifted in, was talking very loud and possibly a little rough and when the ladies came out of the office they came in to say something to us and wound up by giving Jim a little lecture. One asked him what made him talk so loud and he said, "By graneys, I was raised in a mill." They soon left him and when they came again they brought a testament or bible and made him a present of it and asked him to read it.

One day while we were there the yankeys came to the

north bank of the river and began shooting across at the nurses, as they could be seen out and doing their turns, and it was not long till the yellow flag was unfurled. Then they quit shooting and we saw a white flag come down to the edge of the water. Then the doctor went or sent some body over in a skiff or yawl to tell them that the wounded and nurses were all the soldiers there were and our boys come back and the yankeys went on their way.

My arm got so bad that I was in fear of losing it a few days, and the doctors sent me to a little spring that ran out high up in the bank of the river. There was a spout fixed for the water to run out through and I would hold my arm under the spout until that very cold water would chill it thoroughly several times every day and the bad symptoms soon left.

As we got so it was safe enough, we were all furloughed and in about two weeks after I was wounded I left the Florence hospital on a 30 days furlough and I went to the command at Russelville, Ala., where it was taking a well earned rest. As I rode in to camp I saw 6 men of one of our brigade regiments under guard. They were on foot and receiving their punishment for their crime; the penalty was to mark time five minutes and rest five and when they would begin to mark they would sing "How Firm a Foundation" and suit the time to it. They seemed to enjoy it and it attracted the attention of all that could see or hear them.

One thing I over looked that I wish to refer back to. When we were yet in Tennessee and before I was wounded, we lost one of our Co. F. men, T. J. Price. About the time we went into camp one night he became suddenly ill with a severe cramping. I made him a fire and kept it burning for him all night and gave him all the asafoetida I had, but it was not enough. It only partially relieved him a short while. Then I was at my rows end and the doctor we could not find and the next morning we left him at a citizen's house and we never heard of him any more.

I stayed with the boys at Russellville all night and to the middle of the next day when I took my leave of them. That *was the last time I was ever with the 4th Georgia. It was, as I remember, the 18th of September, 1864. Jim Whittle was sent to take me to my uncle, W. P. Shaw, in Franklen Co., Ala. We jogged along till night and stayed with one Mr. Price and the next morning we got to Uncle's by dinner. Jim stayed till the next morning," which was my 20th birthday, when he left me. That was the last time I saw any of the 4th Ga, until a short time before the surrender.*

Now I am left, not with mother, but her sister, Aunt Roda Shaw, Uncle William being away in the army. Their boys portrayed well the character of the boys of that day, that of wrestling with every new boy they met and the largest one at home would take bold of me and throw me about and hurt my wounds so that it took them lots longer to get well. But in two months the tide turned. One Sunday morning he mounted me for a wrestle and I ventured to put my cripple arm to work; then I could burst him on the gravels every time.
A. F. Shaw

IN ARBA'S FIRST DESCRIPTION of his arrival into Florence, he mentions his Uncle Ben Chastain took him to South Florence, and left him in the hospital. But in the next description he describes staying in a hotel at Florence that served as a hospital.

In 1864 multiple buildings were used as CSA Field Hospitals around the town of Florence, Alabama; most were on the north side of the Tennessee River. The two notable ones were the Florence/Elliott Hotel and Pope's Tavern. However from Arba's account, they were being fired on by Yankees who stood on the north bank of the Tennessee River, who had to be told they were shooting at a hospital. This points to a location on the south side of the river known as South Florence. There was a hotel being used as a hospital there in 1864. Today not much remains but hints of foundations to the buildings that were there, now long gone.

Private George Freeman was a new recruit to Company

E, having enlisted at Oxford, Alabama, in April 1864. The records for him are sparse with no report of being wounded in action, though he shows as present in the November and December 1864 muster rolls.[197]

Arba recounted the story of Private Thomas B. Price (1836-1864) who was left behind at a citizen's house near Campbellsville, Tennessee—but Arba did not know what became of him. Union troops captured Price at Campbellsville and then sent him northbound to Camp Chase, Ohio, in late September. He died of smallpox in the northern POW Camp November 19, 1864, and was buried in grave 490 at Camp Chase Confederate Cemetery.[198]

Lieutenant Parkison, who was accidentally shot in the knee by his commanding officer Major Augustus Stewart in North Georgia over three weeks earlier, had to endure multiple skirmishes and battles on the almost 500-mile looping journey through middle Tennessee on horseback before finally getting to a hospital. He was able to rejoin the 4th Georgia Cavalry after staying there a couple of months to recover.

The Edwards brothers—Sergeant James Monroe Edwards (1843-1911) and Corporal William Lumpkin Edwards (1836-1899)—were also with Arba at the Florence field hospital. Bill was the wounded one, having broken his arm in a freak accident when his horse lay down next to him on top of his arm while he was sleeping—one of the many risks of a cavalry soldier.

The Edwards family were from the southern part of Walker County, Georgia, known as Taylor Ridge. The older of the two brothers, Corporal Bill Edwards, enlisted at the same time as his brother on May 15, 1862, at Ringgold, Georgia, as part of the Ringgold Rangers, which became Company K when merged into Avery's 4th Georgia Cavalry during its formation in the fall of 1862.[199] Company K also

---

[197] Private George Freeman, Compiled Service Records.
[198] Private Thomas B., Compiled Service Records.
[199] Sergeant James Monroe Edwards and Corporal William Lumpkin Edwards, Compiled Service Records and family genealogy.

**Sergeant James Monroe Edwards
Company K; 4th Georgia Cavalry
(1841-1911)**

included soldiers from Hamilton County, Tennessee and was led by Captain Hughes H. Burke (1825-1879).[200]

The Edwards family also had an older brother, Richard Marion Edwards (1834-1905), who had enlisted as a Private in Company B of the 44th Georgia Infantry. Richard Edwards became a POW in May 1864 in Spotsylvania County, Virginia.[201]

After his injury, Bill Edwards's rather confusing military records end, listing him as "wounded" in December 1864. In addition, Company K's Captain Burke is shown as wounded on December 4, 1864.

Sergeant Jim Edwards claimed to have been wounded three times during the war. In his Pension Application affidavit from 1897, he was first wounded on September 18, 1863, during the Battle of Chickamauga: "In the right thigh by gunshot wound ranging back and fracturing the bone, disabling the entire right leg, and is one third less

**The Edwards Brothers
(left) Corporal William Lumpkin Edwards; (right) Sergeant James Monroe Edwards**
This image was made in the same photographic portrait sitting as the first single image of James Monroe Edwards.

---

[200] *Chattanooga Daily Times,* (July 23, 1905), Lewis Shepherd, "Story of the Great War of Secession: The Part Taken by Hamilton County on the Confederate Side."
[201] Private Richard Marion Edwards, Compiled Service Records and family genealogy.

its natural size, is painful, rendering the applicant permanently disabled." His second injury came on June 20, 1864, at Kennesaw, Georgia, as the 4th was being pushed backward by Sherman advancing toward Atlanta. He "...was wounded by shell in left leg which has never recovered." So Jim Edwards was likely on some type of light duty just over two months after his second injury; therefore, it was perfect timing to accompany the injured members of the 4th Georgia Cavalry to the field hospital and to act as a nurse to his brother and Arba. Information on Jim Edwards's third war injury was passed down through family history as occurring in March 1865 in Bentonville, North Carolina, though this is not part of his official military records or his Pension Application in 1897.

IN LATE 1864, JIM AND HIS BROTHER BILL Edwards returned to Northwest Georgia with the rest of the 4th Georgia Cavalry and then went rogue. As the war was becoming more futile, he joined the ranks of official soldiers who blurred the lines by working together with the Rebel guerrillas, partisan rangers, and bushwhacker groups—all fighting against the Unionists living in their region, the Tory bushwhackers, and the regular Federal army. To the average citizen living in the chaos around North Georgia, it probably looked like the Rebel soldiers and all the other Rebel factions were one and the same. That's because there was coordination between them.

John Pemberton Gatewood (est. 1845-?) from Fentress County, Tennessee, was originally of the 4th Tennessee Cavalry CSA under Major Baxter Smith. But things dramatically changed for John P. Gatewood following the brutal rape and killing of his teenage sister Sarah Frances "Fannie" Gatewood in April 1862 while he was away with his unit. Fannie was just three or four years younger than her brother John, and by mid-January 1863 Gatewood went rogue, becoming a Confederate bushwhacker to avenge his kid sister's murder. Known as the "Red-Headed Beast," he was perhaps the most notorious of all the bushwhackers, operating in the northeastern Alabama, North Georgia, and East Tennessee region in the latter days of the Civil War.[202] The twenty-year-old Gatewood was a dangerous man; his tactics against his enemies were incredibly violent, bordering on insanity.

Another Rebel guerrilla group in North Georgia was led by twenty-one-year-old Thomas Polk Edmundson (1844-1865). Edmundson had served in the official Confederate Army under General Braxton Bragg and by mid-1864 had achieved a rank of major. His company was left to protect Murray County when Wheeler headed into Tennessee in August 1864.[203] The unit became known as Edmundson's North Georgia Scouts, and their mission was to protect loyal Southerners in the North Georgia mountains. So an official Confederate Army company transformed into a guerrilla force for the remainder of the war, at the behest of the Confederate Army.

Corporal Cicero Smith was a fellow soldier of the Edwards brothers in Company K in the 4th Georgia Cavalry. When he died in 1914, his brother John Henry Smith (1842-1930) wrote in the *Walker County Messenger* about his brother's exploits in the Civil War, which included an alternate view on a famous successful cattle raid that has always been attributed as a John P. Gatewood-run operation, which Edmundson also participated in and which resulted in the deaths of almost fifty Federal soldiers.[204]

Just before Hood started back to Tennessee, Wheeler sent Cicero and other scouts into north Georgia, where they did much service by preventing the Federals stationed at

---

[202] Larry D. Stephens, *John P. Gatewood: Confederate Bushwhacker*, (Gretna, La., Pelican Publishing, 2012).
[203] Zack C. Waters, "Tom Polk Edmundson, The Poet and the North Georgia Scouts" *Georgia Backroads,* (Spring, 2011), 47-51.
[204] Larry D. Stephens, *John P. Gatewood: Confederate Bushwhacker*, (Gretna, La., Pelican Publishing, 2012).

Chattanooga, from raiding through the country.

When Wheeler passed through that country with Hood he left his scouts still in north Georgia. When Hood's army was returning from Tennessee, suffering for the want of supplies, Cicero and 71 other boys went to Missionary Ridge. At just about daylight they ran into a battalion which was guarding beef cattle; they routed and captured the whole outfit, then loaded up the camp outfit into the wagons that were used to haul feed for the cattle. The prisoners and wagons were sent south under guard. The remaining scouts then went down in a cloved field and rounded up 1,100 head of beef steers and drove them to Blue Mountain, Ala where they were shipped to Selma to be used to feed Hood's starving men.

Friday, May 22, 1914
John H. Smith
Walker County Messenger
Dalton, Georgia[205]

DID WHEELER LEAVE SCOUTS IN THE North Georgia mountains, and did those "regular soldier-scouts" collaborate with the "irregular bushwhacker-scouts"? It seems likely.

In an article written on Thursday, April 1, 1915, in the *North Georgia Citizen* from Dalton, Georgia, both Gatewood and Edwards are recounted as acting together during the infamous cattle raid of early January 1865. Also surprising is the account of General Joseph Wheeler in determining the command of the operation:

While Chattanooga was the winter quarters of the Federals, Dalton was the winter quarters of the Bragg-Johnston armies.

Many longing eyes were cast upon the corral of fat cattle at Cloud Springs, located where the fort now stands. They were driven over from Kentucky for the use of the

---

[205] *Walker County Messenger,* (Lafayette, Ga., May 22, 1914), John H. Smith "Sketch of the Death and War Record of Cicero Smith."

Federals. Gen. Wheeler sent for Lieutenant Edwards, who was reared in Catoosa county and knew every path, pass, and road, and asked him if he could get the "beef." Lieutenant Edwards said he would try, and when asked by Gen. Wheeler how many and which men he wanted, said one hundred, and chose Capt. Gatewood's men, who were bold, daring, and fearless raiders and riders. Lieutenant Edwards demurred taking the command over Capt. Gatewood, when Gen. Wheeler settled the matter by putting Edwards in command, with Capt. Gatewood more than willing, having in mind the "beef."

The result was a fight to the finish with a wagon train and an escort of Federals, near Lee and Gordon's Mill, on the old battleground of Chickamauga. Then at daybreak a quick fight and a stampede of a part of the cattle en route to Ringgold and Dalton.[206]

Thursday April 1, 1915
North Georgia Citizen
Dalton, Georgia

There is nothing in the records showing that Jim Edwards was promoted from Sergeant to Lieutenant. However, one thing is clear: General Wheeler left behind some of "his scouts," and Edwards and Smith were part of that group.

Having two separate accounts of the incident published in separate newspapers by different sources seems to corroborate that there was some kind of collaboration between the official Confederate Cavalry and all the other partisan groups.

Also of note was the 4th Georgia Cavalry's Company D under Hamilton County, Tennesssee's Captain William J. Rodgers. Company D had pretty much been on detached

---

[206] *North Georgia Citizen*, (Dalton, Ga., April 1, 1915), "Brief Summary of Campaign Which Marked the Beginning of the End of the War Between the States."

service in Dalton, Georgia, as "scouts" from shortly after the 4th Georgia marched into Tennessee in early 1863 through the end of the war. "Rodger's Scouts" did pretty much as they pleased, detached from the rest of the 4th Georgia Cavalry. Rodger's name appears in multiple incidents in North Georgia and East Tennessee between 1864 until the end of the war. Hamilton County, Tennessee, appears to be the common link between Company D and K, with the majority of their soldiers being from there, so Company D's Captain Rodgers would likely have known Company K's Captain Burke very well.

Sergeant/Lieutenant Jim Edwards had clearly drawn the attention of Union troops in Northwest Georgia. In 1865 a few weeks after the cattle raid came this blurb in the newspaper:

Rebels at Ringgold - On Saturday night last, fifteen guerrillas went to the place of Mr. Nathan Anderson, living near Ringgold, and carried off two negro men belonging to him. The squad was commanded by a fellow named Jim Edwards.

Tuesday, February 9, 1865
Nashville Daily Union [207]

NATHAN ALBERT ANDERSON (1803-1879) was a prosperous farmer living in Catoosa County, and a Union sympathizer whose homestead had been pressed into service as a hospital by Union forces. Anderson does not show as owning any fellow human beings in the 1860 Slave Census, so perhaps these captured men were set free. In the 1850s Anderson had lived near Edwards in Taylor Ridge so they clearly knew each other.[208]

In the *Courier Journal* of Louisville, Kentucky, on Sunday, February 14, 1865, Edward's group was reported as

---

[207] Tuesday, February 9, 1865; *Nashville Daily Union*.
[208] Nathan Albert Anderson family genealogy.

"Jim Edward's gang of guerrillas" in an account of a capture of Meredith Ellenburg, a member of his group by the 6th Tennessee Mounted Infantry. Ellenburg was taken to Chattanooga on Thursday, February 11, following their raid through Catoosa, Walker, and Whitfield Counties.[209] James Joseph Meredith Ellenburg (1846-1904), who was eighteen years old at the time, was from Walker County and never officially enlisted in any Confederate military force.[210]

So the Edwards brothers, Cicero Smith, and Company K of the 4th Georgia Cavalry stayed in Northwest Georgia as scouts through the end of the war. Cicero Smith's brother stated that Cicero "on the 18th of April, 1865...left the scout duty for home."

After the war the Edwards brothers would return to the Ringgold area in Catoosa County, Georgia, and most of the siblings would live and farm on land in proximity to their parents' farmstead. Bill married Mary E. Bryan (1839-1899); the couple had eight children. Both Bill and his wife died in 1899. Jim Edwards was actively involved in 4th Georgia Cavalry reunion functions. He married Louisa Amy Harden (1848-1886), and they had three children together. She died in 1886. Bill then married Sara Alice Cox (1855-1933) in September 1888; they had three children together. James died in 1911 and is buried in the Edwards family cemetery in Ringgold, Georgia.

AFTER AN ALMOST TWO-WEEK STAY at a field hospital in Florence, Alabama, on Saturday, September 17, 1864, Arba, with thirty-day furlough papers in hand, traveled south a little over twenty miles to Russellville, Alabama, where the 4th Georgia Cavalry camped after its wild loop through Tennessee with Wheeler. They were planning on staying camped at Russellville for a thirty-day rest period before they made their way back toward Georgia. The horses needed rest, and the soldiers were exhausted.

---

[209] *The Courier Journal*, (Louisville, Ky., February 14, 1865).
[210] James Joseph Meredith Ellenburg family genealogy.

Rebel Correspondent

All was not well within the command of the 4th Georgia Cavalry. On Friday, September 16, the day before Arba arrived at camp, the 4th Georgia Cavalry's interim commanding officer, Lieutenant Colonel William L. Cook, tendered his resignation in a formal letter sent to General Samuel Cooper (1798-1876), the Confederate Adjutant Inspector General in Richmond, Virginia. Clearly, there had been some issues with Cook's command and leadership during Wheeler's Raid through Tennessee. Cook sent a telegram from the field in Tennessee near Murfreesboro with his resignation to the command in Richmond on August 29. A reply was immediately telegraphed back:

Col Cookes [sic] resignation not accepted
A.T. Cone
Col AAG

BUT COOK HAD LOST THE RESPECT of the commanding officers he was traveling with. So once Lieutenant Colonel Cook got to a place where he could draft a formal resignation letter, it was given to his commanding officer, Colonel Charles C. Crews. There was an immediate hand-written comment attached to that resignation letter by Crews himself on the same day he received it:

Headquarters Crews Brigade
Sept. 16th, 1864

Resp'ty forwarded approved he is not a good disciplinarian
C. C. Crews
Col Cavalry Brigade

THIS FOLLOWED A FEW DAYS later by Brigadier General William W. Allen (1835-1894):
Allen's Cavalry Division
Sept. 20th, 1864

> *Respectfully forwarded and earnestly recommended*
> **William W. Allen**
> **Brig. Gen; Comdg'**

COOK WOULD BE DETACHED FROM the 4th Georgia Cavalry on December 25, 1864, by order of Major General Joseph Wheeler—though, oddly, his resignation was not formally accepted until February 12, 1865, by Wheeler[211]:

> *Respectfully forwarded approved with attention called to endorsements of Brigade and Division Commanders*
>
> **Joseph Wheeler**
> **Maj. Gen.**

IT IS APPARENT THAT after September 16, 1864, Major Augustus R. Stewart was in command of the 4th Georgia Cavalry with the daily correspondence being signed by him as "commanding regiment."

He didn't realize it at the time but Arba would spend his last night in the field with the 4th Georgia Cavalry on Sunday, September 18, 1864. It wouldn't be until the closing days of the war in 1865 when he would see some of them again. The next morning—Monday, September 19, 1864—Corporal Jim Whittle accompanied him twenty-three miles to the west to his Uncle William Patterson Shaw's (1819-1886) farmstead in Seven Pines, Alabama.

Tuesday, September 20, 1864, was Private Arba F. Shaw's twentieth birthday. How long the last two years must have seemed.

AFTER HE LEFT THE 4TH GEORGIA CAVALRY in Russellville, Alabama, in mid–September, Wheeler's Cavalry was quickly called back into Georgia. Crews'

---

[211] Lieutenant Colonel William L. Cook, Compiled Service Records.

Brigade, which included the 4th Georgia Cavalry, reached an area south of Dalton on October 2, 1864, where they would take part in small skirmishes around Rome, Georgia, and along the Alabama state line for about a month. They also seemed to have left behind Company K, which included the Edwards brothers and Cicero Smith. Then the 4th Georgia Cavalry headed southbound, fast on their way to a new task: trying to impede Sherman as he began his March to the Sea. By November15, 1864,[212] they were doing just that 275 miles from Russellville, Alabama, near Macon, Georgia.

November 20, 1902
MY EXPERIENCES
In the War of 1860 Briefly Told.

In Uncle's settlement I found people with a social equality but a small exception. His nearest neighbor was John Ford who had a mill on a small branch, run by its water on a high wheel, and, as the boys said, it was a powerful industrious mill. When it got one grain ground it would jump onto another and if it found a red grain, it would stop and play with it awhile.

I was somewhat inclined to look out among the girls and I found one that I thought would do for me a wife and we came to a mutual agreement not to be made one till the war was over. But after it was over and before I could get fixed, the other fellow had done got her and gone, so I was left.

Uncle lived on the foot hills of Little Bear Creek and his farm was principally in the bottoms and very fertile. There was a narrow below that would hinder a free flow of the high water and by the time it was out of banks it would back and stand on the bottom land.

When my thirty days were out I was not yet fit for service and I reported to a post surgeon and he gave me a

---

[212] Joseph Wheeler letter to Colonel E. L. Drake, "Chronology Summary of Battles and Affairs of Lt. Gen. Joseph Wheeler's Cavalry Command," December 5, 1878.

thirty days exemption ticket and after it was out I had a hard problem to solve. I was hundreds of miles away from my command and what should I do. The resolve was to make the best of it I could, and I went to work. Uncle came home and had the measles and one of his minor sons filled his place in the army and when he was well he went to the bottoms to make rails. We tackled a large white oak whose brace roots made large ridges several feet above the ground. We had to get timbers and build a pen as high as our heads to get us to where the tree was small enough so that we could cut it down. It was a deadened tree of a year and when it fell the thick bark was easily pushed off to the ground to keep our feet off the wet ground. The log was so large we could not cut it in two with an axe with a three foot handle. We cut a notch on each side as far down as we could, then with a saw we would cut it off. We cut four ten foot cuts and four eight-foot cuts and the tree made 800 rails.

There were two widows living in that country of two of my uncles who had given their lives in the cause of our country. One of them had several children and was on a farm of their own and the other was the widow of my youngest uncle who was four years my senior and was not married long before he went in the army.

I went to many all day corn shuckings, and quiltings and house-raisings.

In the bottoms were the cucumber tree, the very large cotton wood trees, and on the second bottom the hackberry was tall, large and straight and as well formed as our best oaks and farmers would make rails of them, but they said the rails were easy to rot. The hackberry is a sap growth. In this country the hackberry is only a crooked, ugly, knotty growth; there the cottonwood took the place of the poplar in the bottoms.

There are many things I remember there I could write about but I pass on.

Bye and bye, I solved the hard problem. I joined the regiment that Uncle's boys belonged to in General Rodgers'

Rebel Correspondent

division. It was Colonel Moreland's regiment at Iuka, Miss., and on the way I stayed one night on Big Bear Creek with a Mr. Southerd. He was as shifty as a coon. He had a good farm on the creek. I believe he had a substitute in the army and he was enjoying home life. He had many bales of cotton and one time when the Yankees were on the north side of the Tennessee river Southerd hauled some bales to them and they bought it and payed in greenback, a good price. Mr. Knight, his neighbor, next below on the creek and on the opposite side, had a gin and the bales of his crop and the toll were all on his hands and it made a large pile and the south could not use it and it had to lie on his hands. Here is what I am driving at. Mr. Knight kept seeing Southerd handling greenback and after a time said: "Southerd, how do you get so much greenback?" Mr Southerd said: "When the Yankees came to the north side of the river, I hauled some bales of cotton over there and they gave me greenback for it." Then Knight said: "The next time they come over there I will take some of my cotton over there and (he stuttered) da, da, dam it, I will have me some green backs, too.

At Southerd's that night I struck up with three government supply men. They were getting up beef cattle and, in fact, any thing soldiers could eat in the line of meat and bread at least that is the way I remember it.

My two uncles were James and Egbert Harden, mother's brothers.

A. F. Shaw

THIS WAS THE THIRD TIME in less than two years that Arba was on medical furlough. In reviewing the events that occurred during the first two furloughs, each came at opportune times. Had he not been on furlough, he could have been exposed to greater risk, based on the intensity of the battles and the number of men lost while he was gone. Then, again, he was furloughed the last two times for being shot so there's that.

It was also convenient that Arba could rehabilitate at his aunt and uncle's homestead, located so close to the field hospital in Florence, Alabama. It would have felt like a small piece of home.

Rhoda Ann Hardin Shaw (1828-1894) was Arba's mother, Harriet Hardin Shaw's, younger sister by four years. Rhoda Ann Hardin, like her older sister, had also married into the Shaw family. Her husband was William Patterson Shaw (1819-1886). Uncle William Patterson Shaw descended from one of Arba's grandfather's brothers. His family had lived in Walker County, Georgia, right up to the beginning of the Civil War when they moved to Seven Pines, Alabama.

When Arba arrived he was greeted by his Aunt Rhoda and a large house full of fourteen Hardin cousins ranging in age from one year to eighteen years.

Uncle William was away in the war, having enlisted in July 1863; he was serving as sergeant in Company A of Moreland's Alabama Cavalry Regiment, which was part of Brigadier General Phillip D. Roddey's (1826-1897) Alabama Cavalry Brigade. The sparse records of this regiment show Sergeant William Shaw in the hospital at the end of August 1864 and, from Arba's insight, his uncle was suffering from rubella. Their two oldest sons were nineteen-year-old James Franklin Shaw (1845-1918) and eighteen-year-old George Mark Shaw (1846-1931). George Mark Shaw does not show up in the compiled military records for Moreland's Regiment but his approved pension records of 1918 do show him in Company A of Moreland's Regiment, serving from June 1864 through May 18, 1865. The Confederate Army at this point in the war began taking both older and younger men to fill their depleted rolls. Next in line was sixteen-year-old Benjamin Cicero Shaw (1848-1898) and fifteen-year-old William Edwin Shaw (1849-1927). With Arba's uncle coming home sick with the measles, perhaps it was one of these two boys who filled in for their father.[213]

Arba began his furlough around September 17, 1864, and after getting a thirty-day extension, by mid-November he was presented with a dilemma that a lot of soldiers that had been wounded and furloughed faced: How do you even find your company when it could be hundreds of miles from where you last saw them?

Arba's solution was to join his uncle and cousins in Moreland's Alabama Cavalry Regiment. Not surprisingly, no records of him show up in the records of this cavalry regiment. He probably just blended in with the rest of the regiment and wasn't noticed, just another tired soldier on horseback.

Lieutenant Colonel Micajah Derum Moreland (1827-1867) was a Mexican War veteran who had served under Colonel George R. McClelland. With the Civil War shuffle of all the Mexican War veterans between the north and the south, Moreland organized Company C in Brigadier General Phillip D. Roddey's 4th Alabama Cavalry in 1862. In 1863 he was promoted and given command of his own battalion of four companies, which by 1864 had grown into a full ten-company regiment.[214] Moreland's Alabama Cavalry Regiment did not have a great reputation. General Nathan Bedford Forest reportedly had made specific complaints about the regiment's discipline and number of AWOL soldiers.

ARBA ALSO MENTIONS TWO UNCLES, his mother's brothers, who lost their lives in the Civil War.

James Mark Hardin (1834-1862) was a Private in Company E of the 16th Alabama Infantry. Having been wounded at the Battle of Shiloh, they moved him to a hospital in Canton, Mississippi, 200 miles south of the

---

[213] Sergeant William P. Shaw, Compiled Service Records and Shaw & Hardin family genealogy.
[214] Lieutenant Colonel Micajah Derum Moreland, Compiled Service Records.

conflict; he died twelve days later on April 18, 1862. The 16th Alabama Infantry lost 162 men in that battle. He was survived by his wife, Martha F. Gains (1832-c1910), and six children.[215]

TWENTY-THREE-YEAR-OLD EGBERT B. Hardin (1842-1865) was the youngest of Arba's mother's brothers. Egbert was a Private in Company B of the 35th Alabama Infantry from Fulton County who died on January 6, 1865, during the Carolina Campaign. Of close to 1,000 men in his regiment, only fifty-five men survive the war. He left a widow, Julia Ann Malloy (1840-?).[216]

November 27, 1902
MY EXPERIENCES
In the War of 1860 Briefly Told.

The night I stayed at Southerd's was a cold night and the negroes had put on two very large round logs of green wood and some little stuff and the little stuff soon burned out and no more was supplied. The negroes all got off and the fire went out and we white folks had to go to bed, but the next morning one of the logs was taken out and split up and it made a good fire.

After that I went on to Iuka and was received into the regiment and had been there about a week when it was ordered up the river and left me and Dock Shaw without any rations or orders, we both being horseless. By the camp was one of the noted Mississippi quagmires. A man would be walking along and unexpectedly drop down like he was in water, possibly to his waist, and if he was not in reach of a shrub that grew promiscuously over the marsh, he could not get out unless some one would help him out. The marsh was

---

[215] Private James Mark Hardin, Compiled Service Records and family genealogy.
[216] Private Egbert B. Hardin, Compiled Service Records and family genealogy.

a low damp looking place and level and occasionally a puddle of clear looking water with somewhat scattering bushes and sometimes a small sapling. I went, in the marsh from tuft to tuft and by springing up and down I could shake everything in sight all around several yards away, even to the largest saplings When man or beast got into it, the more the effort they made to get out of it the deeper they would get into it, until they would go out of sight and drown in the mud and water.

As Dock and I were left without orders and there being no commissary to draw from, we decided to make orders of our own and enforce them; so by the middle of the day orders were for us to go back to his home and we were soon bundled up and on the way, but the weather had moderated and the roads were so muddy that about two miles per hour was all we could make. And when it was getting dark I lost my footing and fell sprawling in the mud. I got a good muddying. It was about 15 miles to Southerd's where we crossed the big Bear and it was late in the night when we get there and the yawl was on the wrong side for us then. We went back to Southerd's shuck house, made a basin in them and lay down and covered with our blankets and slept till twilight, it turned cold in the night and the mud was crusted in the morning and we went to the ford and waded. We pulled off our shoes and socks, pants and slips. The water was swift, deep and cold, it seemed like it would cut us off at the of the water and while we were crossing I slipped and fell and dropped my pants on the water and the way they went and me after them till I caught them. I was good wet all over. We got out, rigged up, and went on to Dock's by 12 where we got breakfast.

After a few days' stay at and about Dock's during which time I helped to rebuild the stick and dirt chimney to his house and to make some new chairs and put bottoms in them, the command came in off of its raid and camped about Uncle's. The Yanks had crossed the Tennessee river and they went to meet them and when they came back they brought me a horse, bridle and saddle. Then I was fixed. After that we started for Dixie.

We went a southwest course and in about twenty miles we reached Smithville in Mississippi, then to Cotton Gin, on Tombigbee river. Down there was the country the North Alabama people called "Egypt." It was prairie country and made lots of corn to sell them when they ran out. We got corn from an over seer of a farm that worked one hundred hands all told. We camped on the east side where it was wooded. The land was rich and he only had corn and potatoes, excepting cotton, for home use. I believe he said they made 130,000 pounds in the summer of 1864 The land was first bottom on the Tombigbee. There were three negro women at the quarter that made clothes all the time for the hands to wear. The first on turned the crank of a machine that took the seed cotton from a slow moving horizontal endless apron. It would gin the cotton then, cord it and spin it and wind it on a half dozen spools before it was ready for handling any more. The next woman would feed the machine when she had time and warp and fill quills and the third woman wove the cloth. That was their every day occupation; they had no other work to do.

When we got down into that country and when the boys went to plantation quarters the negroes would steal the blankets and saddle pockets from the horses where they were hitched. Sometimes they would watch and catch them and there was a clan of white and black in those large wooded swamps that would steal horses. The blacks were run a ways and would stay with the clan, as we learned it.

A. F. Shaw

MISSISSIPPI PLANTATION OWNER Thomas Stephen Southerd (abt. 1801-abt. 1875) was born in Sussex, Virginia. In 1864 he lived in Tishomingo County, Mississippi, where Iuka was located very near to the border of Alabama. One of his sons, James Edward Southerd (1842-1910), was a 2nd

Rebel Correspondent

Lieutenant in Company I of Moreland's Alabama Cavalry. Thomas Southerd had also enslaved thirty-five fellow human beings, including four adult males, eight adult females, and twenty-two children ranging in age from infants to sixteen years old. The records show that Southerd was a prosperous cotton farmer who, before the war began, had a plantation valued at $5,000 and personal wealth estimated at $32,000.

When Arba met him, Southerd was engaged in what would have been the dangerous practice of trading cotton for greenbacks with the enemy. By late 1864 Confederate currency had become almost worthless. A Confederate dollar was worth about three cents to a Federal dollar.[217]

When Arba enlisted in 1862, Confederate privates were paid eleven dollars per month. In June 1864 Privates received a raise to eighteen dollars per month.[218]

After the war in 1870, Thomas Southerd was wealthy no more. His still owned real estate valued at $2,000 but his personal wealth had plummeted to an estimated $800. Listed as living in the Thomas Southerd household, which was likely still operating as a cotton plantation, were ten formerly enslaved individuals. They all had acquired the Southerd last name, now attached to their first names as recorded in the 1870 US Census. Fifty-year-old Julia Southerd, thirty-five-year-old Mary Southerd, and eight-year-old Miranda Southerd were listed as domestic servants. Eighteen-year-old Robert Southerd and fourteen-year-old Jerry Southerd were recorded as farm laborers. Thirteen-year-old Bettie Southerd, twelve-year-old Willie Southerd, ten-year-old Elisa Southerd, eight-year-old Lee Southerd, and two-year-old Ella Southerd were all recorded as "at home."[219]

Moreland's Cavalry made its way from Iuka approximately fifty miles south to Smithville, Mississippi. It

---

[217] *The New York Times,* (September 28, 1864), "Grant's Army. Gold out of sight in Richmond. Rebel paper absolutely worthless."
[218] Mark M. Boatner, III, *The Civil War Dictionary*, (New York, D. McKay Company, 1959).
[219] Southerd family genealogy.

was late November 1864, and they would soon to be looking for a place to camp for the winter.

December 4, 1902
MY EXPERIENCES
In the War of 1860 Briefly Told.

We caught one darkey, said to be the most dreaded of any and he was whipped almost all he could bear with dogwood bushes with their tough nibs on and hung time and again to make him tell who was with him in his stealing, but not a word would he tell, only implicate some negroes that never failed to prove themselves clear. Don't know what was done with him. He was kept in our guard house several days.

I have ran ahead a little. We went from the cotton gin south and crossed the Bertahacee river, an eastern tributary of the Tombigbee. It was a wet time. The banks were level full and we ferried across and were in a great deal of flat country. Sometimes we would see large bodies of water, often not so deep but what we could ride through it anywhere dry shod with our feet in the stirrups. We stopped at Dr. Broiles' place and went into winter quarters that had been built by some other command. There were pine pole cabins covered with boards with stick and dirt chimneys. We stayed there possibly a month. The doctor had an ever flowing artesian well. He said it was 650 feet deep. It was chalybeate and in cold weather seemed perfectly warm. About his place was an immense amount of China trees loaded with berries and there was a large drove of Robin redbreasts there all the time eating the fruit. It was not uncommon to see a robin fall dead from the wing. The doctor said the berries killed them.

While we were there the wagons went off a day's drive to a town to get commissaries and it rained and got the waters up and they had to stay about a week. When those Mississippi waters were swollen they run so slow that it took them 3 or 4 days to run down as much as our streams do in one day. Our commissaries gave out, then we began to rustle the fat biters that were continually in the way at feed time. One evening Polk Miller and I went out and found one in an old pine field and be with the gun charged with the hollow of the minnie ball full of powder was to shoot and me stick. So here goes, the biter fell and squeeled, but not loud. I ran, and Polk said, "Stick it, stick it, stick it." With these words Polk heard some one coming and said run, and tore off like a scared rabbit, and stooping down over the hog could see it was two of my mess, Will Daniel and Tom Patterson. I called Polk back and in less time than it takes to write it that hog was skinned. We hung it, head up, and split the hide down and stripped it it down in strips about four inches wide. The balance was soon done and quartered up. Then we decided to replenish our beds, and we cut broom-sedge and wrapped the pork up and took it in.

By this time it was late and when dark came the pork was put upon the roof of the cabin above one of the water holes and next morning when we were frying for breakfast Colonel Moreland smelled the fry. It was the strong kind any way and he said: "Boys, there is fresh meat in the camp" and he sent a posse to hunt it and we had an eye out and saw them coming. Ben Shaw took what was in the pan and lit out to the evergreens in the near by swamp, frying pan and all. The posse came in and searched and found no meat.' The hog on the cabin was covered with evergreen brush and the evergreen bushes grew up to hide the west side of the roof as they came up and the door was in the east side and we had a good chance to conceal our meat.

I want to go back awhile.

When I was in Franklin county and Mark Shaw and I were at our aunt Martha's, one day I was on foot and Mark on his horse and as he mounted his horse, I said, "Mark, I can beat your horse to the branch." It was about eighty yards, and right then the race started, and just at the water the horse struck my head and I fell on the other side of the little stream. As it happened I was not hurt and it was great fun to us.

As we left Alabama we stopped once and scoured around on detail to catch some of the boys that had gone home and stayed too long. We scoured around and got up all we could and one morning we started out and saw a man in the distance running. We were on top of a hill and the horse I was on in running down the hill and at the foot of the hill be failed to make allowance for the flat and fell. He swapped ends and when I struck the ground I was about a rod further along the road than the horse and my gun was about a rod ahead of me. I was hurt a little but I got up and got my gun and went back before the horse got up. He was strained up some, but he got up and I mounted and went on but our man was not caught. The day before my squad caught a man and saw some others that saddled up and went without any trouble.

A. F. Shaw

BY DECEMBER 1864 MORELAND'S CAVALRY had found winter quarters in Monroe County, Mississippi, near the plantation of Dr. Erasmus Senaca Broyles (1815-1883) and close to the town of Aberdeen. Conveniently, they took over quarters built by another group of soldiers from the previous winter.

Dr. Broyles was born in South Carolina and moved to Mississippi when he married Abigail Virginia Moore (1833-1895). The couple would have five children together. Dr. Broyles had also enslaved eight fellow human beings, including three adult men, three adult women, and two children under sixteen years old.

Private Polk Miller, Private Will A. Daniels, and Private Thomas Patterson were all three members of Company A in Moreland's Cavalry. They had all enlisted on the same day, Wednesday, July 1, 1863, in Dickson, Alabama. Privates Miller and Patterson each had periods of time in 1864 when they were AWOL but had then come back to the regiment. Patterson had taken an "extended vacation" from service from April 1 to July 14, 1864. Everything with this group was loosey-goosey, and now Arba was part of the company.

The soldiers all seemed to be biding their time, taking it on the slow and enjoying Moreland's Cavalry's lax discipline. Why were they hidden in central Mississippi, hundreds of miles away from any conflict? The obvious answer is that it was safer for them all. Things had gone very bad for the Confederacy, and they must have seen the handwriting on the wall, though most of the members of Moreland's Cavalry were illiterate.

December 11, 1902
MY EXPERIENCES
In the War of 1860 Briefly Told.

Our last installment was the last of our hunt for deserters and the father of one of our crew was living in that vicinity, His name was John Miller and Polk took us home to stay with him that night. 7 in all. His father was in a still house making liquor that night. It rained the cross out and rained till 12 the next day, and in the morning, when we started, four of the boys bought a quart and the other three bought a pint and my partners would pass the bottle to me often and I would take a little dram and pass it back. I soon found that I was getting funny. They would turn up the bottle every time and only taste and I found they wanted to get me drunk and when they passed it again I didn't drink and soon met the regiment and gave the balance to Col. Moreland and told him I had enough. That was the nearest drunk I ever was on.

Now back to winter quarters.

While we were there we saw a grist and a saw mill that was supplied with steam of water from an artesian well. It ran high enough above the ground in a wooden pipe to fill a tank 10 or 12 feet above the ground.

One night John Bailey's horse was stolen. He was our blacksmith and his horse was fine. He never had anything to do only when we marched. The next morning possees went out to hunt; at night they returned with no trace or clew and the second day's hunt was attended with the same result and yet Bailey went out the third day, one man with him. He went on a thrown up road through a large swamp and he saw horse tracks that had left the road and went off into the jungle. They resolved to follow the tracks and sure enough it was the horse wanted. The two men concealed themselves to wait for the thief and late in the evening their waiting was rewarded. The man came to feed the horse and while he was feeding Bailey shot and killed the thief and went into camp with his horse.

One morning while we were in that same camp, but it was not in the shanties, I had watered and curried my horse and was feeling rather tough and made a pallet by the fire and Mark Shaw went and fixed his horse and I happened to eye him as I lay down. He was eyeing me in a sly way and when he was done with his horse he stalked toward the fire and when he got close to my pallet he made a spring at me for a ground scuffle which he was good in and hard to turn. As he sprang I threw up my hands and bended knees and he went over and as he went over I grabbed him, and when he struck the frozen ground I was across him and took the Indian hug on him and stayed across him till he thawed the ground under him. If he had been successful in his leap he would have held me down. I could throw him, but he was as good in a ground scuffle as I was.

Now we are going for Alabama. We went to the Black Warrior River and camped on the foothills near a ferry, 10 miles west of Tuscaloosa, Ala., and we stayed there, I believe, two nights and a day. On the river was an abundant supply of cane of all sizes up to 25 feet tall. We would go and cut turns for our horses and give them the leaves and play with the canes by putting them in the fire to get hot and then warp them around trees to make them pop. There were so many at it that it would sound like guns in a battle. When we left we went to the ferry and were ferried across in groups in a long ferry boat by an old darkey. He said he had been the ferryman at that place for 40 years and said he was then eighty years old. He used side oars. The river was very slow and ferrying was easy. It took him half of the day to set us over and after I was over and waiting I saw one of the boys put his feet on the sides of the skiff so his weight would sink the rear some the lowest and by certain motions he could run the skiff without a paddle. I also saw three men on a flat boat. It was loaded with corn. They said they had bought it 110 miles down the river from home. They said 10 miles a day was all they could row up the stream. They were fixed for wet weather. They were landed and cooking breakfast and had rowed some distance that morning before breakfast.

All across and on to Tuscaloosa. It was there I saw, in a store, my first pumpkin yam. That was the finest looking city I saw in all my rounds; out a piece we camped and then went on to the place where Birmingham is now There was only a blast furnace there then and some tram way about a large hollow. The pig iron was freighted to market on wagons.

A. F. Shaw

December 18, 1902
MY EXPERIENCES
In the War of 1860 Briefly Told.

We stopped at Birmingham possibly three hours. Our eyes were full looking at the, to us, strange devices. We saw how they moulded the pigs in trenches moulded in sand, then the pigs were loaded on tram cars, as much as two mules could pull on the wooden tram-way to the stock house by the public road, which ran on top of the ridge west of the furnace The two mules worked one in front of the other between the track rails and the ore was mined in that section and was trammed in by mules to the furnace. That was the first we ever saw of the process of getting the iron out of the ore.

I don't remember where we went next from Birmingham, but we camped several days by a good farm. The man treated us nicely; he had plenty to live on and to spare. In his yard there was a tall rail pen full of peas in the hull. He gave me a mess for myself and the boys of my mess. I asked him what he was going to do with so many peas? He said; "Plant and eat them. Peas and bacon would make little n----s grow faster than anything he could feed them on; and while I was conversing with him a flock of geese came up around us and among them was one that was much taller than the others and was gray like the goose and I said, "What sort of a goose is that?" He said, "it is a wild gander," and said his father shot

into a flying flock of wild geese eighty years ago and brought that one down by breaking his wing. He broke it close to the body and he was only left a short stub.

Don't know how long we stayed at that place, but we had in circulation much of the fun that kept the soldiers from having the blues. But for the fun we would have become despondent and worthless.

Now we have orders to move, and as I remember, went south in the direction of Montevallo on the Selma, Rome & Dalton R. R. On the way we went into camp one evening late and the forage master took from each company a detail to go for forage. An old-time darkey was with us and the officer that he was serving sent him along. His name was Jo—we called him old "Uncle" Jo. He, as I remember, was the property of the Alexandria that used to own the farm where Col. Clark Gordon now lives and had lost his master, or whoever he was serving in the army, and couldn't get home and was staying with us for protection. Poor fellow, he had been in General Hood's fatal raid to Nashville and Franklin, and his toes were frozen off. He had to go with his feet muffled up with rags. He had a good time with us and had a good horse to ride and attend to and the one the officer rode was in his care in the camps and when we got to the place to *get the corn the forage master told a soldier and Jo to get in the crib and every man tell how many horses he wants corn for and put in 20 ears for every horse. They got in and went to counting and the old gentleman and lady of the place were among us and protesting strong against our getting the corn all the time. The man was so wrathy about it that he started to the house to get his gun to shoot us, so he was promptly put under guard. Meanwhile the soldier and Joe were counting out the corn. Of course, every eye there was on the old man and when be was put under guard our eyes and ears went back to the old lady's clash and behold! she had got a pole and was punching Joe through a crack. We used no violence but soon there were enough strong hands ahold others to loose her grip and take the pole from her. She vainly kept trying to get sticks to punch Joe but we would not let her; she could not stand the idea of the black man going in the crib and when we all got our allowance of corn the forage master appointed men to go to the fodder stacks in the crib lot and give out two bundles of fodder to each horse. Now that we are all supplied we all mounted and rode away in the dark.*

The next morning we went on to our destination— Montevalla, Ala, it was. There I, through curiosity as I did many other things, visited two old darkeys— a man and his wife that were 118 years old. They were almost blind. The man was trying to plat shucks to make a foot mat and the woman was trying to wash their clothes and cook dinner. They told me they served old master till they were 80 then he set them free and gave them the house they were living in. it was in the town and as long as he lived after their freedom he saw that they were provided for and after his death, his sons had kindly kept them supplied with what they needed. They looked very feeble and their eyes looked hazy white.

A. F. Shaw

MORELAND'S CAVALRY HAD BROKEN winter camp when

the food supplies were diminished. They then headed east and leisurely made their way into Alabama in February 1865. Though they were probably all beginning to get hungry, they seemed to be in no particular hurry. They were wandering in no particular direction toward no particular enemy.

Foraging became the rule of each day to find enough food for the soldiers and their horses. It was a cold, hard winter for those trying to survive in Central Alabama as the war headed for its logical conclusion. The rural population's limited food supplies were being foraged by a passing cavalry regiment of at least 500 men and horses. Those food supplies could be the difference between life and death to the farmstead owners along their path. The army that was there to defend them was now not looked upon so kindly. Trying to defend your property from a large band of armed men was futile.

December 25, 1902
MY EXPERIENCES
In the War of 1860 Briefly Told.

While we were in camp at Moutevalo, we had an easy time There were no yankees for us to look after and no bush whackers, and supplies were shipped to us on the railroad. We had but little to do but sorter go as we pleased.

One day I was in the town and as I was passing a shop where a barber was shaving a man, not a soldier, the barber said, "Come in and have a shave, and I said, "I don't need it." My beard was only fuzz, but was growing a little and when he got the done be was on, they said, "Take a shave " I sat down in the chair and the-customer paid for his chair and mine, too. I had the money and aimed to pay for my shave.

There was a foundry in operation there and it was another wonder to us. I went in and saw men setting up moulds in sand. They had the sand dampened so it would pack together and when they got the moulds shaped, they would dust powdered charcoal over the parts that the melted iron would come in contact with when it was poured in. They were moulding a general line of old time cooking utensils—pots, kettles, turning plows and so forth.

There was in that country many soldiers that, like me, had been left by their commands in North Carolina and Virginia, and we naturally preferred our own command. On application to General Roddy, he kindly provided papers for all that made application and I was one of the applicants and some time in the first of March I boarded a south-bound train at Montevalo headed for Selma, Ala., and got there late in the evening and went to the boat landing on the Alabama River and found there was no boat going up to Montgomery until 9 o'clock the next day. Then I had to stay all night. The next morning there was a boatload of three thousand yankee prisoners that bad been exchanged, landed at Selma and got off the boat and when they came to the landing they rushed to the landing side and came very near making the boat dip water.

When I was going down to Selma the seat I rode on was not cushioned and I put my overcoat on the seat and when I went out at Selma I forgot my coat and walked away a steps and went back at once but some fellow had done got it and gone.

At the wharf was the finest and largest boat I ever saw. It's name was Southern Confederacy; don't remember it's dimensions. Nine o'clock came and the little Cherokee steamed away for Montgomery up the river. It was 340 feet long and, I believe, 60 feet wide. I saw the process of steering the boat. There were two engines that ran a side waterwheel each and had a rope fixed to each engine so it could control the steam; then they went up through the boat to the pilot house on top, and a round beam with pins of wood to turn the beam, and the turning would make one rope shorter and the other longer. That would throw more power on one wheel and less on the other and by that easy process boats are steered in their course. That was the easiest riding I ever did. One inside would scarcely know the boat was moving. There were men on the boat that would shoot wild ducks from the running boat. Of course they never got them.

The long gray moss was quite a show to us. It was hanging from the limbs of the trees several feet long and waving in the breezes. I was more the color of a tree frog than anything I can now think of.

The boat made 10 miles per hour up the river and only stopped to exchange mail and possibly let off and take on passengers and about 10 p.m. we landed at Montgomery, 110 miles from Selma. We soldiers had to stay in the-car shed in waiting for the Opelika train the next morning where we were to get on

the Columbus railroad, but I ran the gauntlet and went to West Point to get off and went to aunt Susan Holoway's and stayed a week and went back to West Point and boarded a train for Opelika where I changed cars for Columbus, Ga. There we staid in the car shed again all night in waiting for a train to go to Macon and the next morning the train rolled into the shed and we were soon steaming toward Macon. As I stepped on the ground a news butch met me with a newspaper that told of the fall of Richmond, Va., and I gave him a 25 cent shinplaster for it.

Then I went to the Post Commandant to get my directory fixed for the balance of the journey and who should I see in command but my old Colonel I. W. Avery, and Sam Latimer, his orderly. The Colonel directed me out two miles.

A. F. Shaw

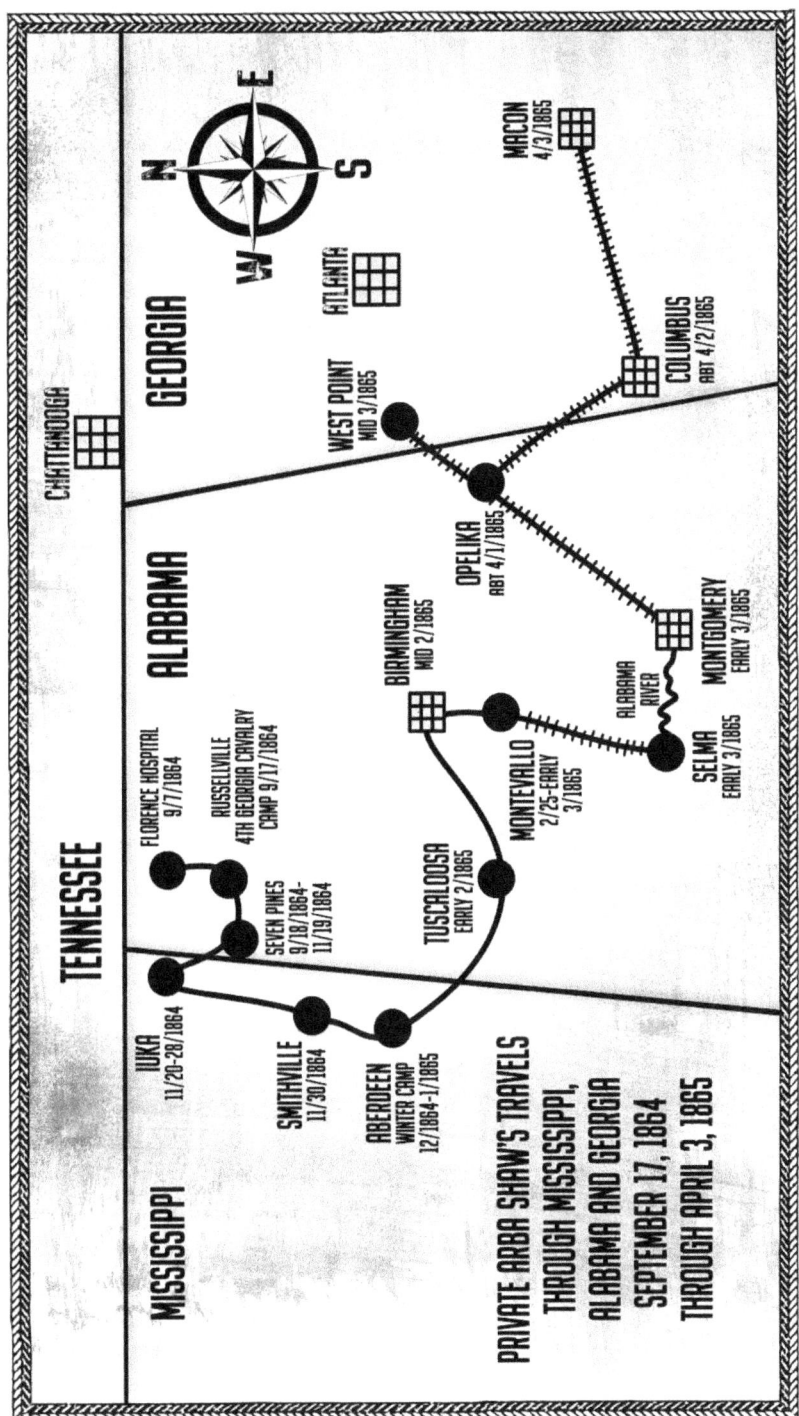

HIS ODD SIDETRACK FROM THE 4TH Georgia Calvary had come to an end. The time with Moreland's Cavalry Regiment was now up. So with papers in hand once again, Private Shaw's great adventure returns him to Georgia. He impressively manages to employ three modes of transportation to get there: horseback, riverboat, and rails. The memories so many years later of actual dates are slightly off when analyzed against the known historic date of the fall of Richmond, which was April 2, 1865.

Perhaps the date he actually left Moreland's camp in Moutevalo, Alabama, was a little later. Or perhaps he stayed with his Aunt Sou at La Grange, Georgia, a little longer than he remembered.

When he made it to Selma, Alabama, he likely boarded the first steamship he had ever traveled on in his life. The "Cherokee" would have regularly traveled up and down the Alabama River between Mobile and Montgomery with lots of other boat traffic. If he estimated the "Cherokee" at 340 feet long and sixty feet wide, how much bigger was the "Southern Confederacy"? The infamous "Sultana" that plied the Mississippi River and was just over a month from its tragic moment in history that would claim the lives of upwards to 1,500+ soldiers was 260 feet long with a beam (width) of forty-two feet. Since this was his first trip via steamboat, this impressive mode of transportation must have felt much bigger to Arba than it probably was.

The average size of steamboats in Alabama in that era was 200 feet long and thirty to forty feet wide, and most of Alabama's antebellum steamboats were side-wheelers. Alabama's rivers were shallow and narrow. The cotton economy so important to the South was all made possible by steamboat transportation. In 1865 there were more than 200 landings along the banks of the Alabama River[220] from Mobile to Montgomery.

---

[220] Robert O. Mellown, *Encyclopedia of Alabama*, "Steamboats in Alabama," http://encyclopediaofalabama.org/article/h-1803.

Scene on the Alabama River
Alabama Historical Society, Volume 2 – 1898

The Montgomery and West Point Railroad left Montgomery at 8 a. m. and arrived in West Point, Georgia at 4:30 p. m.[221] Arba's description of "running the gauntlet" meant he was headed toward the Federal troops, then located in northern Alabama. He would not have known exactly where they were so when Arba took the train to West Point, he was taking a risk. Ironically, some of those Union troops were the very ones he had skirmished with at Campbellsville, Tennessee, when he was wounded in September 1864.

So in mid-March 1865 Arba visited familiar family members, then at the start of April jumped on a train southbound toward Columbus, Georgia, with a connection in Opelika, Alabama. The Union troops converged on the area right after he left. The Battle of West Point would take place on April 16, 1865, seven days after Lee surrendered at Appomattox.

Finally, on and around April 3, 1865, Private Shaw stepped off a train in Macon, Georgia. He was greeted with the news that the Confederate capitol of Richmond had fallen the day before.

---

[221] *Montgomery Daily Mail*; April 1865.

After Private Shaw left the 4th Georgia Cavalry in Russellville, Alabama, they and the rest of Wheeler's Cavalry were called back into North Georgia. They would eventually head south past what remained of Atlanta. On November 14, 1864, they participated in the Battle of Bear Creek Station near Griffin, Georgia, fighting Union Col. Smith D. Atkins (1836-1913) 2nd Cavalry Brigade.

This was the beginning of Crews' Brigade shadowing Sherman's army during the March to the Sea. From this point until the war's end, Crews' Brigade was made up of the 1st, 2nd, 3rd, 4th,[222] and 6th Georgia Cavalry.

On November 16, 1864, Crews' Brigade was on the east side of the Ocmulgee River at Macon, Georgia. On November 27, Company E of the 4th Georgia Cavalry was skirmishing in Lawtonville, South Carolina.

December 4, 1864, saw them among more than 4,000 Confederate Cavalry soldiers defeated in the Battle of Waynesboro, Georgia, against Sherman's Cavalry commanded by General Judson Kilpatrick. On December 20 and 21, 1864, the 4th Georgia Cavalry was part of the Confederate forces in the evacuation of Savannah, Georgia. By the afternoon of December 21, 1864, Sherman's troops occupied the city. The 4th Georgia Cavalry then retreated north along the Savannah River to regroup their forces.

The start of 1865 saw Crews' Brigade under General William W. Allen's Division of Wheeler's Cavalry Corps. They reorganized their remaining forces around Augusta, Georgia. There was a lull waiting to see where Sherman would go next.

Finally, in late January 1865 Sherman showed his hand and began his move into the Carolinas. The 4th Georgia Cavalry would take part in skirmishes that sent them from Augusta, Georgia, northeast into South Carolina.

On February 11 they took part in the Battle of Aiken, South Carolina. Less than a week later on February 17 and

---

[222] The 4th Georgia Cavalry was officially renamed as the 12th Georgia Cavalry on January 30, 1865.

Rebel Correspondent

18, 1865, they were on the banks of the Saluda River burning a railroad bridge on the northwest outskirts of Columbia, South Carolina, as it was captured by Sherman. Much of Columbia was burned.

With each skirmish and battle, the casualties began to cut down the overall size of the entire Cavalry Brigade. On March 10, 1865, Wheeler's diminished cavalry forces attacked a sleeping Union Camp and achieved a small victory, in what would be known as the Battle of Monroes's Crossroads near Fayetteville, North Carolina—a location now in the present-day Fort Bragg Military Installation.

March 19 and 20, 1865, marked the last major battle of the Civil War, fought at Bentonville, North Carolina. It is a Rebel loss with a cavalry detachment left at the rear guard as General Joseph Johnston retreated. There were 239 Rebels killed in the battle.

Once off the train in Macon, Arba went looking for a place to check in. Headquarters known as "Wheeler's Absentee Bureau" was located in Macon, Georgia, and would have been the logical place to go for a Private who had been absent from his unit for more than five months. By April 1865 Colonel Isaac W. Avery, though technically the commander of the 4th Georgia Cavalry, was still recuperating from wounds he had received the same day as Private Arba Shaw at the Battle of New Hope Church.

IN THE ELEVEN MONTHS SINCE THEY had both been wounded in the same battle, Colonel Avery had also been evacuated to a hospital in Atlanta. He would have likely been a patient at Fairgrounds Hospital No. 1 or No. 2, though no records show the soldiers who were there in late-May 1864. Soon after the evacuated both hospitals south to Macon, which might explain how Colonel Avery ended up in Macon. His wounds were much more serious than Arba's, who was in and out of the Atlanta hospital in just a few days. He spent

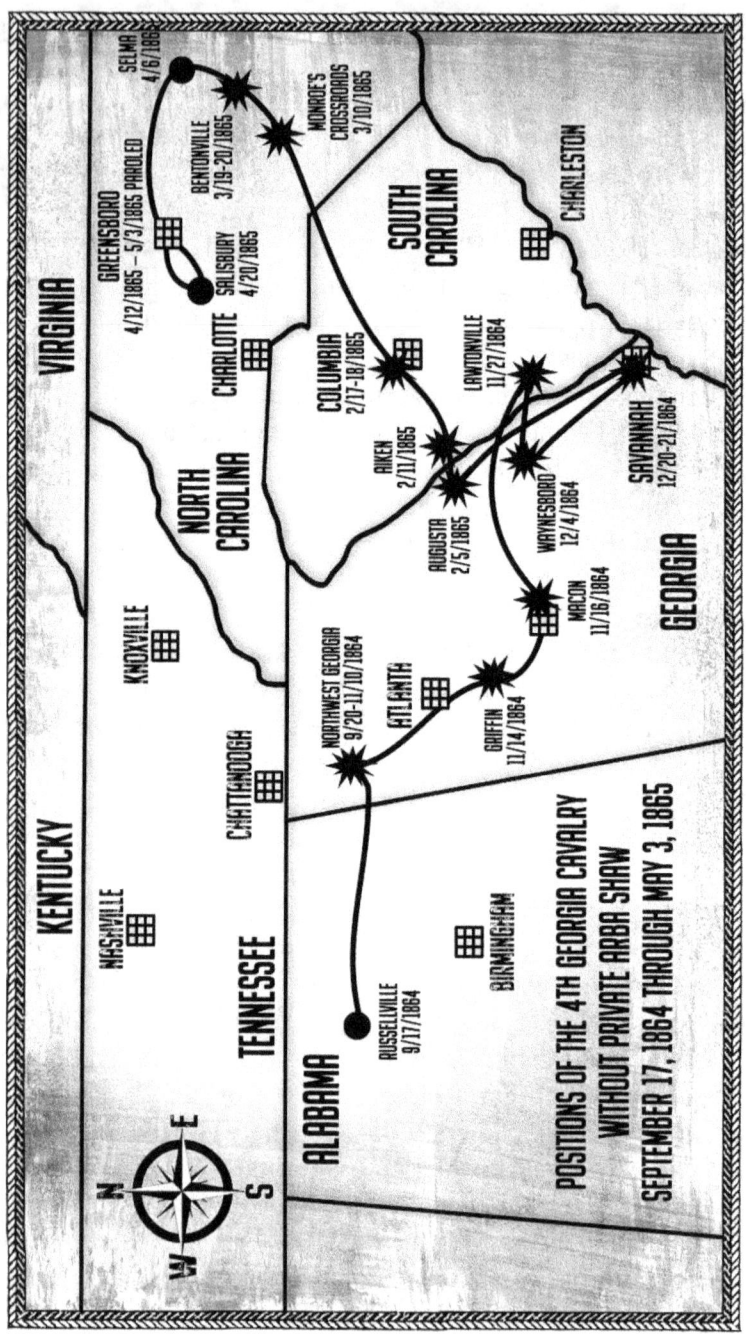

the summer of 1864 convalescing at his mother's home in Sandersville, Georgia, [223] writing in a letter to General John T. Morgan on June 26, 1864: "staying at mother's, my wound was a very severe one and the Post Surgeon at Macon said it would take three months."

No doubt Avery took longer to recover and, in fact, he would walk with a cane for the remainder of his life. On September 2, 1864, the date that Atlanta fell, Colonel Avery penned a letter from Sandersville, Georgia, some sixty miles east of Macon to Lt. Colonel and Assistant Adjutant General Samuel W. Melton in Richmond, Virginia, where he mentions being "wounded severely three months ago."[224].

ON NOVEMBER 15, 1864, COLONEL Avery penned a letter to the Confederate Secretary of War, James A. Seddon (1815-1880), from Jonesboro, Georgia. This location is important because on that date the main body of the 4th Georgia Cavalry was located just to the south near Griffin, Georgia, so Avery had rejoined his regiment, though not actively commanding it "in the field."

Confederate Secretary of War Seddon had been a two-term member of the U. S. Congress from Virginia prior to the war and was now serving as Jefferson Davis's 4th Secretary of War, a position he held from November 1862 to February 1865.

Jonesboro, GA November 15, 1864
Hon. James A. Seddon
Secretary of War
Richmond, Va.

Sir:

I command a Regiment of the Georgia Cavalry in the Army of Tennessee and have the honor to request the authority to increase my command and raise a Brigade of

---

[223] Isaac Avery Papers, Book 30, 21-47, Lewis Leigh Collection, U. S. Army Heritage & Education Center.
[224] Colonel Isaac W. Avery, Compiled Service Records.

Cavalry for the War.

I shall be unable for field duty for two or three months in consequence of a severe wound and while unable for field service I can benefit the cause by raising troops. I have served since the beginning of the war, and have commanded Cavalry for three years, two years of which I have commanded a Regiment, and I have had considerable experience in commanding a Brigade.

I have assurances of success in raising a Brigade. I can get many recruits from territory once occupied by the enemy and many Reserve troops are desirous of entering the regular Confederate Cavalry service.

**I have the honor to remain
Very Respectfully,
I.W. Avery
Col 4th Ga Cav.**

THE LETTER WAS ENDORSED BY General Joseph Wheeler who highly recommended Avery, claiming him "competent at his position." General Pierre Gustave Toutant-Beauregard could not recommend Avery's idea because, in his opinion, there were already too many Cavalry Brigades; but he wanted Avery to go after all the stragglers and deserters. In fact, Beauregard was very enthusiastic on having Avery find these absent soldiers. General Alfred Iverson weighed in with comments to allow Avery to raise a Brigade.

Ultimately, General Beauregard's suggestion won the day as Colonel Avery was soon located at what he referred to as the headquarters for "Wheeler's Absentee Bureau" in Macon, Georgia—although his application to raise "Avery's Brigade" continued to bounce around within the command of the Confederacy into early 1865.

There is no recorded official response to Avery's proposal from Confederate Secretary of War Seddon. In addition, no record can be found that officially states the forming of an organization known as "Wheeler's Absentee Bureau"—it only appears on a letter in Colonel Avery's handwriting where he appends his proposal to raise a Brigade in January 1865. So it appears the official office of "Wheeler's Absentee Bureau" may have been a name manufactured by Colonel Avery himself.

Hd 2nd Wheeler's Absentee Bureau
Macon, Ga. Jany 11, 1865
Hon. James A. Seddon
Secretary of War
Richmond, Va.

Sir:

I have the honor to apply for authority to raise a Brigade of Cavalry in North Georgia in territory overrun by and exposed to the enemy, In that section are many informal organizations already raised, which are engaged in protecting the people from Tories and scouting among the enemy. Almost as many men can be raised there by authorizing new organizations, as General Forrest obtained in West Tennessee, and without some step of this kind these men will not be secured to the Confederate service except as Guerrillas.

There is also a fine field to operate upon the enemy's lines in North Georgia and Tennessee and I could do good service and recruit a Brigade of Cavalry if ordered there for that purpose and put in command of this section.

I append a copy of an application similar to this, made two months ago, and containing endorsements of Generals Beauregard and Wheeler showing their estimate of me as an officer.

I have the honor to be
Very Respectfully,
I.W. Avery
Col 4th Ga Cav.
Comdg.

AVERY'S FAMILY ALSO RECORDS HIM at this time as the commander of the Macon Georgia Home Guards from 1864 to 1865. He was very much itching to get back in the fight. But the fight was fizzling out.

So when Private Shaw walked into the building with the "Absentee Bureau Headquarters" sign hanging next to the front door, he was greeted with the friendly faces of twenty-seven-year-old Colonel Avery and his faithful orderly, twenty-four-year-old Private Samuel Carpenter Latimore (1840-1901).

The 5' 10" tall Private Latimore sported a light complexion and hair with grey eyes; he was from Sweetwater in Monroe County, Tennessee, located midway between Chattanooga and Knoxville—which, coincidentally, the 4th Georgia Cavalry had fought and skirmished at in 1864. He was first mustered into Company E of the 4th Georgia Cavalry but soon was given detached service alongside Colonel Avery for his entire stint in the Civil War. Prior to the war in 1859 the Latimore family was prosperous enough that Sam was able to attend the preparatory school at Emory and Henry College in Washington County, Virginia, which helps explain his qualifications to act as Colonel Avery's aide.

After the war Latimore returned to Monroe County, Tennessee, and worked with his father, Daniel Webster Latimore (1812-1888), on the large family farmstead. Sam Latimore married Nancy Isabella Cunningham (1845-1880), and they had three children together before her death from pneumonia in 1880. He would marry a second time to Catherine Elizabeth Robinson (1843-1927) and continue working the family farm until his death in 1901.[225]

After catching up on the specifics of where Private Shaw had been since September 5, 1864, they sent him up the road. Arba's journey was heading for its conclusion.

---

[225] Private Samuel Carpenter Latimore, Compiled Service Records and family genealogy.

CHAPTER TWELVE
Endgame

January 1, 1903
MY EXPERIENCES
In the War of 1860 Briefly Told.

And as I went out to the two miles away camp from Macon I saw a man in the distance who had on a top-heavy load of "hoopee" and he was going this way and that way for the right way. Soon I overtook him and asked him if he could tell me how to find camp direction and he said, "Yes, I am going there." He was a soldier. He got hold of me and said: "I will take you through all right, if you will help me." Then he said, "What state do you live in?" I said, "Georgia." He said, "Your name is Georgia. I live in Arkansas. My name is Arkansas." "Georgia," he said, "do you know how I got my start? I will tell you. I got it by toting pine at $5 a load." He would repeat it often in the same words. He would go out in the forest and split and tie rich pine in bundles and tote and roll it in Macon for kindling at five dollars a load as he called it.

Bye and bye we got to the camps and took him to his camp and turned to go to the Georgia boys and, behold, who but my Captain Horn. He saw me come in with the drunk man from Arkansas and was coming after me to stay with him. Of course, I went.

The Captain since he came off of the raid had been shot in battle through the chest and was worse for wear. I had not seen a man of my regiment since I left them at Russellville, Ala., in September. It was a joyful meeting; the Colonel seemed awful glad to see one of his old boys and he praised me for being faithful.

The next morning there was a company of us organized and put in charge of a Lieutenant to go to Augusta. We marched out early to Macon, where we boarded a train toward Atlanta and at Jonesboro the railroad was torn up and we left the train and hit the grit across the country for Covington. We camped on the way at Woodstock one night. When we started from Jonesboro, the Lieutenant, whose name was Mo Somebody, (I don't remember his name,) turned his cunning Irish face and eyes back on us and said, "Follow me, boys." Then he cut the sand at a mile-to-ten-minutes rate. He had a pair of new boots on his feet and they soon blistered his feet and he began to fall back and soon we boys began looking back at him and saying, "Follow us Lieutenant." It was not much funny to him but he would grin and endure our guys, and before we got to Covington, as I remember, he was toting his boots on his shoulder.

At noon of the day we left Woodstock, about three of us boys and the Lieutenant went into a citizen's house to get some dinner and he drew the old time demijohn on us and and one of us three boys let his taste overbalance his judgment and he drank so much it made him so boozy he wanted to lie down and sleep. The Lieutenant told me to stay with him and see that he came on and I lay down on the roadside and took a nap as he slept and in a few minutes I was awake and wanted to go on and I began to call and shake him to get him up and he would grumble and say many abusive words. After a while he rose for fight and I shoved him off and picked up a withe and said, "I will wear you out if you don't go on*" He was not so drunk, but he wanted to be contrary and do as he pleased, but be went on all right when he was convinced. The reason I was left to bring him up was because be was a man of the 4th Georgia and we were all the 4th Georgia men in that Company. We got to Covington all right and the Company had done camped when I got my man in.

The next day we got to Augusta late in the night. Trains did not run fast like they do now and when they got to *stations they would stand a long time before starting. The average soldier would grow impatient and want to know why they didn't go on. Then the railroads were in bad condition; the track rails were made of iron and many places in them were mashed in scallops and splinters frayed off—a thing that now is of the past, since our railroads are railed with steel.*

Don't remember where we stayed the balance of the night after our late arrival at Augusta. Anyway we were assigned to another camp of direction, which was a mile from Hamburg on the S. C. side of the Savannah river, by an alligator swamp, where we staid a few days in waiting for enough companies to come in to make a regiment.

A. F. Shaw

CAMP WRIGHT WAS THE CONVALESCENT camp on the east side of the Ocmulgee River near Fort Hawkins in Macon, Georgia. The camp had been under the command of Colonel Stephen H. Colmes (1819-1874) of the 50th Consolidated Regiment, Tennessee Infantry, since October 1864.[226] The Kentucky-born Colmes himself was seriously wounded during the Battle of Chickamauga in 1863. The primary purpose of Camp Wright was for soldiers who were "fit for garrison and guard duty, and who are temporarily disabled for field duty on account of wounds, or disease, received or contracted in the service."[227] So as commander of the post at Camp Wright, Colonel Colmes himself was continuing to serve, even as he was disabled on account of his wounds. An attorney before the war, Colmes would return to practicing law in Sparta, Tennessee, but would take his own life in December 1874 because of the lingering results of his injuries.

Captain Felix Grundy Horne (1838-1903) was a

---

[226] Richard W. Iobst, *Civil War Macon – The History of a Confederate City*, (Mercer University Press, 2009), 350.
[227] *Macon Daily Telegraph and Confederate*, November 28, 1864.

prominent leader in Arba's Company F. Since the last time Arba had seen him—when Horne had likely saved Arba's life with his quick thinking—Horne had been promoted to Captain. He began the war as a Sergeant in Company F and was promoted as positions became available, a phrase that usually meant the prior occupant was wounded or killed.

Captain Horne himself was seriously wounded in December 1864 at the Battle of Waynesboro, Georgia, and likely returned to the hospital in Macon, followed by entering Camp Wright for rehabilitation. Captain Horne was born in Tennessee but moved to Georgia and lived in Tunnel Hill, Georgia, before the war. Horne had married Susan M. Whitten (1843-1899) in September 1861 during the early days of the war, and they would have at least five children, three of whom survived to adulthood. They promoted him to Captain at the war's end. After the war Horne returned to his family, farming near Tunnel Hill until his death in 1903.[228]

ARBA ARRIVED AT CAMP WRIGHT on approximately April 3, 1865, and immediately became part of an unarmed group of convalescents, led by Colonel Colmes, being sent toward North Carolina in what was an exercise in futility. Within a few days they had passed through Augusta, over the Savannah River, and into Hamburg, South Carolina. At about that same time, what remained of the 4th Georgia Cavalry was located over 275 miles to the east in Selma, North Carolina.

On April 6, 1865, the last remnants of the Confederate Army gathered at the Everitt P. Stevens plantation in Selma, North Carolina, for what would be the last Grand Review. Crews' Brigade, which included the 4th Georgia Cavalry with General Joseph Wheeler and General Joseph Johnston in attendance. Johnston would soon leave and head approximately 100 miles northwest to Greensboro, North Carolina, for a meeting with Confederate President Jefferson

---

[228] Lieutenant Felix Grundy Horne, Compiled Service Records and family genealogy.

Davis, who had escaped Richmond a few days earlier.

Three days later, on April 9, 1865, Robert E. Lee would surrender to Ulysses S. Grant at Appomattox Court House in Virginia. The war was over, but it would take several weeks until Arba and his regiment of convalescents got the news.

THE NEXT INSTALLMENT OF ARBA'S reminiscences, published on January 15, 1903, begins with a short comment by then editor of the newspaper Nathan Campbell Napier, Jr. (1878-1923), the son of the man who had first hired Arba to write for him twenty-three years earlier. The elder Napier had passed away on January 21, 1902, shortly after the start of the serialization of Arba's Civil War account in the *Walker County Messenger,* with only a few articles published. He would have read the part of Arba's manuscript, no doubt encouraging him to complete his writings. Coincidentally, Nathan Campbell Napier, Sr. was a Captain in Company K of Colonel John Hart's 6th Georgia Cavalry and was likely at the last Grand Review of the Confederate Army at Selma, North Carolina on April 6, 1865.

January 15, 1903
Walker County Messenger
OUR VETERAN CORRESPONDENT.

We doubt if any paper in the state can make the boast the Messenger *can—of having a correspondent who has furnished the news of his community continuously for twenty two years. Such is the record of our able correspondent at Cooper Heights - Mr. A. F. Shaw, who with last week's issue begun his 23rd year as correspondent for the* Messenger.

The Messenger congratulates itself upon having retained the valuable services of such interesting writer and good friend for almost a quarter of a century and we trust it will be in the far distant future before the readers of this paper will look in vain for the weekly letter from his entertaining pen.

Steve Procko

January 15, 1903
MY EXPERIENCES
In the War of 1860 Briefly Told.

While we were there I would secure passes to go in to Augusta and in my mess was a young Chamberlain of an Alabama command who was a Catholic and at his suggestion I would go of evenings with him to Augusta to their every evening service. When we went into the house we found on the right and left basins—within them holy water for all persons when they came in to dip a finger and with that fingertip the forehead and drop to one knee on the floor before being seated They had many other formalities performed by servants at the rostrum under the lighted candles and the many rich pictures—so called—of Christ and others of His visible days. The formal service was done in obedience to the priest as he stood before them in his long black gown. And when the formal was done for the time, the priest went into an altar and those that desired him to pray their sins away would go into another and through a small window would confess their sins to him and he, as they believed, prayed them away. Chamberlain went in and when we went back to camp he was cursing as usual and I said: "Chamberlain, do you think you can ever get to heaven and swear like you do?" He put on a solemn look and with upturned face and uplifted hands said, "Yes, my name is written in God's book of life."

When I was in Augusta I visited the city watch tower. It was said to be 130 feet to the floor. The night watchman stood on to turn in fire alarms by ringing a very large bell that was over his head. I went up by way of the winding stairs.

Then I went to the south market house and we went up to the city clock where I could see all of its parts. It was a strong structure and had four dials that one could tell the time a mile away and one mile north was another market house, but I never was at it.

Rebel Correspondent

While we were in this camp John Fricks was in a camp with some convalescents of his—White's—Battery south of our camp and we were together all we could be. He would visit me and I him and in his camp the boys had climbed two limbless pines, took up a pole and fastened it about 60 feet from the ground and tied the two ends of a long manilla rope to the pole to make a swing. When one wanted to swing he would get in on his feet and start the swing by his forward and back motion until he went as high as be wanted to, then hold fast (or an easy swing until it stopped.) The rope was one they used to tie from tree to tree to hitch their horses to.

One day while we were there news came to us that the yankees were making a raid by way of, I believe, Columbus, Ga. Some of the boys that were the most zealous in our cause made some speeches in favor of going to Augusta and pressing a train and going to meet the enemy and compel him to retreat his step. Of course they met with opposition as we were all unarmed convalescents and one of their opponents, a very small lad, made a speech. He told them that they were unarmed and it would be useless for them to try against the odds in arms in Augusta and if they bad been successful in getting a train they would be no good when they were in front of the enemy with out guns and he wound up by saving: "You can't do any such thing. You haven't got the power of a tumble-bug" and so on. A lot of the boys went over to Augusta after dark but they met defeat; some of them turned back before they went far and they kept dropping out and before they got to the depot there were only a few of them and they were soon all in camp again and the others were guying them.

The little lad that made the protesting speech was named Byron.

At last orders were for us to draw three days rations and be ready to start by day the next morning to the front in North Carolina. The day came and off we went—10 companies of us, all convalescents and unarmed, on force march forty miles per day. We were commanded by one

Major Combs. He was all right and his boots took the hide off of his heels as large as silver dollars. This march was made after Lee's surrender, but we did not know it until we got to 96 in Upper South Carolina, when we met Lee's men coming in and they told us it was all over. Then Major Combs said; "Boys, I surrender you all now. We will go back to Augusta and be paroled and go home." That was in the last week in April. Some of the boys wept because we lost our cause.

96 was a Fort thrown up in the war of 1812 and from the south east the British started a tunnel to undermine and blow it up, but it went under a ravine and caved in and was detected.

A. F. Shaw

BACK IN NORTHWESTERN GEORGIA, the last remnants of Company D of the 4th Georgia Cavalry totaled just a few dozen from an original force of more than 100 soldiers raised by the company's Captain William Jefferson Rodgers[229] from Hamilton County, Tennessee. On April 3, 1865, Captain Rodgers' company and a few other "official" Confederate Army companies were working alongside Thomas Polk Edmundson's North Georgia Scouts. Federal forces, which included the 6th Tennessee and 14th Illinois Mounted Infantry led by Lt. Colonel Verner Wilhelm Printzlau Bjerg (1831-?), had been tracking Edmundson. A skirmish began south of Spring Place, Georgia, near the Coosawattee River. At times they fought each other at close range in hand-to-hand combat. In the last part of the skirmish a charge led by Edmundson fell into a trap set by Lt. Colonel Berg, and Edmundson would fall dead with fatal wounds.[230]

---

[229] *Chattanooga Daily Times,* "1865 – The Battle of Coosa Wattee," July 3, 1905.
[230] Zack C. Waters, "Tom Polk Edmundson, The Poet and the North Georgia Scouts," *Georgia Backroads,* (Spring 2011), 47-51.

Rebel Correspondent

Bjerk was a Danish-born immigrant who moved to St. Croix in the early 1850s and then immigrated to New York in 1859, where he first enlisted in 1861 in the New York 1st Infantry as a Captain. He resigned that commission in November 1862, and soon after moved to Chicago. He reenlisted at the start of 1865 in Dalton, Georgia, in the 14th Illinois Mounted Infantry as a Lieutenant Colonel—Bjerk certainly got around. He was dishonorably discharged after the war on June 2, 1865, for reasons not contained in his military records, and moved back to St. Croix soon after.

In a report to headquarters dated April 8, 1865, a few days after the incident, Lieutenant Colonel Bjerk filed this report:

...while crossing the river, we were attacked all afternoon by the whole gang of guerillas, composed of Major Edmonson, Captain Rodgers, Captain Willraur, Captain Tate, Captain ---, Lieutenant Ring & company. They made several charges upon us, but were driven back each time. In one of the charges, Major E, who was in command of the gang, was killed, having received two wounds, one through the face and one through the back.

CAPTAIN RODGERS AND WHAT WAS left of Company D were soon paroled, then Rodgers disappeared into history with no records found documenting his life after the war. As a Confederate officer who lived on the edge commanding a Confederate Cavalry Company employing guerrilla tactics, he is likely to have gone west to Arkansas or Texas after the war.

Confederate President Jefferson Davis and General Joseph Johnston met in Greensboro, North Carolina, on April 12, 1865. Lee had already surrendered but Davis was looking for options. Johnston reportedly said to Davis, who was preparing to head to Charlotte, North Carolina, and eventually flee into Georgia: "Our people are tired of the war, feel themselves whipped, and will not fight. Our country is overrun, its military resources greatly diminished, while the enemy's military power and resources were never greater and may be increased to any extent desired...My small force is melting away like snow before the sun."[231]

Two days later on Friday, April 14, 1865, at shortly after 10 p. m., President Abraham Lincoln was assassinated by John Wilkes Booth at Ford's Theatre in Washington, D. C.

IN THE LAST DAYS OF THE WAR, Arba was in Augusta sightseeing. He offers an account of climbing the circular stairs of the Augusta Fire Observation Tower, known to the people living in Augusta as "Big Steve." The tower built in 1860 must have offered a remarkable view of the surrounding area and had surprisingly survived the war. During this time he was also testing the waters with other forms of Christianity by attending services in a Catholic Church. Arba's father was a primitive Baptist minister; for Arba, attending a Catholic mass must have been a culture shock. The primitive Baptist religion he was used to would have embraced a very straightforward, "pure Bible" approach to religion, which would have been in stark contrast to the Catholic rituals of the time including preaching to him in a foreign language—Latin.

Arba had grown up with twenty-one-year-old Private John Dickson Fricks (1844-1882) as a neighbor, whose father's farm was right next door to his own father's farm in Walker County before the war. Besides farming in the valley known as McClemores Cove, Arba's father, William, and John's father, John Fricks, Sr. (1809-1876), were both preachers. John Fricks, Jr. had enlisted in the 4th Georgia Cavalry shortly after Arba on December 15, 1862, mustered into service by Captain Helvenston at Dalton, Georgia. Two weeks later he was part of White's Horse Artillery Battery and served with the battery through the entire war, following

---

[231] Alan Axelrod, *Generals South, Generals North: The Commanders of the Civil War Reconsidered*, (Lyons Press, 2011), 25.

alongside the 4th Georgia Cavalry. After the war he returned to his father's farm in McClemores Cove and married Sarah Clementine Lee (1854-1891) in 1875. They would have a daughter together before his death at just thirty-eight years old 1882.[232]

So in the latter part of April 1865, ten companies of ragtag, unarmed convalescents under the command of Colonel Colmes left camp from Hamburg, South Carolina, and began their march about fifty miles northward to Ninety-Six, South Carolina. They got word the war was over some two weeks after the actual surrender so they resupplied themselves, turned around, and marched back to Augusta, Georgia. It must have seemed anticlimactic.

January 22, 1903
MY EXPERIENCES
In the War of 1860 Briefly Told.

On the home stretch now.
A lot of us were taking in 96 Fort when we were surrendered. We had stopped at noon the third day to rest and the Major took us on further north where we could draw three days rations and get it cooked. How could we cook and nothing to cook in was a hard problem. If we could get bread cooked we could manage the meat; the bacon we ate raw or broiled, as we chose, and we could broil the beef. I believe we got women to cook our meal into bread at their homes and when it was all done we started back to the camp. We had left two and a half days before and in two and a half days more we were back in the same tents. We made the round trip in five days. We went two miles north of 96 which made 196 miles round trip.
On the day we were giving our names, so the officers would know who and how many to print paroles for, our old

---

[232] Private John Dickson Fricks, Compiled Service Records and family genealogy.

comrade came up and said put down J. D. Strange there. That was the first time I knew of his being in that part, so he was paroled by Major General B. D. Fry, post commandant, Augusta, Ga., and which was given out to us May 3rd, 1865.

While we were waiting for our paroles the government stores were thrown open to us and there was a general charge made on them. J. D. Fricks quit his battery after the surrender and came and stayed with me and the day the charge was made we were all aiming to go and John said if I would stay and take care of our things he would bring me a new suit and I said all right. I was suffering with sciatica anyway and he went and did what he said he would. He said he never thought about women being so strong till that day when they were toteing off such loads of cloth and goods of any kind they could get hold of and in the rush they broke down a gas jet and that broke up the frolic. Lots were stifled down before they could get out.

Next, on the morning of the third of May, we were called up to have our paroles signed. The blanks had come and when they were fixed we all met at the car shed by noon to board the train for home and while we were waiting, Bill Dale, of Company A, 4th Georgia, was there and told about going to Colonel Cruse once to get leave to shoot off his pistol and reload it. Colonel said, "What do you want to do that for?" and he said; "I have tried every barrel and it won't shoot." The Colonel said: "What were you trying to shoot?" Bill told him a hog and the Colonel said, "That is the reason; you wait till you get in a fight and see if it won't shoot." And sure enough he said the first fight he was in it fired as clear as it ever did.

The next thing of note. There was a nicely dressed woman with a watch suspended by a nice cord standing among the men that were waiting for the train. Meantime I had got on top of the car to sit down to rest and was watching the woman's shines and big talk and passing on her pedigree when I saw some of the men shove her out of balance and take the watch from under her belt, the cord *being around her neck. She did not know her watch was gone until she had got squarely on foot again and it was not long after that she preached the funeral of any set of men that would treat a lady that way. Then she left.*

We were kept waiting and the length of the train was being added to every once in a while until it was about a half mile long and about sun down the announcement was made "All Aboard," and all were in motion and soon aboard— every car fall inside and on top. Then an engine steamed to the rear and gave the starting signal and was answered back by the one in front. Then they both began the tug finally the cars moved homeward and as soon as we felt the first forward move we gave Augusta her farewell rebel yell.

Soon night fall was on us and all quieted down, but in the night the car I was on caught on fire at the truck-bearings and was cut out and left on the siding and all the men that were on it. A freight train came along and we thought we would go on it, but it never stopped and it and a southbound freight made a head end collision up the country. I stayed awake all night watching for a train.

The next morning there came a mixed train and we boarded it.

A. F. Shaw

WHEN THEY ARRIVED BACK IN Augusta on May 3, 1865, Arba and his fellow soldiers were paroled from the Confederate Army by Major General Birkett D. Fry (1809-1876). They would have been required to sign a loyalty oath pledging their allegiance to the United States of America and agreeing to never take up arms against it again.

The last members of the 4th Georgia Cavalry still in active duty, which on January 1, 1863, marched north out of Georgia with more than 1,000 men, surrendered the day before Arba on May 2, 1865, in Greensboro, North Carolina. The ranks of the 4th Georgia Cavalry at surrender and parole totaled less than 100 men.[233] In August 1888 Lieutenant Colonel William L. Cook reported that number to be just fifty-eight men.[234] They surrendered as a tiny part of General Joseph Johnston's army, which on that day totaled 89,270 soldiers, making it the largest surrender of the war.

Arba joined up with John Fricks and a couple of other neighbors from Walker County—James Doreseth Strange (1843-1920) and William L. Dale (1835-1903)—and boarded a train for home. He would meet up with additional friends and neighbors along the way and stay with relatives as he went, spending a night here, taking a meal there, and surely telling the tale of his adventures. Many of these friends and neighbors were also fellow soldiers all on the same mission: to get home. It would take him eleven days to do so.

January 29, 1903
MY EXPERIENCES
In the War of 1860 Briefly Told.

After we boarded the train I set down upon the steps of a passenger couch, and locked my hands after running my left arm around one of the upright supporters that held up the hand rails and went to sleep while the train was standing, and when it started and was getting in headway, I fell and was tumbling down a high fill when I woke up, and the boys were giving me the Rebel yell, I got up and went back to the top and there was a flat car with some wagons on it and I jumped up and caught a spoke in a wheel and the boys got hold my hand and pulled me up. They were in the wagon Then I was on board again and I stayed awake that time.

The train ran on all right until it got to the wreck where the two freights headed together and and were tom into splinter chunks and the track torn up. A crew was there at

---

[233] *The Dalton Citizen*, (March 3, 1911), "A Short History of the 4th Regiment Georgia Cavalry," by A. C. Gunz; 1st Lieutenant; Company I.
[234] *The North Georgia Citizen*, (Dalton, Ga., August 8, 1888).

work. The boss told us there would be a train to leave the next station in one hour and a half and it was 9 miles; if we could make it there in that time—90 minutes—we could go on. We lost no time. There was a good walk between the rails and a mile for every ten minutes to make connection. We knew how to get there. We would walk a while and then we would double-quick awhile and we made it all right. We boarded the train and got to Atlanta before night—in time to draw meal and good old Ned to do us three days. I went to one of the very few houses that had not been destroyed in 1864 and the kind lady cooked the bread for me and her husband said I could stay all night and I did. At, that time Atlanta looked like a dilapidated brick yard.

Soon the next morning we were footing it homeward. The railroad had not been rebuilt from Atlanta to Chattanooga. We got to Big Shanty the first night and as I remember to the Etowah river by noon the next day. There I decided to paddle my own canoe and took to my left and went down the river and soon came to a place with a well in the yard. I went in to get some water and went in the hall to rest and was noticing the old lady, and I said "Ain't you a daughter of Uncle Buck Shaw's" and she said "Yes." Then I said, "My name is Shaw; we are kin," and that I was a son of Wm. Shaw, of McLemore's Cove. She knew him. Then she said, "You will stay with us tonight," and I stayed. Soon her young folks began to come in and we had us a good time.

The next morning I went to see Uncle Buck and Aunt Becky, the last time I ever saw them, and after dinner I went up to Eaharlee and stayed with Elbert Shaw and the next day, Sunday, I got to Captain E. L Cooper's on Spring Creek and went with Miss Sallie to a singing, and Monday I started to go on home and within two miles I found Jake Hale and Anderson Bryan at Squire Gilbert's and, I believe, Jasper and Pat were there, too, and they being old chums said I had to stay with them a day and would not agree to anything else. I stayed and I had a letter from a young woman that had married a Tennessee man and I believe he belonged to

White's battery and when he found that I was going to pass by where she lived he asked me to take it to her and I did so—she lived close to the Gilbert's. She had picked up a strange soldier to her sorrow. She seemed to be bad hurt, but it was too late then as it was with many other poor girls who shared the same fate.

The next morning I started home by way of Rome, Ga., and directly I started I fell in with Uncle Ben, the father of our efficient Dr. Jones, who lives now at Pond Spring, Ga., and we traveled all day together. We crossed the river at Rome, Ga. and I stayed with Dr. Sam Hamilton in Dirttown Valley that night and the next morning I left early to go to where father was teaching school at the Sand Mountain Academy. It was about five miles and I soon was there, Father was standing up hearing a lesson and I stepped in front of the door where I could see him and said. "What are you doing here?" and he was surprised and whirled around quickly, as if he was scared and said, "Yes, what are you doing here?" And I said, "I am going home." Then I went in and he said, "Children, this is one of my sons that has come home from the army." I was seated until dinner and after dinner I studied with the school and after dinner we went on little Sand Mountain to stay all night at Granney Quin's.

A. F. Shaw

February 5, 1903
MY EXPERIENCES
In the War of 1860 Briefly Told.

On the morning of May 12, 1865, I left father in his school Friday morning and started home. I went by father Johnston's and called a few minutes. My wife was then a little girl of 13 and was carding cotton into rolls to be spun into thread. In that day people made the clothes they wore at home, now that is a thing of the past.

By noon that day I got to a Mr. Fitzpatrick's house. He was a son in law of Alex Shaw, of LaFayette, as I now remember, and in a farm at the foot of Taylor's Ridge in West Armuchee valley and near where the Smith Gap road started across. He was a prudent man; I was but a lad of 20 and he gave me some good advice that has been worth a great deal to me. He cautioned me to never be too hasty and several things that were wise in counsel. He gave me dinner and I started on for home and when I got to the top of Taylor's Ridge and for the first time since October 1863 could see the Pigeon and Lookout Mountains and reflecting on the many bad reports of the acts of scouts in all of the country between those mountains and especially in McLemore's Cove where my home has always been, it brought a shudder to me. I stood on top of Taylor's Ridge several minutes in meditation whether I should try to go home by myself or not.

Finally I ventured and got down to the Phipps tan yard in LaFayette, Ga, at sundown. Some scouts had just left; the little fires the left had not burned down. Mr. Phipps, Jo's father, told me I had better stay with him that night. He said it was the best for me to do my traveling in daylight for if the scouts found me traveling in the dark they might kill me. I had about 45 minutes then to dark and four miles to Uncle George Shaw's and I thought I could make it and that will put me four miles closer to mother and I started on a double quick on the levels and a fast walk up the hills and made the four miles in day light. The next morning I went on, paused with Uncle Mercer Shaw a few minutes and about 9 a.m. on May 13, 1865, I landed home and met a fond mother who had given two of her sons up for service of her country and had scarcely heard from us in more than a year. Father was forced away too, but he, being a cripple of white swelling, was exempt.

On Sunday, the 14th, I went to a singing and one of the yankee scouts, Bill Bailey, was there and I asked him if it would be safe for father to come in and he said, "Yes, I will guarantee it." Bill and I were brought up together.

About 2:00 Sunday the 14th, brother Jim came in. He

was surrendered I believe 9 miles east of Raleigh, N.C, and I got home 29 1/2 hours before he did. Now mother is all right; her boys at home alive and father can come home.

On Monday, the 15th, I went back after father and on the 17th we got back home. As the soldier often said, "When this cruel war is over and I don't get killed and the yankees don't bind me, I will go back to the girl I left behind me."

The little boys at home has scraped around and done a little fence and had about six acres planted in corn and a little old sore-back pony that belonged to R.F. Shaw's wife. Her children were all girls at that time and brother LaFayette Shaw was to plow their crop for the use of the pony to plow his and when we got home father bought some rips of horses and in June we planted more corn but the season was too dry for it but he cut it for feed and the nubbins helped out lots.

Our orchard was laden with fruit and it was no hard task to get $40 for a two-horse load of apples and peaches in Chattanooga that summer. Father bought four sides of bacon from Mr. Hans Robbins at the place Dr. Crowder now lives at, for 30 cents per pound and they average $15 per side, $60 for the lot.

The yankees had failed to get one pig and one young cow and an old warty-head hen and her brood. They left her because of her warts and after so long a time four sheep came out of the jungle where they had escaped death. They came in sight of the house and refused to be coaxed or driven any closer and would run off and again they would come back to the same place and some of the children found the bell that had been worn by one of the flock and had it at the house and some one of the family suggested the idea of ringing their bell. As soon as they heard the sound of the bell they ran to it as quick as they could get there and were as gentle as ever. The bell was put on one and they assumed their usual contentment. The young cow was giving milk when we got home and from one little pig there was a fine bunch of shoats and a nice lot of chickens from wart head.

One thing I wish to mention that I overlooked at the beginning. At Fayetteville, Tenn., J. M. Henry, one of my Co F, essayed to cross Elk River at the ford below the stone bridge, The river was so swollen that it was swimming, but it was narrow and the water was calm and Mr. Henry, as I remember, wanted to see if his horse could swim. He rode in and his horse would go to the bottom and then leap as high as he could and kept on that way until the river was crossed. It was a serious affair to the rider, but he got out about as much dead as alive and is here yet, one of my neighbors, but his life race is almost run. He is 76.

(Since the above writing, J.M. Henry has died on January 12th, 1903.)

A. F. Shaw

February 12, 1903
MY EXPERIENCES
In the War of 1860 Briefly Told.

Now I have gone through and at home again and if I can I want to give a review of the whole affair.

I will say that in the army is the best place to measure and weigh men. It seemed that some men liked the service because they were provided for at the expense of others and some because they could make money trading, and some because they were natural born soldiers and many were there because the laws required them to be there, and they felt that for the sake of a good name and good character they could, by so doing, bestow upon them and their descendants, that they would not try to shun the 'loathsome and hazardous task.' And there were men there because they could escape the execution of the civil law by joining the army.

And on the other hand men for various reasons deserted; some because they were not born soldiers and had rather bear reproach than to take the risk there was in the army of being killed and did not want to be subject, to orders.

And some were deserters because of the deplorable condition of their family. I knew one man to desert because he had made repeated efforts to get a furlough and was denied to go to the aid of his sick wife and children, who were out of anything to live on, and soon after he left his last application was signed all right, but it was too late; he was gone to return no more. It is the best to listen to the cries of the poor. And I knew some other men to desert because their officers took their good horses from them for other men to make a special trip on. They said "We don't want to give up our horses; we are willing to go ourselves," but they were forced to give their horses up and the result was, they with one accord deserted.

And others quit because they passed their homes and they tho't their cause was as good as lost anyway and there was no use for them to struggle on. And still others did not have the weight of the cause impressed upon them and wanted money, which they could get by falling back behind the lines of the enemy.

In the Confederate service we were not getting much money for our service. I do not remember how much money I drew at two drawings, and at the surrender they were about two years behind and I got that at Augusta, but it was not worth a penny only for a relic as it was after the surrender.

So you see we had men of all grades with us and to put men in the army they are under military restraint and where they can be more closely watched by the authorities than when under civil rule and they nearly all will seek some way to beat the law, so the more restraint the greater is the per cent, of violation.

We had a class that would go and call for meals and when they would get done eating would steal a knife, fork or spoon. Of course they were useful in the camp kitchen, and a class that would steal provisions from a brother soldier or blankets, shoes, boots, bridles and would even take the halters off of our horses and turn them loose in the camps.

And as I was coming home I was on top of the car that caught fire and I had my new suit in my saddle pockets and my new shoes tied to them and I called a man in whom I had full confidence and asked him to take them down and be said all right and took them down and when I got down, I in the darkness, could not get an answer from him. So we never knew when we were meeting a slick duck.

And we had many slick ducks who would beguile good girls and marry them and when their command left that place they would leave to return no more. The truth is such men's character was black and they had blasted the future hope of possibly a fair, innocent maiden for life.

Now I will close by giving a few words to the dear girls of today and advise them to watch all strangers. It is as I have already said: We never know when we are going to meet a slick duck that ought to have his neck broken.

This series finished the 25th day of February, 1902, almost 40 years after I joined the army and it is all entirely from the memory that was impressed on my mind and retained yet.

Written by A. F. Shaw, Co. F, 4th Ga. Cavalry

CHAPTER THIRTEEN
Afterwards

ON SATURDAY, MAY 13, 1865, Arba arrived home and embraced his mother, who he had not seen in more than a year. Her oldest son was now home; it must have been a very happy reunion.

His brother James B. Shaw arrived home the next day, Sunday, May 14, 1865. It was the second Sunday in May, a day that in 1914 would begin to be celebrated as Mother's Day. In 1864 it was definitely Mother's Day for Harriet Hardin Shaw. James was in the last group of less than 100 remaining men of the 4th Georgia Cavalry that was there at surrender and parole in North Carolina. As soon as Arba fetched his father home, a few days later, the family was whole again: the Reverend William M. Shaw, his wife, Harriet, and eight of their children who had miraculously survived the war. It was late spring, and they began to pick up the pieces, trying to return normalcy to their farmstead and planning for a future harvest.

THURSDAY, FEBRUARY 12, 1903, MARKED the last of the articles by Arba F. Shaw, Co. F, 4th Ga. Cavalry, titled by the *Walker County Messenger* as "My Experiences In the War of 1860 Briefly Told." He began writing his manuscript in early December 1901 and, a little over ten weeks later, completed its more than 40,000 words on Friday, February 25, 1902—a date he recorded in the last paragraph of his personal account of the war.

The *Walker County Messenger* began serializing Shaw's writing as soon as he started writing; for the first couple of months the series did not publish on every Thursday. All told, his work was broken down into fifty-four separate articles published between 1901 and the beginning of 1903. During those fifteen months in which his memories were serialized, he also continued to write his regular weekly column on the goings-on in Cooper Heights, the small farming community in McClemore's Cove where he and his family lived. Arba's account was well received by the locals in Walker County, with several comments published in the newspaper at its completion. But, after several weeks, his account began to recede into the past and soon was mostly forgotten.

In his remaining years, he would write and celebrate the events of day-to-day life on his family and neighbors: anniversaries, births, deaths, crop reports, visitors to his small part of the world, and more—all carefully noted in his weekly letter to the *Walker County Messenger's* editor, which was promptly mailed two days before either the Thursday or Friday publication date. Arba relished the annual summertime reunions with his comrades of the 4th Georgia Cavalry, as well as the big picnic thrown by the *Walker County Messenger* for its correspondents, of which he was a senior member; at one time he served as vice-president of this group. The yearly event began in 1904 and was attended by close to 1,000 Walker County residents each year, including Arba and his wife.

On January 5, 1906, he would mark his twenty-fifth anniversary as a correspondent for the *Walker County Messenger*:

I have been writing to the Messenger a quarter century and since I began there have been many remarkable changes in the county. Then the Messenger was a four page paper; our courts lasted one week or less, now three; LaFayette was then a little dull village, now it is growing into a city, proud of its two cotton mills and its many other enterprises; when there was not a foot of railroad in our county, now two line run through length-wise and one cross-wise from Crawfish Spring to the coal field on Lookout Mountain, where mining is done on an extensive scale. Estelle is getting to be an iron mining center and is growing into an extensive town and Blowing Spring has a tile manufactory and Rossville is flourishing with two mills, one woolen and the other a hose mill and the Chickamauga park is the most noted place in the county for sight-seers. All of these make a demand on laborers, the mines, the tile works and park for athletic men, while the mills are a boon for afflicted men with families and widows who are left with children. These things keep it impossible to get good farm hands, unless we pay public work rates, and nearly all the young men, that don't want to do hard labor and the girls, are going to town's or teaching school. But that is all right, we don't all want to be farmers; if they were, where would be the consumer for our farm products that are for sale.

A. F. Shaw
January 5, 1906

AS THE FIRST DECADE OF THE twentieth century progressed, Arba began to suffer from a lifetime of hard labor and his wounds from the Civil War, requiring him and his wife to move from the farm they had lived in since the 1870s to his daughter Sarah Elizabeth (Lizzie) Shaw Leath's (1874-1947) farm in Kensington, Georgia, near where his parents' original farmstead was located:

The good woman and I moved on the 22nd of March. Now we live in my native valley at the east base of the Lookout mountain and one mile north of my parental domicile and Sunday we were greeted by quite a crowd of comers and goers whom we were glad to have.
My writing arm was prostrated four days last week and is weak now.

A. F. Shaw
March 30, 1906

HE ALSO RECORDED A VISIT by his youngest sister,

REBEL CORRESPONDENT

Parthena Shaw Whittle (1863-1937), who was born during the Civil War when Arba was a soldier. He first met his new infant sister when he came home sick on his first medical furlough from Cherokee Springs Hospital near Ringgold, Georgia.

My youngest sister, Parthena Whittle of Keith, Ga., and her son, William, are with us at this writing, it being the first time since August, 1890, when our father was on his bed in the affliction that proved to be fatal. Then father and mother were living at the home where they brought us all up and where they lived to see and know that their children who lived to be grown were married and where they were born, except your humble servant. And here I will say that the old cabin is standing at Shaw, Ga., that I first saw light in, 62 years since. Sister is the eleventh born of our parents and on the 11th day of July, 1863. Then I was a soldier boy and came home on a furlough; that the only time till it was over. We have tried to make her stay enjoyable while she was with us. She stayed at the old home two nights and a day and we are all ever so glad she came.

Parthena Shaw Whittle
1863-1937

A. F. Shaw
August 24, 1906

A FEW WEEKS LATER HE WOULD write to deliver the sad news of the death of his granddaughter Mary E. Leath (1899-1906). Mary was the daughter of Arba's third daughter, Lizzie, and her husband, Jeremiah M. Leath (1869-1927).

STEVE PROCKO

Jeremiah H. Leath and Mary Elizabeth Shaw. "Lizzie" was one of the two daughters of Arba who lived into adulthood.

We have been called on to part with our little Mary E. Leath at 3:30 in the morning of this September 12, 1906. She was born August 8, 1909, and lived seven years, one month and four days. She had Laryngitis and when the risings broke we hoped the worst had passed, but her system was so poisoned that medicine failed to bring a reaction...Mary had never been to school any but she showed an aptitude in studies. Her mother was teaching her in a common school course and she was in third grade...her course in life was solemn. Always a matter of fact manner...Before she got sick she talked of dying; she asked her grandmother if she would cry if she died and yet before she was sick she asked her mother where she would bury her if she was to die. Of course her mother was dumbfounded. Then Mary said "I want you to bury me close to the house so you can keep flowers on my grave..."

A. F. Shaw
September 21, 1906

HE AND HIS WIFE CELEBRATED their twenty-ninth wedding anniversary, along with the readers of the *Walker County Messenger*:

Rebel Correspondent

Twenty-nine years, this 31st of July, the preacher pronounced the good woman Mrs. A. F. Shaw. She was young and pretty good looking then, now she is old and really good looking to me.

A. F. Shaw
August 1, 1907

ALL THROUGH THE PROCESS OF researching the life and writings of Arba F. Shaw, there was a constant search to find a photograph of the man. Nothing seemed to have survived. His descendants did not recall seeing a photograph of him later in life, let alone as a Confederate Private.

Photographs of his siblings were found, including a few of his younger brother Dr. James B. Shaw, who served with him in Company F of the 4th Georgia Cavalry. Finally, after a trip to McClemore's Cove and the cemetery where he was laid to rest to meet two of Arba's 2X great-grandsons, they mentioned that they had heard of a picture of him and his wife in the *Walker County Messenger* from way back when he was alive.

Photographs printed in the newspaper during the first decade of the twentieth century are rare so this one had to be for a special couple celebrating a special day. Published on Friday, November 15, 1907, the image was likely taken on or around the day of their twenty-ninth wedding anniversary. Arba was sixty-three years old, and his wife, Rebecca, was fifty-five years old. His paralysis-prone right hand grasps his cane, and he wears his Confederate veteran's "Cross of Honor" over his heart.

"UNCLE ARBA AND THE GOOD WOMAN"

MR. AND MRS. A. F. SHAW, of Cooper Heights.

Mr. Shaw has been a regular correspondent of the Walker County Messenger for the past twenty-seven years, and in point of service is probably the oldest correspondent of which any country weekly in the state can boast. His bright, newsy and entertaining letters to this paper have made him known to every reader of the Messenger. He was a brave Confederate soldier and worthily wears the cross of honor. His wife is in every particular entitled to be known as the "Good Woman," as Mr. Shaw affectionately calls her in his letters.

When this cruel war is over and I don't get killed and the yankees don't bind me, I will go back to the girl I left behind me.

A. F. Shaw

BY 1908 ARBA'S HEALTH WAS deteriorating. He had to get about on two canes, but he was willing to share his

Rebel Correspondent

garden and farm tips in his weekly column. It reads like an excerpt from Jerzy Kosiński's "Being There" and could even be interpreted as a statement on politics written way before its time:

Kensington, Rfd. 2, March 18 ...I will try to give you a few garden and farm hints but I expect you to know as much as I do about it. I know but that is not all there is to it for if we can't keep it in good trim there is not much profit derived from it; but a garden well seed and properly the spring and summer through and in the early fall turned is a beautiful thing to look upon or the same if remanured and planted in turnips for winter. Now for the planting and utility of the products we are generally governed by our own likes or dislikes; as to what we plant it is common to plant onions first and garden peas and various vegetables that are valuable more than for the kitchen and all wholesome for the pigs as for us. Save the mustard for the pigs, but it will kill the cows. We will upon trial find that a few onions are good for hogs and that the large lettuce and the large white radishes are easily grown in large quantities on rich beds, so you can save much corn by feeding them daily to your hogs. To be sure they will do better with a little corn each day, so if you have hogs you will help to consume a great surplus of onion, peas, turnips, beets, lettuce, radishes and Irish potatoes, and they should all be planted now and later the cabbage plants more than you eat. Don't let them stand an rot but divide with hogs and see how they will thank you for them and see how healthy they will be. The best way I find to feed the hogs so they will always seem glad feed time is coming when you go to feed.

I am improving and can go to the lot on two sticks and shuck corn for the good woman while she feeds. Paralysis is slow about turning loose.

A. F. Shaw
Walker County Messenger
Friday, March 20, 1908

Steve Procko

THOUGH WRITING FOR HIM became a struggle, he would continue this job as a columnist for the *Walker County Messenger* into 1909; his last column was published on Friday, March 19, 1909, written two days before and placed into his mailbox to be delivered the next day, deadline day to the *Walker County Messenger* offices—like he had done for over twenty-nine years.

Kensington, Rfd. 2, March 17 - Last week it took me two days to write my little scroll all tangled up...

Sunday we were well pleased to have our brother-in-law and his wife, Mr. and Mrs. R.C. Boss and their daughters, Misses Irene, Georgia and Rita. Theyu stayed all night and Monday they went home. Sunday there were 22 of my friends came to see me. How I do appreciate their appearance. They spread all the sunshine and they hope I will soon be up and out, but I tell them I do hop so too, but all my hope seems to be against poop prospects for the better, as I continue to be forced to stay where I am left and not improve. All my muscles are getting more and more insensitive to touch, gouging and pinching more insensitive to any other parts mentioned and each day I get more and more unable to dress and undress on account of loss of strength in my arms and legs.

We would be blessed with luxuriant Jap clover that we can have on all vacant places just for the annual burning, and the beggar weed and have free liberty to the bountiful mast that frequently falls and that would be annually increasing by the burnings. The old timber is mostly our and the young has gone into business.

A. F. Shaw
Walker County Messenger
Friday, March 19, 1909

Rebel Correspondent

IN THE NEXT COUPLE OF WEEKS, his condition continued to deteriorate. On April 2, 1902, readers were apprised of his condition with a front-page article.

Mr. Shaw's Condition Is Much Worse–
Feeble and Helpless

Kensington, Rfd. 2, March 17 - *By request I will try and write a few lines for A. F. Shaw, as he is unable to write this week. He is very weak and feeble. He can't help himself much, so he stays where he is left until he's moved again. He has almost lost the entire use of his limbs and his eyes are failing so fast that he can read very little, and his nerves have given down so he can't write to do any good.*

He has written so many welcome letters to the Messenger that they will be missed by its many readers.

The health of his good woman is very good, considering. Mr. Shaw wants all his kin and friends to come to see him. Mrs. J. H. Pryor, his daughter, is with him at this writing.

Among the many friends that called on the old veteran Sunday were Uncle John Leroy, C. C. Boss and wife, S. R. Tucker and wife, C. R. Johnson and wife, and many others too tedious to mention. Come again, you are all welcome at any time.

W. H. McGuffey
Walker County Messenger
Friday, April 2, 1909

WILLIAM HOUSTON MCGUFFEY (1867-1928) was a neighbor living two households down from Arba's daughter Lizzie Shaw Leath's home. A week later saw the delivery of another—more grave—bulletin published on the front page:

Walker County Messenger
Friday, April 9, 1909

At the home of his son-in-law, J.M. Leath, at Cooper

Heights, Mr. A, F. Shaw, the veteran correspondent of the Messenger and the president of the Correspondents' Association, is lying at the point of death, his dissolution being but the matter of a few hours. This news will carry sadness into the home of every subscriber of the paper. During the past week, Mr. Shaw's condition has gradually grown worse.

Helpless from a number of paralytic strokes, since last Thursday Mr. Shaw has lost the power of speech, visitors at his home Sunday finding it impossible to understand him. Wednesday night it was reported that he was in a state of unconsciousness and that the spark of life was slowly flickering out. Mr. Shaw has received devoted attention since his condition became so critical, his physician, Dr. J. .T. Johnston, having been at his bedside almost constantly for the past week.

TWO DAYS LATER, ON SUNDAY, April 11, 1909, Arba F. Shaw died. It was early Easter morning.

A little over a month later, one of Arba's relatives would pen a final tribute to him in the Friday, May 14, 1909, edition of the *Walker County Messenger*. The article was signed with the initials "P. B. S.," an unknown close relative who clearly knew Arba F. Shaw well:

"Daddy Shaw"

On September 20th, 1844, in a little log cabin near the foot of Pigeon mountain our dearly loved Uncle Arba Shaw opened his eyes to this bright and beautiful world.

As the mother fondly cared and prayed for a noble career for her boy, little she dreamed that a life of patriarch and romance awaited him, but such was to he. So he lived and grew in the knowledge and strength of the Lord.

He was only a lad of seventeen at the beginning of the war of the sixties. which proved so disastrous to the fair southland of ours. Though so young, he knew his party's need. In the second year of the war, be enlisted and served as a brave Confederate soldier who was not afraid to die. Bravely and courageously he fought through the remaining three years of the war; with pride he wore the cross of honor and as long as he lived the old and young never tired of gathering around his cottage door to hear his wartime tales. But to every sweet comes the bitter, and the bitterness and sorrow the war brought to him was a wound which disabled him in a manner for life and perhaps caused an early death.

On a balmy summer evening while the land was stained with blood, some soldier boys with coats of grey stopped at a wayside well to quench their thirst. As did Rebecca of old to the servant of Isaac, a maiden fair stooped to draw the water and lifted the pitcher of cool water and bade each drink. This face was not forgotten by one of the soldiers true. When the war was over he searched for his loved Rebecca, who proved to be Miss Mandy Bradley, and they were married in the year of 1868.

Times were not well during the days of reconstruction, but to this happy pair all the world was forgotten and they made their little home on a farm near what is known now as Cooper Heights.

To them were born four children—Lula, Ida, Lizzie and Hattie. Ten years passed and all went well. But, alas! a reaper visited the green earth and took the kind mother and wife away. Oh, how sad for the poor motherless children! A brokenhearted father was their only comfort, but he kept them all with him and was a mother as well as a father to them. Later he married Rebecca Johnston, who in every way could not have been excelled by their angel mother in training and caring for the children.

Time passed away beautifully with him and the good woman, as he affectionately called her, a title which she in every way well deserved. But in its turn an angel came and took their sweet loving daughters, Hattie and Ida, to dwell in the golden city. The dear father and mother could only say, "Thy will, oh Lord, not mine, be done."

Shortly after this occasion Mr. Shaw's correspondence with the Messenger began, which made him famous throughout his native country. Some of his pieces were copied in the New York Herald, thus being circulated everywhere.

The two other daughters lived to comfort them in their old age, married honorable respected men and have raised families who were the ride of the grand father's heart.

The old home was sold and they moved to the farm of his son in-law a few short years ago in hopes it would benefit his ill health, which the cooling breeze from Lookout mountain did for awhile. Although life was sweet and full of hope, it seemed that he had all that heart could wish for but health—a priceless gem. For many months, the many friends gathered around him.

Devoted attention was given by all, but to no avail. Continued strokes of paralysis weakened bis frail body, and we saw he soon must go and how sad, how sad! It did not seem like we could ever give him up. He was so good. The last talk he had before losing consciousness he laughed as merrily as a youth and his face bore an angelic expression.

He was greatly loved by the young. All the children lovingly called him "Daddy" Shaw.

Time and tide wait for no man. On Easter morning he left us. Sleep sweetly on, dear brother, we would not bring you back if we could for you are at rest. We will meet you at the pearly gate, where there will be no more parting.

Throughout his life he was a faithful member' of the Primitive Baptist church. To dear, heart-broken "Mammy" Shaw, as she was called, weep no for it will only be a short while until that happy day when you shall meet him where parting will be no more.

P. B. S.
Walker County Messenger
Friday, May 14th, 1909

CHAPTER FOURTEEN
The Tale of Two 4ths

**Isaac Wheeler Avery
1837-1897
Colonel; 4th Georgia Cavalry**

*Carte De Visite by
J. H. Van Stavoren; Nashville, Tennessee
David Wynn Vaughan Collection*

There are no known photographs of Duncan Lamont Clinch, Jr. (1826-1890), likely due to a fire that destroyed his plantation home at Waynesville, Georgia, in 1883.

THERE WERE ACTUALLY TWO SEPARATE 4th Georgia Cavalry Regiments. One was under the command of Colonel Isaac W. Avery, and the other was under the command of Colonel Duncan Lamont Clinch, Jr. And yes, it makes researching both of the 4th Georgia Cavalries confusing,

So why were there two 4ths—and wouldn't it have really screwed up their mail? Well, the answer to the first question is that there were two 4ths because of one big Confederate military snafu that didn't get formally corrected until the war was almost over. The answer to the second question is yes. Mail to each respective regiment was often being confused.

Besides having Cavalry regiments with the same numeric designation, Isaac Wheeler Avery and Duncan Lamont Clinch, Jr. also share the state in which they were born. Clinch was born on November 18, 1826, in Pensacola, Florida, and Avery was born eleven years later in St. Augustine, Florida, on May 2, 1837.

DUNCAN LAMONT CLINCH, JR. was a Mexican War veteran who lived in the shadow of a famous father. Brevet Brigadier General Duncan Lamont Clinch Sr. (1787-1849) served as a U. S. Army officer from 1810 to 1836, commanding forces in the First and Second Seminole Wars in Florida. After he resigned from the Army, he was elected in a special election to serve in the Congress from Georgia in 1844, serving out the term caused by the death of John Millen (1804-1843), the prior office holder. He ran for reelection to Congress but lost by a narrow margin and retired to his plantation. He died in Macon, Georgi,a in November 1849. His son Duncan Lamont Clinch, Jr.'s first Civil War service was as Captain and Volunteer Aide-de-Camp to Brigadier General Alexander R. Lawton (1818-1896). He was promoted to Major when given "Cavalry Command of the Altamaha River," formed between late 1861 and early 1862. By mid-1862 they added more companies to become the 3rd Georgia Cavalry Battalion.

With Clinch now promoted to Lieutenant Colonel, his battalion was composed of six companies with soldiers recruited mainly from southeast Georgia. Their task was primarily to act as resistance to Federal forces in the area between the Altamaha and St. Mary's River, as well as scouting, picketing, and running courier duties.[235]

AVERY'S 4TH GEORGIA CAVALRY came together in late 1862 and officially accepted its numeric designation in January 1863. Its roots came from a single company called the Georgia Mountain Dragoons, originally formed in January 1862 with its soldiers recruited from Whitfield County, Georgia. The Dragoons left for Bowling Green, Kentucky, on January 1, 1862, but were ordered to stop upon arriving at Nashville. They were ready to get into the fight. Writing to Adjutant General Samuel, Cooper on February 24, 1862, Avery commented: "The war spirit is rife here now, a enlistments brisk. We will get this company and arm them with guns. I will by [sic] and get them sabres like my own."[236] They finally took part in battle during the fall of Fort Donaldson on February 14, 1862, and then they traveled to Mississippi where the Dragoons would soon see action at the Battle of Shiloh.[237]

After Shiloh, the Georgia Mountain Dragoons conducted reconnaissance near Corinth, Mississippi, through much of May 1862, capturing the attention and praise of General Pierre G. T. Beauregard. Then on June 1, 1862, Captain Isaac W. Avery was captured between Booneville and Baldwin, Mississippi, by Federal forces.[238] A few weeks later he returned to the Dragoons in a prisoner exchange for Union Captain Benjamin Crabbe (1821-1906) of Company

---

[235] O. J. Hickox, *A Brief History of Clinch's Regiment, 4th Georgia Volunteer Cavalry.*
[236] Colonel Isaac W. Avery, Compiled Service Records.
[237] *The Dalton Citizen*, (March 30,1911), First Lieutenant A.C. Gunz, Company I, "A Short History of the 4th Regiment Georgia Cavalry."
[238] *OR*, sr. 1, vol. XXII, pt1, 733.

H, 7th Iowa Infantry. Before the war Benjamin Crabbe was a hotelkeeper in Iowa, eventually being promoted to Colonel of the Iowa 19th Infantry. He would survive the war, returning to his previous occupation as a hotelkeeper in Nebraska.[239]

After the prisoner swap, they sent Avery back to North Georgia with the orders to raise a battalion of five companies using the Georgia Mountain Dragoons as their nucleus.

By the fall of 1862, Avery was having outstanding success recruiting men from northwestern Georgia, and had ideas of something bigger.

Dalton, Ga. Oct 12, 1862
Gen Geo W. Randolph Secry. of War
Richmond, Va
General
Under authority from you I increased my cavalry command to a Battalion.

I have almost enough troops to make a Regiment. To get enough will be to simply gratify good men over thirty five, who have fine homes and prefer the cavalry service.

I have been in the service since the war began, and had an independent cavalry command for the last eight months in the West. I beg to call your attention to an endorsement by Maj Genl Hardee on an application I sent to you some two months ago.

My command is regular Cavalry, and I design to make it what our Generals claim we much need - a well-drilled organization that can be used to purpose on the battle field

The expense of a corps of officers for a Regiment is very little more than for a Battalion while the efficiency of the organization is greatly increased.

I respectfully request the authority to increase my Battalion to either a Regiment or a Cavalry Legion of ten Dragoons companies, & one company of light Flying

---

[239] Colonel Benjamin Crabbe, Compiled Service Records and family genealogy.

Artillery, all the gunners to be mounted - the most effective combination in our country.

**Very Respectfully
I.W. Avery
Lt. Col. Bat. Geo. Dragoons**[240]

A DAY LATER, THE REQUEST was endorsed by General Pierre G. T. Beauregard, and Avery was given authority by the Confederate Secretary of War four days later on Friday, October 17, 1862. Colonel Avery would, by January 1, 1863, have eleven companies totaling close to 1,500 men[241] when his newly minted 4th Cavalry regiment would leave camp west of Dalton and head into Tennessee.

BY JANUARY 1863 Clinch was also given new orders to recruit more men and form a regiment using the six companies of the 3rd Georgia Cavalry Battalion as a nucleus. The newly minted Clinch's 4th Cavalry was soon made up of close to 1,000 men in ten companies.

Clinch's 4th spent approximately eighteen months, from January 1863 to July 1864, operating primarily in southeastern Georgia and northeastern Florida. In early 1863 more than 500 miles separated Clinch's 4th from where the Avery's 4th was operating in Tennessee. No one noticed the conflicting numerology.

Avery's 4th Georgia Cavalry would spend the first half of 1863 in Tennessee as part of Colonel C. C. Crews' Brigade of Wharton's Division in Wheeler's Cavalry Corps. Finally, in the summer of 1863, Colonel Avery came to what must have been the surprising realization that there were actually two 4th Georgia Cavalry regiments.

---

[240] Colonel Isaac W. Avery, Compiled Service Records.
[241] *North Georgia Citizen*, (Dalton, Ga., August 8,1888), I. W. Avery, "Fourth Georgia Cavalry – Proceedings of the Meeting of the Cavalry on the 17th Instant-Letter from Colonel Avery."

Hdqrs. 4th Geo. Cav.
Crews Brig. Whartons Div.
Wheeler's Corps. Braggs Army
Calhoun, Geo. Aug 10, 1863
General Samuel Cooper
Adjt. & Inspr. Genl. C.S.A.
Richmond, Va.

General
I have the honor to call your attention to the following facts.

My Regiment and Col. Duncan L. Clinch's have both been designated the "<u>4th Geo. Cav.</u>". His was organized on the <u>15</u>th January 1863, and mine the <u>30th Jan 1863.</u> His is therefore the legitimate <u>4th</u>.

I respectfully request that my Regiment, which has been serving under General Bragg in Tennessee, be properly and permanently designated.

I have the honor to remain
Very Respectfully,
Yr Abt. Svt.
I.W. Avery
Col. 4th Geo. Cav

THIS LETTER FROM COLONEL AVERY clearly explains why there were two 4ths: They were formed at almost the same time and, by the luck of the draw, Colonel Clinch's 4th was the first 4th. So, in being first, Colonel Avery concedes the mistake and states Clinch's 4th is the "legitimate" first 4th. Now if only the Confederate Army could figure out what exactly to do about it.

From Colonel Clinch there are no records or letters responding to the snafu to give history any idea of what he thought of this matter. Perhaps he was unaware of the situation, or perhaps his correspondence were just lost in the mail.

The war didn't stop just because of a numerical mix-up,

and both 4ths continued to fight their respective fights. On February 20, 1864, Colonel Clinch was wounded at the Battle of Olustee in Florida. He would then retire for a few months to convalesce at his Brooks County, Georgia, plantation.

Four months later on May 25, 1864, Colonel Isaac W. Avery led his 4th Georgia Cavalry in a charge through the driving rain at the beginning of the Battle of New Hope Church. Colonel Avery was wounded severely: "Shot through the body, the ball entering the left-side at the stomach and passing out grazing the spine. Wound declared mortal at the time."[242]

By June 1864 things were not going well in Georgia. General Joseph E. Johnston and his army had their backs to the wall with Union forces slowly pushing toward the inevitable in Atlanta, and both 4ths were missing their Colonels. Colonel Avery's letter regarding the two 4ths from the prior August was still rattling around in the Confederate bureaucracy.

Finally, ten months later, the Confederate War Department replied to an issue regarding another officer that offered them an opportunity to state their point of view regarding the facts, as they knew them, regarding the two 4ths:

Lt. Chappell does not appear in the records of this office as an officer in the 4th Reg. Ga. Cavalry; nor does I.W. Avery appear as Colonel in that regiment. The 4th Georgia Cavalry as known at this office, is commanded by Colonel D.S. Clinch, and is serving in the Dept of S.C, Ga & Fla. Col Avery appears as Lt. Colonel of the 23rd Ga. Battalion. If that Battalion has been made into a Regiment this Department is not aware of that fact.

---

[242] 1889 Isaac W. Avery Pension Application.

A report as to the Regiment commanded by Col Avery is requested, that the status of the Regt may be fully understood, and that the field officers appointed to it...

**By Com'd Sec. of War
Samuel W. Mellon
Lt. Col & A.A.G
June 16.64**[243]

SECOND LIEUTENANT WILLIAM B. Chappell, who was in Avery's 4th's Company L, had tendered his resignation on May 17, 1864, because of a permanent disability likely from being wounded in action.[244]

Though permanently disabled, Colonel Avery himself would never admit it. His recovery from the minnie ball passing through his stomach and hitting his spine would cause him constant pain. He would need to walk with a cane for the rest of his life. The correspondence from Lieutenant Colonel and A.A.G Mellon didn't reach him until September 2, 1864, the day that Atlanta fell.

*Sandersville, Georgia
September 2, 1864
Lt Col Samuel W. Mellon
A.A.G C.S.A
Richmond, Va*

I have the honor to state that I have just received a paper from the War Department, dated "June 16th 1864, A.S. & G. O." marked "EB 244" stating that I do not appear as Colonel of the 4th Ga. Cav, but as Lieutenant-Colonel of 23rd Bat. Ga. Cav; that the Department is nor aware that the 23rd Ga. Bat. Cav. being made into a Regiment; and calling for a Report as to the Regiment commanded by me, that its status may be understood and its Field Officers appointed.

---

[243] Ibid.
[244] 2nd Lieutenant William B. Chappell, Compiled Service Records.

Rebel Correspondent

In reply I have to communicate that the delay in finishing the information is owing to my having been wounded severely three months ago, and being still unable for the field the paper has been forwarded to me.

I was authorized to increase the 23rd Ga. Bat. Cav. to a Regiment by the authority of Gen. Geo W. Randolph Secretary of War, date Oct 17th 1862.

The 23rd Bat. Ga. Cav. was organized into a Regiment at Fayetteville, Tennm January 30th, 1863, by order of General Braxton Bragg commanding Army of Tenn and was designated as the 4th Ga Cav from ignorance that there was any higher numerical designation of Georgia Cavalry than "Third" (3rd). Capt. Wm L. Cook, Senior Captain was recommended as Lieutenant-Colonel. and Capt D J Owen, Co "I" as Major.

The muster rolls and organization were forwarded to the War Department immediately. A reply was received that there were but (9) Muster rolls, but that as soon as the Tenth Muster roll was sent on the organization would be recognized. This was immediately done.

This Regiment has done the service in the Army of Tennessee as the 4th Ga. Cav. since then - a period of nineteen months - and received numerous official papers from the War Department recognizing its existence. It has been Inspected, Mustered & Paid a number of times, and the Muster rolls forwarded to the Department.

W is now in the Georgia Brigade of Cavalry, commanded by Brig Gen Alfred Iverson, Martins Division, Wheelers Corps, Hoods Army.

Its field officers are I.W. Avery, Colonel; Wm. L. Cook, Lt. Col; and Augustus R. Stewart, Major. Major D. J. Owen was the first Major resigned, and his resignation was accepted by the War Department, February 19th 1864, as will be seen in General Order No 51 A.S. & G. O. June 10th, 1864 and Capt A R Stewart, Senior Captain was recommended for promotion as Major.

Some time after the organization of this Regiment, it was

ascertained that there was another 4th Ga. Cav. in the Department of Ga, So Ca & Fla, and much confusion ensued from papers meant for one Regiment being sent to the other. At length I addressed the Department some time in August, 1863, calling attention to the dual designation, and requesting an official settlement of the matter, but no response has been received

The Muster Rolls of the Regiment have been forwarded to the War Department in accordance with Military Law.

I respectfully request that my Regiment be properly and authoritatively designated.

I send this in duplicate one copy through the regular channels of official communication, & the other through the mail, in order that there be no uncertainty in its reception.

I have the honor to remain
Very Respectfully
Yr abt svt
I.W. Avery
Col. 4th Ga. Cav[245]

COLONEL AVERY SEEMED A LITTLE frustrated that the War Department had not recognized his efforts in providing an explanation a year earlier, which confirms that the confusion of the two 4ths had indeed resulted in mix-ups of correspondence between the two regiments of the same number.

At this point of the war in September 1864, Colonel Clinch and Colonel Avery could have crossed each other's path and met face to face.

Colonel Avery was in convalescence in Sandersville, Georgia, where he was staying with his family and where after the war he would run a business supplying cross-ties to the Central Railroad.[246] But shortly after the September 2, 1864, letter to Lieutenant Colonel Samuel W. Mellon,

---

[245] Colonel Isaac W. Avery, Compiled Service Records.
[246] *Atlanta Constitution*, (September 1897), Isaac W. Avery Obituary.

Colonel Avery would be in Macon, Georgia, running what he called "Wheeler's Absentee Bureau" next to Camp Wright, a convalescent camp for Rebel soldiers.

In September 1864 Colonel Clinch was hospitalized in Macon, Georgia, at either the Floyd House or Ocmulgee Hospital.[247] He likely could have ended up in Camp Wright, which is how the two Colonels of the two 4ths could possibly have met each other—no doubt trading mail. Clinch would weeks later head down to southern Georgia, returning to his Brooks County plantation to continue his convalescence.

What remained of the soldiers in the two 4th Georgia Cavalry regiments possibly crossed paths in late 1864. In November Avery's 4th was near Jonesboro, Georgia, and the records note Clinch's 4th as being "near Atlanta." Avery's 4th took part in a skirmish at Jonesboro on November 15, 1864. If Clinch's 4th wasn't in that battle, they were close by. The skirmish at Jonesboro marked the beginning of Sherman's March to the Sea, and both 4ths flanked Sherman, mixed together as part of Wheeler's Cavalry.

On December 3rd, 1864, the Confederate Department of War finally got around to responding to Colonel Avery's original August 1863 letter, in which he first presented the facts on the tale of the two 4ths:

The 23rd Ga. Battalion Cav'y—has been recognized and the rolls of five companies have been on file in this office.

It appears from the accompanying papers that Col. Avery was authorized by the Secretary of War, Octo 17, 1862, to enlist men not liable to conscription at that date, organize them into companies, and increase his battalion to a regiment - The authority is herewith filed. These companies were raised, and Col. Avery states that, by order of Genl. Bragg, the regiment was organized by the addition

---

[247] Colonel Duncan L. Clinch, Jr., Compiled Service Records.

of these companies to the battalion.

Col. Avery states also that the companies were regularly mustered into service, and that rolls were forwarded to this office - but they have never been received; consequently no steps have been taken to determine the status of the command.

The fact of the organization of the regiment is confirmed by Maj. Genl. Wheelers endorsement to which the attention of the Hon. Secretary of War is invited.

The rolls now sent forward are not original rolls.. Col. Avery states that all the rolls of the regiment have been captured; and, as the rolls originally forwarded to this office have never been received, it is not practicable to ascertain whether the enlistments were in strict accordance with the authority of the War Department.

It seems now that there were eleven (11) companies in the regiment - rolls for only ten are presented - one being on detached service, from which no roll could be obtained.

It is recommended, as this regiment has been in active service since January 1863, that its organization should be recognized by the Department in orders, with a proper numerical designation.

The field officers now on duty with the regiment are:

I.W. Avery Colonel
Wm L Cook Lt Col
DJ Owen Major

If the organization of the regiment is confirmed, it is desirable that the field officers be appointed as above, to date, from the organization of the regiment by Genl. Bragg - say Jan'y 30th 1863 -

Lt. Col Averys claim to the Colonelcy is based on the fact that he raised the additional companies under the authority granted him by the Department.

Wm. L. Cook was Senior Captain, and therefore entitled to

the Lieut-Colonelcy by seniority, in the event of Avery's appointment to the Colonelcy. The Majority in the Battalion has never been filled, and that position in the regiment may be regarded as an original vacancy. Capt. D J Owen of Company I has been serving in that capacity, and his appointment is recommended. He is not senior in rank, but it is presented he was selected because of his fitness for the position.

**By order of
Jno. Blair Hoge
A.A.G.
Orgn. Office
3 Dec 64**

Respectfully referred to the Appt. Office, for action in reference to appointment of the field officers of this regiment.

The regiment has been formed by S O _____ _____ to take effect
30 Jany 1865, and is known as the 12th Regt. Georgia Cavy.

**By order of
Jno. Blair Hoge
A.A.G.**

THE ORDER BY MAJOR JOHN BLAIR Hoge (1825-1896) was endorsed by the Secretary of War of December 31, 1864, with this note attached:

Secretary of War, approved with the condition that the number of Cos. be limited to ten, as authorized by Con. The other Co. may be attached to the Battalion now in service -
JAS

THE INITIALS "JAS" STOOD FOR THE Confederate Secretary of War James S. Seddon (1815-1880); this would be one of his last official acts as he resigned on January 1,

1865. To the hand-written order was the additionally attached single line:

AG - Has the President's endorsement and to order.
3 Jany 1865 JAS

SO WITH THAT FINAL PEN STROKE, Colonel Isaac W. Avery's 4th Georgia Cavalry was redesignated as the "12th Georgia Cavalry" officially on January 30, 1865. The designation "4th Georgia Cavalry" was formally now under the command of a single Colonel, and that was Colonel Duncan L. Clinch, Jr. The confusion of the two 4ths would soon be over, along with the war—which both 4ths and everyone else in the Confederacy had lost.

After the war Duncan Lamont Clinch, Jr. returned to Camden County in southeastern Georgia and returned to the life of a planter at his plantation known as "Cedar Hill." He had married Susan Ann Hopkins (1835-1879) prior to the war in November 1855. They would have five children who survived into adulthood. He died on October 28, 1890, and is buried in Brunswick, Georgia.

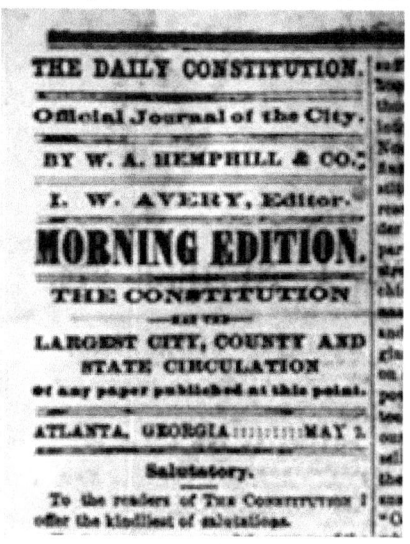

The Constitution
May 2, 1869
I. W. Avery, Editor

Isaac W. Avery would marry Emma Bivings (1851-1914) on January 1, 1868, in Dalton, Georgia. The couple would have three children who survived into adulthood. Avery worked for the railroad immediately after the war, then became a journalist and one of the first editors of *The Constitution* in 1869, which is today known as the *Atlanta*

Journal-Constitution. In 1881 his critically acclaimed book *The History of the State of Georgia* was published. It covered the period from the decade before the Civil War through Reconstruction. Avery was active in the reunions of his beloved 4th Georgia Cavalry. Increasingly frail in later life, an accident in September 1897 when he fell off his porch at his Kirkwood home, a suburb east of downtown Atlanta, proved fatal.

TO THE INDIVIDUAL SOLDIERS who served in either Avery's 4th or Clinch's 4th, they would forever be known to their brother-in-arms as members of the 4th Georgia Cavalry. Though to further continue the confusion, early official U. S. Government sanctioned headstones to mark the grave for any soldier in Avery's 4th and Clinch's 4th had the same designation chiseled in the white marble: "4th Ga. Cav." Later headstones would switch the chiseled designation of Avery's 4th Georgia Cavalry to "12th Ga. Cav."

IN 1888 AVERY WOULD WRITE on his 4th Georgia Cavalry: *record for steadiness, dash and discipline. For sturdiness, fighting quality, and endurance it was not surpassed. On the march or in attack, in charge or repelling assault, under fire or on picket, its men were ever reliable and brave.*
The general outline of this rare body of officers and soldiers is perhaps all that is proper to give now. Speaking for myself personally, the most cherished memory of my life will be that I raised and commanded this superb regiment in the great revolution of 1861-5, and for each and every one of its heroic members I shall entertain the warmest regard and feel the deepest interest.
I.W. Avery[248]

---

[248] *North Georgia Citizen*, (Dalton, Ga., August 8, 1888), I. W. Avery, "Fourth Georgia Cavalry – Proceedings of the Meeting of the Cavalry on the 17th Instant-Letter from Colonel Avery."

CHAPTER FIFTEEN
4TH GEORGIA CAVALRY, COMPANY F

THERE ARE SPARSE MILITARY RECORDS for the 4th Georgia Cavalry including Company F, which was made up of men from Walker County, Georgia. Company F was formed from Company G of Avery's 23rd Battalion Georgia Cavalry. The 23rd Battalion's ranks were originally formed beginning September 20, 1862, with Company A and B. Company D, E, F, and G were added on October 4, 1862. Company G was added on November 1, 1862. Then on January 5, 1863, the Battalion was increased to a Regiment size, and the companies were reorganized and renamed the 4th Georgia Cavalry. The 4th Georgia Cavalry became the 12th Georgia Cavalry on January 11, 1865, with all of the same officers and companies as of that date remaining the same.

The following appears in the record for the movements of the company. Arba's account provides a much more accurate timeline to where Company F was from its founding in January 1863 through the end of the war:

15 Dec 1862 - Georgia Dragoons 23rd Battalion - Capt Jos E. Helverstein
June 30 - Dec 31, 1863 Camp near Sevierville, Tenn
to Nov 14, 1864 Camp near Fayetteville, GA
Nov & Dec, 1864 Camp near Lawtonville, SC

OFFICERS

CAPTAIN - Helvenston, Joseph E. (Name also appears as Helvenstein and Helvinston)(Born May 19, 1825 - Died September 16, 1863 in Battle) Enlisted and was the officer who formed the original Company G, 23rd Battalion Georgia Cavalry - Killed during a charge at Catletts Gap, Georgia near Gover's Ford - K.A (Ann) Davis (Born May 14, 1837 Georgia - Died December 12, 1863 Whitfield County, Georgia) Wife Keziah Ann Davis (Born May 14, 1837 - Died December 12, 1863 Whitfield, Georgia) married September 23, 1852 Whitfield County, Georgia. His wife died three months after Captain Helvenston was killed leaving three children who were raised by their grandmother Elizabeth Hannon Davis.

CAPTAIN - Horn, Felix Grundy. (Born July 28, 1836 - Died 1876-1880 Georgia) Rank In: Sergeant; Rank Out: Captain. 12/4/1864 wounded in chest while in battle, sent to hospital - Occupation: Farmer - Wife Susan M. Whitten (Born June 4, 1843; Georgia - Died December 12, 1899; Tunnel Hill, Whitfield County, Georgia) married September 26, 1861- Eight Children.

CAPTAIN - McCutchen, Cicero Decataur (Born October 21, 1824 Hall County, Georgia - Died 1898 Dalton, Whitfield County, Georgia) Enlisted with the original Company G, 23rd Battalion Georgia Cavalry - Rank In: 1st Lieutenant; Rank Out: Captain. Became Capt after death of Captain Helvenston - resigned 4/17/1864 because he was elected to Georgia Senate 43 District. Occupation: Lawyer - Wife Frances Cornelia Kelly (Born January 19, 1834 Wilkes County, North Carolina - Died November 29, 1920 Dalton, Whitfield County, Georgia) - Eight Children

FIRST LIEUTENANT - Allen, Isaac David (Born May 2, 1829 Rutherford County, North Carolina - Died November 26, 1910 Chattanooga, Hamilton County,

 Tennessee) Originally enlisted June 12, 1861 in the 9th Georgia Infantry; Company G - Rank In: Second Lieutenant Rank Out: First Lieutenant - Resigned June 13, 1862 due to ill health. Reenlisted December 15, 1862 by Lt. Colonel I.W. Avery - Captain Helvenstein's Co. 23 Battalion Georgia Dragoons which became the 4th Georgia Cavalry June 30, 1863 - Rank In: First Lieutenant - June 30, 1864 Captured while on a scout near LaFayette in Walker County, Georgia. POW at Johnson Island, Ohio until the end of the war. Released June 14, 1865. Occupation: Grocer in LaFayette, Georgia and then Chattanooga, Tennessee - Wife Elizabeth Vickery (Born May 6, 1837 - Died October 2, 1916 Chattanooga, Hamilton County, Tennessee) - Six Children

SECOND LIEUTENANT - McCutchen, Augustus Raymond (Born October 31, 1836 Flinstone, Georgia - Died November 31, 1887 Atlanta, Fulton County, Georgia) Rank In: Sergeant Rank Out: Second Lieutenant - Brother of Captain Cicero Decataur McCutchen - Occupation: Professor/Geologist - Wife Martha Elizabeth McCulloh (February 22, 1848 Alabama - December 30, 1932) Lee, Alabama) - Four Children

SECOND LIEUTENANT - O'Neal, John W. (Born November 8, 1824 Green County, Georgia - Died May 23, 1884 Savannah, Georgia of Hepatitis) Enlisted with the original Company G, 23rd Battalion Georgia Cavalry - Rank In: Sergeant Rank Out: Second Lieutenant. Resigned on surgeon's certification due to Chronic Hepatitis and Dyspepsia January 22, 1864, August R. McCutchen succeeded him. Occupation: Farmer. Wife Ellen - Eight children.

SECOND LIEUTENANT - Sloan, Jackson Boyd (Born December 19, 1824 Blount, Tennessee - Died July 15, 1870 Lawrence, Arkansas. Enlisted with the original Company G, 23rd Battalion Georgia Cavalry - Resigned September 30, 1863 on surgeon's certificate dated August 25, 1863 due to chronic bronchitis and Rheumatism was succeeded by Felix G. Horne. Occupation: Farmer - Wife America H. Pittman (Born 1828 Georgia - Died 1870 Lawrence, Arkansas) married on March 8, 1846 Murray, Georgia - Six children.

COMPANY F - ENLISTED SOLDIERS

Alexander, Mellville C. - Private - (Born July 23, 1840 Georgia - Died May 30, 1912 Walker County, Georgia) Enlisted October 20, 1862 Dalton, Georgia. Occupation: Farmer. Unmarried

Atwood, Greenberry B. - Private - (Born September 5, 1826 Georgia - Died December 30, 1896 Walker County, Georgia) Enlisted January 4, 1863 Chattanooga, Tennessee. Occupation: Farmer. Wife Elizabeth Ann Hobbs (Born November 29, 1829 - Died June 6, 1901 Walker, Georgia) married in 1850 - Eight children.

Baily, Benjamin W. - Private - (Born November 28, 1824 Tennessee - Died March 22, 1904 Ringgold, Catoosa County, Georgia) Enlisted December 15, 1862 Dalton, Georgia. AWOL April 19, 1864 Occupation: Farmer. Wife Margaret Elizabeth Cole (Born May, 1850 Graysville, Catoosa County, Georgia - Died September 5, 1939 Chattanooga, Hamilton County, Tennessee) - Two children.

Baldwin, Green B - Private - (Born 1826 South Carolina - Died February 28, 1864 Rock Island, Illinois of Variola) Enlisted December 15, 1862 Dalton, Georgia. Captured September 14, 1863 in Walker County, Georgia.

POW at Rock Island, Illinois died in prison. Occupation: Farmer - Wife Matilda (Born 1828 Tennessee) - Four children.

Barnes, William - Private - (Born 1830 Wilke County, North Carolina - Died March 30, 1863 Fayetteville, Tennessee hospital of pneumonia/fever) Enlisted December 1, 1862 Murray County, Georgia. Killed in action March 30, 1863 Occupation: Farmer - Wife Matilda Ann Pearcy (Born 1830 Cocke County, Tennessee - Died 1905 Ellijay, Gilmer County, Georgia) married July 20, 1854 Gilmer County, Georgia - Four children.

Bates, Joseph Isaac - Private - (Born June 6, 1827 Greenville County, South Carolina - Died February 14, 1909 Mount Vernon, Whitfield County, Georgia) Enlisted May 1, 1863 Dalton, Georgia. Wounded June 30, 1863 Tullahoma, Tennessee Occupation: Farmer - Wife Mary Elizabeth Richardson (Born November 5, 1828 Union County, South Carolina - Died March 3, 1909 Whitfield, Georgia) married July 25, 1850 - Twelve children.

Beers, Robert A. - (Born 1826) provided James England as his substitute.

Biggerstaff, John B. - Private - (Born October 25, 1834 Rutherford, North Carolina - Died August 9, 1889 Sunshine, Rutherford, North Carolina) Enlisted November 1, 1862 Dalton, Georgia. August 20, 1864 wounded severely at Sweetwater, Tennessee and left behind - supposed POW. Occupation: Farmer - Wife Elizabeth Putnam (Born 1836 Georgia - Died 1878 North Carolina) married January 1,

1868 Rutherford, North Carolina - Four children.

Biles (Boiles, Boyles), David - (Born November 21, 1825 Lincoln, North Carolina - Died February 21, 1897 Walker County, Georgia) Enlisted December 19, 1862 LaFayette, Georgia. Occupation: Farmer/Minister - Wife Mary Amanda Cassidy (Born About 1828 Tennessee - Died 1925) - Nine children.

Boss, Enoch Judson (Jack) - Corporal - (Born November 25, 1825 - Died December 29, 1903) Enlisted December 15, 1862 Dalton, Georgia. Captured at Catlett's Gap, Georgia on September 17, 1863 (Same event where Captain Helvenston was killed). POW at Camp Douglas, Illinois until June 15, 1865 - Occupation: Farmer - Wife Maranda Ann Jackson (1823-1894) married July 29, 1847 Walton, Georgia - Five children.

Branham, William C. - provided Shadrick Farmer as his substitute.

Brock, William E. - Private - (Born March 17, 1838 South Carolina - Died October 16, 1909 West Chickamauga, Georgia) Enlisted October 20, 1862 Dalton, Georgia. Wounded at Catlett's Gap, Georgia on September 17, 1863 (Same event where Captain Helvenston was killed). Taken as POW in Gordon County, Georgia July 18, 1864. Took Oath of Allegiance and remained north of the Ohio river until the end of the war. - Occupation: Farmer - Wife Anna Zima (Born May 15, 1832 South Carolina - Died March 1, 1914) married in 1859 - Two children.

Carry, (Corry) James Alexander - Private - (Born February 2, 1821 Morgan County, Georgia - Died February 13, 1865 Indianapolis, Indiana) Enlisted August 27, 1863 Dalton, Georgia. October 2, 1863 - Captured Sequatchie Valley, TN. POW Camp Morton, Indiana. Died there

February 13, 1865 of 'inflammation of the lungs'. Buried at Green Lawn Cemetery; Indianapolis, Indiana, reinterred in Ringgold, Georgia after the war. Occupation: Engineer - He was part of the construction of the Western & Atlantic Railroad in 1848 from Atlanta to Chattanooga. Wife: Mary Roane Ramsey (Born July 22, 1823 Tennessee - Died December 28, 1859 Ringgold, Georgia) Married May 12, 1843 in Greene, Georgia. Mary was the granddaughter of Archibald Roane (1759-1819) the second governor of Tennessee who was a sergeant under George Washington and was present at the surrender of General Cornwallis. - Four children.

Chastain, Benjamin Lafayette - Sergeant - (Born January 22, 1825 - Died September 16, 1906 Rock Spring, Walker County, Georgia) - Enlisted March 8, 1863 Pulaski, Tennessee. Rank In: Private Rank Out: Sergeant. Promoted to Sergeant March 6, 1864. Occupation: Farmer - Wife: Eliza Patience Harwell (Born August 4, 1834 - Died November 18, 1920 Rock Spring, Walker County, Georgia) married 1858 Ringgold, Georgia - Nine children. Arba Shaw mentions him as his Uncle multiple times in his writings regarding the civil war.

Conley, John Fletcher - (Born October 19, 1827 Burke, North Carolina - Died May 24, 1917 Rock Spring, Walker County, Georgia) provided Harrison E. Hamilton as his substitute - Occupation: Farmer - Wife: Sarah Ann Elizabeth Willbanks (Born November 6, 1829 Georgia - Died July 4, 1928 Rock Spring, Walker County, Georgia) - Three children.

Cooper, John Ervin - Private - (Born about 1823 White County, Georgia - Died November 15, 1863 Indianapolis, Indiana) Enlisted October 20, 1862 Dalton, Georgia. October 2, 1863 - Captured Sequatchie Valley, TN. POW Camp Morton, Indiana. Died there November 15, 1863 Pneumonia.

Buried in grave number 500 Greenlawn Cemetery, Indianapolis, Indiana. Reburied in a mass grave called 'Confederate Mound' in 1931 Crown Hill Cemetery, Indianapolis, Indiana. Occupation: Farmer - Wife: Martha C. Williams (Born February 8, 1819 Gwinett County, Georgia - Died December 24, 1888 Ringgold, Georgia) - Five children.

Dalton, Harrison - Private - (Born October 28, 1825 Greenville, South Carolina - Died August 23, 1884 Pond Springs, Georgia) Enlisted December 15, 1862 Dalton, Georgia. Reported as wounded in chest in the fall of 1863 per Arba F. Shaw's account. Reported as deserted before May 1, 1864 though wounded in battle is not mentioned. Occupation: Farmer - Wife: Caroline Lowery (Born December, 1827 - Died after 1900) - Nine children.

Dorsett, James F. - Enlisted December 15, 1862 Dalton, Georgia - No further information in military records.

Dorsett, John K. - Recorded as member of Company F -No Enlistment Date or further information in military records.

Drew, Thomas - Private - Recorded as member of Company F - No Enlistment Date - Signed Loyalty Oath May 19, 1865.

Dupree, John S. (Du Pré) - Private - (Born October 27, 1835 Georgia - Died June 17, 1918 Whitfield County, Georgia) - Enlisted December 15, 1862 Dalton, Georgia - Detailed as a courier for General St. John Richardson Lidell (1815-1870) who was a schoolmate of Jefferson Davis August 29, 1863. Occupation: Farmer - Wife: Delara Martha Main (Born February 16, 1846 - Died July 7, 1935 Dalton, Georgia) married January 14, 1869 - Seven children.

Edwards, A. B. - Private - (Born ? - Died ?) - Recruited November 10, 1864 Lagrange, Georgia - Paroled at Charlotte, North Carolina May 3, 1865.

England, James Lee - Private - (Born February 5, 1817 Burke County, North Carolina - Died February 5, 1905 Georgia) - Enlisted December 15, 1862 Dalton, Georgia as a substitute for Robert A. Beers. Sent to hospital May 10, 1863. Furloughed to Dahlonega, GA June 14, 1863. Dropped AWOL April 19, 1864 Pension claim states he was in Compton, Georgia hospital until the end of the war - Occupation: Farmer/Miller - Wife: Elizabeth A. Largent (Born 1816 - Died ?) married about 1839 - Five children.

Faith, Abraham - Private - (Born 1828 Henry County, Georgia - Died August 7, 1863 Georgia) - Enlisted December 1, 1862 Dalton, Georgia - Killed in action August 7, 1863 - Occupation: Railroad Track Hand - Wife: Sarah Jane Owens (Born November 5, 1838 Whitfield County, Georgia - Died January 15, 1923 Dalton, Georgia) married July 31, 1854 Whitfield County, Georgia - Two children. Brother Josiah Gresham Faith.

Faith, Josiah Gresham (Gusom D.) - Private - (Born 1837 - Died ?) - Enlisted February 1, 1862 Dalton, Georgia - Occupation: Farmer - Wife: Elizabeth J. Flemon (Born ? - Died ?) married June 24, 1866 Whitfield County, Georgia - Brother Abraham Faith

Farmer, Shadrick (Shadric) - Private - (Born 1837 Floyd County, Georgia - Died October, 1863 Georgia) Enlisted December 15, 1862 Dalton, Georgia as a substitute for William C. Branham. Occupation: Farmer - Wife: Annie Virginia Johnson (Born January 7, 1843 Union County, Georgia - Died November 23, 1926 Gordon, Georgia) married January 17, 1861 Floyd County, Georgia - One child.

REBEL CORRESPONDENT

Fricks, John Dickson - Private - (Born June 9, 1844 Walker County, Georgia - Died February 2, 1882 Walker County, Georgia) Enlisted December 15, 1862 Dalton, Georgia. Was also part of Captain B. F. White's Battery of Horse Artillery May 30, 1863 - wars end. Occupation: Farmer - Wife: Sarah Clementine Lee (Born September 1, 1854 Cassandra, Georgia - Died February 15, 1891 Cassandra, Georgia) married 1875 - Two Children.

Hamilton, Harrison E. - Private - (Born ? - Died ?) Enlisted December 15, 1862 Dalton, Georgia as a substitute for John F. Conley. Left sick at Resaca, Georgia September 1, 1863. Listed as AWOL April 19, 1864

Hamilton, James Harrison - Private - (Born September 15, 1844 Alabama - Died June 16, 1925 Martha, Oklahoma) Occupation: Farmer - Wife: Sarah Elizabeth Kemp (Born September 7, 1845 Georgia - Died 1902 Georgia) married in 1865 - Twelve Children. Note: it is possible that this soldier is the same as Harrison E. Hamilton. He is the brother of Wiley Taylor Hamilton.

Hamilton, Wiley Taylor - Sergeant/Acting Chaplain - (Born October 23, 1838 - Died August 3, 1902 Greensboro, Georgia) Enlisted December 15, 1862 Dalton, Georgia - Captured September 5, 1864 near Franklin, Tennessee. POW at Camp Chase, Ohio. Took Oath of Allegiance May 15, 1865. Occupation: Minister - Wife: Parizade Ware (April 3, 1841 - November 22, 1887 Greensboro, Georgia) - Six children. He was a methodist minister, and was the first pastor after the civil war, of the Mt. Carmel Methodist church in Walker County, Georgia. He is the brother of James Harrison Hamilton.

Henry, Josiah M. - Private - (Born May 4, 1826 Haywood County, North Carolina - Died January 12, 1903 Walker County, Georgia) Enlisted December 15, 1862 Dalton, Georgia - Took Oath of Allegiance in Chattanooga, Tennessee March 24, 1864. Listed as AWOL on Comapny F records April 19, 1864. Occupation: Teacher/Farmer - Wife: Hannah Elizabeth Dickey (Born January 28, 1844 Walker County, Georgia - Died April 1, 1920 Walker County, Georgia) - married April 20, 1858 Walker County, Georgia - Thirteen children.

Keener (Kiener?), John H. - Private - (Born ? - Died ?) Enlisted December 15, 1862 Dalton, Georgia.

Kirby, Elijah - Private - (Born January 4, 1826 Murphy, North Carolina - Died March 16, 1890 Dalton, Georgia) Enlisted December 15, 1862 Dalton, Georgia. AWOL April 19, 1864 Occupation: Farmer - Wife: Serepta Caroline Phillips (Born September 27, 1835 North Carolina - Died September 27, 1913 Dalton, Georgia) married December 24, 1857 - Eight children.

Lively, John - Private - (Born 1842 - Died ?) Enlisted December 15, 1862 Dalton, Georgia.

Loyd, Hiram Spicely - Private - (Born January 20, 1826 North Carolina - Died) July 10, 1892 West Armuchee, Georgia) Enlisted January 25, 1863 Fayetteville, Tennessee. Captured near Blain and Roads, Tennessee December 10, 1863. Oath of Allegiance Dec 4th-16th 1863 sent to Kentucky. Dropped for Desertion April 19, 1864 - Occupation: Farmer - First Wife: Catherine I. Miller (Born 1831 Virginia - Died November 11, 1869 Walker County, Georgia) married November 8, 1849 Walker County, Georgia - Seven children. Second Wife: Elizabeth Lawrence (Born June 30, 1845 Chatooga, Georgia - Died September 10, 1910 West Armuchee, Georgia) married 1871 Peavine, Georgia - Six children.

Loyd, W. Alvis - Private - (Born ? - Died ?) Enlisted July 25, 1863 Calhoun, Georgia. Left company without leave February 4, 1864 - dropped for desertion April 19, 1864.

Hugh P. Lumpkin - Private (Born March 19, 1846 Walker County, Georgia - Died September 25, 1915 LaFayette, Georgia) Enlisted April 1, 1864 Oxford, Alabama. Also was First Lieutenant, Captain Taliaferro's Company of Mounted Infantry, Floyd Legion State Guards August 1, 1863 - February 1, 1864 (6 month period) Rome, Georgia - Occupation: Lawyer (Admitted to the bar in 1868) - Wife: Emma Black (Born 1848 Georgia - Died 1934 Walker County, Georgia) married 1868 Walker County, Georgia - Three children.

Massey, William Alexander (Asa) - Private (Born 1823 Homer, Banks County, Georgia - Died July, 1899 Homer, Banks County, Georgia) Enlisted December 15, 1862 Dalton, Georgia. Captured at Burnt Hickory/Altoona, Georgia May 26th, 1864. POW Rock Island, Illinois. Occupation: Farmer - Wife: Elizabeth Ann Lawson (Born 1836 Alabama - Died ? Taylor, Williamson, Texas) married September 5, 1849 - Six children.

McClure, Ezekiel A. - Corporal (Born - Died) Enlisted December 15, 1862 Dalton, Georgia. Left at Covington, Georgia with disabled horse August 10, 1864 - afterwards wounded while on duty under General Iverson.

McCracken, James M. (Also listed as McCrackin, McCracker, Joseph) - Sergeant (Born 1825 - Died) Enlisted October 20, 1862 Dalton, Georgia. Occupation: Farmer - Wife: Mary A. (Born 1836 Georgia - Died ?) - Three children.

McWhorter, A.H. - Private - (Born ? - Died ?) Enlisted December 22, 1862 Gordon Springs, Georgia. Detailed by order of Brigade Surgeon to carry wounded to hospital December 5, 1864

McWhorter, James Hamilton - 1st Sergeant - (Born August 24, 1844 Pickens County, South Carolina - Died August 24, 1908 Walker County, Georgia) Enlisted December 6, 1862 Gordon Springs, Georgia. Rank In: 1st Sergeant Rank Out: 3rd Sergeant. Occupation: Farmer - Wife: Amelia Edwards. (Born December 29, 1837 Henderson County, North Carolina - Died March, 1915 Chattooga County, Georgia) Married 1865. No children.

Moore, Francis McF (McFarland) - Quarter Master Sergeant - (Born ? - Died ?) Enlisted December 15, 1862 Dalton, Georgia. Detached Reserve Camp July 15, 1864

Rebel Correspondent

Murphy, Henry - Private (Born ? - Died ?) Prisoner of War, Signed Loyalty Oath Thomasville, Georgia May 15th, 1865

Nash, Joseph Peyton - Private (Born July 4, 1845 Walker County - Died June 16, 1931 Chattanooga, Tennessee) Enlisted July 22, 1863 Calhoun, Georgia. Deserted May 26, 1864. Occupation: Clerk in Dry Goods Store/Salesman - Wife: Annie M. Whitman (Born November, 1854 Georgia - Died April 7, 1916 Chattanooga, Tennessee) Married 1876. No children.

Nesbet, Franklin M. (Nisbett) - (Born 1837 - Died ?) Enlisted December 15, 1862 Dalton, Georgia. Transferred from Company A.

Odom, John Henry (Odam, Odum, Oldham) - Private (Born ? - Died June 18, 1874) Enlisted December 15, 1862 Dalton, Georgia. Captured at Burnt Hickory/Altoona, Georgia May 26, 1864. POW Military Prison, Louisville, Kentucky Died in Hospital Typhoid Fever June 18, 1864; buried at Cave Hill Cemetery; Louisville, Kentucky (Grave 89; Range 2)

Oliver, J. S. - Private (Born ? - Died ?) Enlisted April 1, 1864 Dalton, Georgia. Paroled at Charlotte, NC May 3, 1865

O'Neal, Jesse Crawford - Private (Born April 29, 1827 Green County, Georgia - Died February 27, 1910 Catoosa, Rogers County, Oklahoma) Enlisted December 15, 1862 Dalton, Georgia. Captured near Knoxville November 22, 1863. Dropped for Desertion April 19, 1864 - Occupation: Farmer - Wife: Catherine Matthew Relley (Born July 29, 1851 Arkansas - Died November 26, 1916 Catoosa, Rogers County, Oklahoma) Married September 13, 1868 Arkansas. Ten children.

Palmer, Joshua C. - Private (Born ? - Died ?) Enlisted December 15, 1862 Dalton, Georgia. Transferred from Company A- AWOL June 19, 1864

Parks, Lewis Jefferson - Private (Born March 19, 1938 Lumpkin County, Georgia - Died September 2, 1901 Brookside, Alabama) Enlisted December 15, 1862 Dalton, Georgia. Captured Missionary Ridge November 25, 1863 (Noted as General Walkers Escort) Discharged to Rock Island, Illinois December 8, 1863 Occupation: Miller - Wife: Cinderella (Cinderilla) Amanda Fowler (Born June 17, 1850 Anderson, South Carolina - Died July 21, 1900 Brookside, Alabama) Married November 17, 1867 Dalton, Georgia. Twelve children.

Phillips, George Washington - Private (Born January 28, 1844 Murray County, Georgia - Died October 21, 1911 Catoosa County Georgia) Enlisted December 15, 1862 Dalton, Georgia. - Occupation: Farmer - Wife: Sarah Ann Rodgers (Born 1841 - Died 1911) Married March 14, 1867 Whitfield County, Georgia. Eight children.

Powell, Watson F. - Private (Born 1835 - Died ?) Enlisted December 15, 1862 Dalton, Georgia.

Price, Thomas B - Private (Born 1836 South Carolina - Died November 19, 1864 Camp Chase, Ohio) Enlisted December 15, 1862 Dalton, Georgia. Captured September 5, 1864 near Campbellsville, Tennessee. POW died of smallpox on November 19, 1864 at Camp Chase, Ohio - Grave number 490

Ransom, Reuben Jefferson - Private - (Born December 3, 1825 Georgia - Died April 2, 1873 McLemores Cove, Georgia) Enlisted December 15, 1862 Dalton, Georgia. AWOL April 19, 1864 Rank In: 1st Sergeant Rank Out: Private. Occupation: Farmer - Wife: Hannah Caroline

Owings (Born August 15, 1828 Laurens, South Carolina - Died September 9, 1897 Walker County, Georgia) Married 1850. Seven children.

Risener, Jasper Newton - Private (Born February, 1837 Tennessee - Died Before 1910 Whitfild County, Georgia) Enlisted December 15, 1862 Dalton, Georgia. Transferred from Captain D. J. Owens Company A in which he originally enlisted in 1861- Occupation: Farmer - First Wife: Sarah C. Ellison (Born 1843 Georgia - Died 1897 Whitfield, Georgia) Married August 5, 1862 Whitfield, Georgia. One children. First Wife: Nora C. Cornelison (Born October, 1870 Canton, Georgia - Died 1955 Clarke, Georgia) Married August 29, 1897 Whitfield County, Georgia - One child.

Roberts, William M. - Private (Born 1825 or 1828 South Carolina - Died Before 1890) Enlisted December 15, 1862 Dalton, Georgia. AWOL September 15, 1863.- Occupation: Farmer - Wife: Margaret Elizabeth Mills (Born 1836 Walker County, Georgia - Died 1881 Walker County, Georgia) Married 1853 - Four children.

Rogers, Joseph F. - (Born 1841 Likely Tennessee - Died ?) Enlisted December 15, 1862 Dalton, Georgia. Transferred from Captain D. J. Owens Company A in which he originally enlisted in 1861

Rogers, William Henry (Rodgers) - Private (Born August 2, 1844 Duplin, North Carolina or Georgia - Died September 18, 1893 Thomas County, Georgia) Enlisted December 15, 1862 Dalton, Georgia. Captured Burnt Hickory/Altoona, Georgia May 26, 1864. Volunteered for Union service but rejected June 6, 1864 took Oath of Allegiance. Occupation: Farmer - Wife: Adella Jackson (Born April 14, 1862 Georgia - Died September 27, 1949 Georgia) Three children.

Saxson, William H. - Private (Born 1836 - Died ?) Enlisted December 9, 1862 Gordon Springs, Georgia. AWOL May 26, 1864

Shaw, James Benjamin - Private (Born January 26, 1848 LaFayette, Georgia - Died May 23, 1920 Grant, Arkansas) Enlisted July 29, 1864 LaGrange, Georgia - Parolled May 3, 1865 Charlotte, North Carolina - Occupation: Physician - First Wife: Jane Bradley (Born 1848 South Carolina - Died 1889 Grant, Arkansas) Married 1870 Walker County, Georgia - Five children. Second Wife: Martha Ann Holiman (Born October 13, 1858 Arkansas - Died May 8, 1941 Grant, Arkansas) Married October 4, 1889 Belfast, Arkansas - One child. James Benjamin Shaw was Kirjath Arba F. Shaw's younger brother.

Shaw, Kirjath Arba F. (Arby) - Private (Born September 20, 1844 Walker County, Georgia - Died April 11, 1909 Cooper Heights, Georgia) Enlisted December 15, 1862 Dalton, Georgia. Wounded in the thigh on May 25, 1864 at the Battle of New Hope Church, Georgia. Wounded a second time in the arm September 5, 1864 near Campbellsville, Tennessee - Occupation: Farmer/Newspaper Correspondent - From December 19, 1901 through February 12, 1903 Arba's account of his experiences in the Civil War was published in the *Walker County Messenger*, He wrote the account of over 40,000 words between December, 1901 and February 25,1902 the newspaper then cut it up into more than 50 articles - First Wife: Amanda M. Bradley (Born

September 7, 1841 Greenville, South Carolina - Died January 2, 1878 Walker County, Georgia at Shaw Cemetery in LaFayette, Georgia) Married Arba in 1868 - Four children Second Wife: Rebecca Frances Johnson (Born September 10, 1852 Chatooga County, Georgia - Died February 22, 1920 Walker County, Georgia at Singleterry Cemetery in Walker County) Married Arba in 1878 - No children.

Shaw, Robert Franklin (Frank) - Private (Born March 17, 1824 Green, Georgia - Died March 12, 1902 LaFayette, Georgia) Enlisted December 15, 1862 Dalton, Georgia. Captured near Burnt Hickory/Altoona, Georgia May 26, 1864. POW at Rock Island, Illinois released June 20, 1865. Occupation: Farmer - Wife: Mary Francis McWhorter (Born February 11, 1833 LaFayette, Georgia - Died July 2, 1890 LaFayette, Georgia) Married 1849 Walker County, Georgia - Ten children.

Sims, H. L. - Private Enlisted October 8, 1863 Resaca, Georgia.

Smallwood, Clayton - Private (Born 1828 Carrol, Georgia - Dies April 3, 1865 Camp Chase, Ohio) Enlisted December 15, 1862 Dalton, Georgia. Captured July 13, 1864 LaFayette, Georgia; Died of Pneumonia Camp Chase, Illinois April 3, 1865 Buried in Grave 1814- Occupation: Farmer - Wife: Mary Kelley (1831 Bradley, Tennessee - 1891 LaFayette, Georgia) - Eight children

Smith, Abraham Overall - Private (Born 1824 Marion County, Tennessee - Died October 3, 1863 Sequatchie Valley, Tennessee) Enlisted December 15, 1862 Dalton, Georgia. Killed in Sequatchie Valley, Tennessee October 2, 1863 during Wheeler's Raid - buried Cedar Grove Cemetery; Walker County, Georgia - Occupation: Farmer - Wife: Phebe Theresa Holloway (Born September 23, 1824 Marion, Tennessee - Died May 27, 1894 Walker County, Georgia) Five children

Smith, Jesse W. - Private (Born 1825 South Carolina - Died April, 1863 Tennessee) Enlisted December 15, 1862 Dalton, Georgia; Joined White's Battery Horse Artillery; Died of measles April, 1863 in Central, Tennessee - Occupation: Farmer - Wife: Hannah Pare (Born 1833- Died After 1910 Logan, Arkansas) Married April 25, 1847; Gilmer County, Georgia; Six children

Springfield, H. - Private (Born ? - Died ?) Enlisted May 6, 1862 Robertsville, Tennessee; Wounded at Catlett's Gap September 17, 1863 sent to hospital. 1864 - Detached as Acting Forage Master for Captain Moore (AQM) Reserve Camp Ft. Browder, Alabama - Paroled Bainbridge, Georgia May 20, 1865.

Springfield, R B (Bob) - Private (Born ? - Died ?) Enlisted August 1, 1861 Knoxville, Tennessee Records thru end of 1864

Tanner, Thomas Langley - Private (Born November 26, 1826 Hall County, Georgia - Died August 6, 1907 Tilton, Whitfield County, Georgia) Enlisted December 15, 1862 Dalton, Georgia; Captured while on scouting duty June 30, 1864; POW Rock Island, Illinois; Had four other brothers in war, one who was killed - Occupation: Farmer - First Wife: Margaret Allright (Born April 26, 1828 Jackson County, Georgia - Died June 20, 1894 Sugar Valley, Gordon County, Georgia) Married September 4, 1844 Hall County, Georgia; Eight Children - Second Wife: Nancy H. Tomlinson (1843-1929) Married 1895, Whitfield County, Georgia - No children.

REBEL CORRESPONDENT

Taylor, Soloman L. - Private (Born abt 1825 - Died February 20, 1864) Enlisted December 15, 1862 Dalton, Georgia; Died February 20, 1864 while on sick furlough.

Thornton, Pleasant Lawson - Private (Born November 5, 1831 - Died March 4, 1907 Grayson County, Texas) Enlisted October 20, 1862 Dalton, Georgia - Had been recommended as a cadet applicant for U.S. Military Academy in 1851 Occupation: Farmer - Wife: Harriett Graham (Born May 31, 1829 Tennessee - Died November 27, 1928 Sherman, Grayson County, Texas) Married April 5, 1853 Bradley, Tennessee Five children.

Warren, John Turner (Johnnie) - Private (Born March 30, 1826 Stone Mountain, Georgia - April 24, 1915 Sugar Valley, Georgia) Enlisted December 1, 1862 Resaca, Georgia; Captured while on scouting duty June 30, 1864 Marietta, Georgia; POW Rock Island, Illinois - Occupation: Farmer - First Wife: Mary Jane Russell (Born 1829 Sugar Valley, Georgia - Died 1862 Sugar Valley, Georgia) Married about 1850; Five children - the children went to live next door with their maternal grandmother until their father returned. Second Wife: Sarah Ann Turner (Born 1830 Georgia - Died 1895 Sugar Valley, Georgia) Married September 15, 1865 Gordon County, Georgia; Four children. Third Wife: Night?; Married 1910?

Whitworth, William Drummond - Private (Born September 9, 1825 Habersham County, Georgia - Died February 9, 1876 Georgia) Enlisted December 15, 1862 Dalton, Georgia; Paroled May 3, 1865 Charlotte, North Carolina - Occupation; Farmer - Wife: Charlotte E Phillips

(Born March, 1839 Georgia - Died December 7, 1902 Blount County, Alabama) Five children.

Williams, H. J. R. - Private - Enlisted May 1, 1862 Jacksonville, Georgia; Detailed courier for General Lydell August 29, 1863; Courier Brigadier General Govan February 1864 (1 month)

Williams, Jesse - Private - (Born abt 1834 - Died ?) Enlisted December 15, 1862 Dalton, Georgia; Transferred from Captain D. J. Owens Company A in which he originally enlisted on January 10, 1861

Wilson, Thomas Posey - Private (Born August 6, 1839 Alabama - Died November 22, 1918 Whitfield County, Georgia) Enlisted December 15, 1862 Dalton, Georgia; In hospital June 27 - July 23, 1863 Chronic Diarrhea ;Left sick Chickamauga September 21, 1863; AWOL April 19, 1864. - Occupation: Farmer - First Wife: Mary Minerva Whitten (Born March 21, 1836 Tennessee - Died June 18, 1890 Whitfield County, Georgia) Married December 29, 1861 Whitfield County, Georgia; Three children. Second Wife: Orlena L. Grady (Born December 27, 1857 Tennessee - Died May 2, 1917 Whitfield County, Georgia) Married November 25, 1891 Whitfield County, Georgia; One child.

Woods, John Allen - Private (Born December 30, 1829 Georgia - Died March 19, 1899 Walker County, Georgia) Enlisted December 15, 1862 Dalton, Georgia; Also in Captain White's Horse Artillery Battery, transferred August 4, 1863 - Occupation: Farmer - First Wife: Sarah E. Price (Born January 22, 1828 Rutherford County, North Carolina - Died January 16, 1880 Walker County, Georgia) Married September 7, 1854 Walker County, Georgia; Two children. Second Wife: Louisa Caroline Adams (1846 Georgia - October 26, 1927 Lafayette, Georgia) Married April 17, 1881 Walker County, Georgia; Widowed. Two children.

Acknowledgments

THIS BOOK BECAME MY CORONAVIRUS 2019 (COVID-19) PANDEMIC PROJECT during the time some of us were locked down and quarantined in 2020-2021. Had a similar quarantine occurred twenty years earlier, I could not have undertaken a book such as this. I would have had to travel in person to do the research. Instead, almost all of the research was done through the internet—a painfully slow connection piggybacked on a telephone cable cradled on telephone poles meandering over mountainous terrain before finally venturing underground to emerge at a log cabin looking down onto Stanley Creek near North Georgia's Rich Mountain. Still, it was the perfect time and place to immerse myself in deep research.

I give thanks for the online archives with their vast collections of rich sources just waiting to be discovered: Ancestry.com, Newspapers.com, the Library of Congress, and the Georgia Historic Newspapers Archive, which is a project of the Digital Library of Georgia and a part of Georgia's Virtual Library GALILEO based at the University of Georgia Libraries.

I also thank the various folks who were contacted via email and phone and actually took the time to respond back out of curiosity to help me discover more information on a story of historical importance. These people include Carol Smith at the LaFayette-Walker County Public Library, David Boyle of the Walker County Historical Society, and Jim Staub of the Martin Davis House in Chickamauga, Georgia; the Martin Davis House was owned by a distant relative of Arba Shaw and is close to the site of the cabin where Arba was born.

My thanks to the Probate Court at the Walker County

Courthouse for allowing me to access their archive of the *Walker County Messenger*. Although cameras are not permitted into the courthouse, I was given special permission by the judge to photograph select articles that were missing from my original cache of Arba's writings, including the critical one describing when he returned home from the war to his mother on May 13, 1865.

My thanks to the Georgia Battlefields Association and their knowledgeable associates for helping me sleuth the story around Resacca and Lay's Ferry. These associates include Charlie Crawford, Marvin Sowder, Jeffrey Wright, Ken Padgett, and Tony Patton.

My thanks to Dan Roper of *Georgia Backroads* magazine.

My thanks to Travis McDaniel, descendant of Fannin County Georgia's William Clayton Fain, for interviews and discussions about his ancestor for a documentary I am still working on, which led me to find Arba Shaw in the first place.

My thanks to John Randolph Poole, author of *Cracker Cavaliers, The 2nd Georgia Cavalry under Wheeler and Forrest,* and to David Wynn Vaughan and his amazing collection of photographs, several of which are included in this book.

My thanks to Lamar Williams for loaning his great image of James E. Burton.

To David Summerford, a fellow North Miami Senior High School alumni for his insight into the Primitive Baptist religion.

From the many descendants of the Shaw family I was able to locate, I particularly thank Retha Williams, who was the first descendant I was able to connect with through Ancestry.com and who, in turn, connected me with Alicyne Roth whose great-grandmother Parthena Shaw Whittle (1863-1937) was Arba's sister. I thank Betty Anderson Smith and Art Coburn who descend from Arba's daughter Sarah Elizabeth Shaw Leath (1874-1947) and June Keith

Johnson who descends from Arba's daughter Lula Jane Shaw Prior (1869-1944). June put me in touch with Arba's great-great grandsons Rick Keith and Joe Pryor, and we met at Arba's grave to exchange family stories and photographs. Rick's daughter Alyse Keith is a talented, emerging artist who created the pen and ink illustration of the 3X great-grandfather she had never really known about—placed at the beginning of this book. Tim Day, another of Arba's descendants, searched for photographs of Arba for me from other Shaw descendants. Additionally, Linda Leath Currie and her sister Karen Leath Bell both 2X great-granddaughters of Arba descending through his daughter Sarah Elizabeth Shaw Leath.

My thanks to book cover designer Eric Labacz for taking my initial rudimentary idea and making it shine. The pen is mightier than the sword. And thanks to my editor Karen Hodges Miller—another fellow North Miami Senior High School alumni. Mrs. Hicks would be proud.

Finally, thanks to my daughter Melissa Procko, research librarian extraordinaire who proofed my early chapters and offered valuable suggestions. And thanks to my wife, Lauren, for enthusiastically reading about Arba chapter by chapter, over and over again—with a smile.

A Final Note

At Arba F. Shaw's Grave in Singleterry Cemetery
(left to right) Steve Procko and Arba's
2X Great-Grandsons Joe Pryor and Rick Keith

In completing this book, it is the desire of the author to continue researching the history of the Colonel Isaac W. Avery's 4th Georgia Cavalry. To help the continuing endeavor, the website RebelCorrespondent.com has been created not only as a website for this book, but also as a clearinghouse for information on the 4th Georgia Cavalry.

The plan for this website is to create a complete list of all the members of each Company within the 4th Georgia Cavalry as well as any photographs, biographical, and military record details that come to light.

About the Author

Steve Procko never thought of himself as a Confederate history buff, let alone a biographer. He does love history; however, he particularly loves learning about the small, everyday events in the lives of little-known people and the small towns they lived in.

A documentarian and photographer, Steve was sleuthing for stories for a series he has developed—the Emmy-nominated series entitled "There's History Around Every Bend" currently available on YouTube—when he came across the writings of Private Arba F. Shaw.

The down-to-earth accounts of the everyday life of a lowly private struggling to survive one of the greatest events in American history fascinated Steve. As he read the series of articles, mostly unread since they were published in a small, North Georgia newspaper between 1901 and 1903, he began to realize that this was a remarkable cache of history.

A native of Florida, Steve, along with his wife, Lauren, and their dog, Rigby, splits his time between a mountain log cabin nestled next to Stanley Creek near the town of Blue Ridge, Georgia, and a home in Ocala, Florida.

He opened a commercial film production company—Steve Procko Productions, LLC—in 1984. His Emmy award-winning financial literacy program entitled "Talkin' Money Minutes" is available on more than 100 public television stations nationwide. His company has also won three additional Emmys as well as several Addy Awards, Telly Awards, and two Promax awards.

When he's not behind a video camera or researching the archives for his next documentary or book, Steve explores remote areas throughout the United States and Canada as a fine art photographer. His work has been displayed at The Carnegie Institute in Pittsburgh, Pennsylvania, and The Museum of Art in Ft. Lauderdale, Florida, as well as featured in various solo and group exhibitions throughout the United States.

Steve's second book, *Captured Liberty*, will be published in 2022. He also plans to develop documentaries about *Rebel Correspondent* and *Captured Liberty*.

www.ingramcontent.com/pod-product-compliance
Lightning Source LLC
Chambersburg PA
CBHW071803080526
44589CB00012B/658